The Incidence of Female Criminality
in the Contemporary World

The Incidence of Female Criminality in the Contemporary World

Edited by
Freda Adler

New York   New York University Press   1984

Library of Congress Cataloging in Publication Data
Main entry under title:

The Incidence of female criminality in the
contemporary world.

Includes bibliographical references and index.
1. Female offenders—Addresses, essays, lec-
tures.   I. Adler, Freda.
HV6046.I48   364.3'74   81-2495
ISBN 0-8147-0576-6   AACR2
ISBN 0-8147-0577-4 (pbk.)

Manufactured in the United States of America

To
Gerhard O. W. Mueller
who, as Chief of the United Nations Crime Prevention
and Criminal Justice Branch has promoted the open and honest
exchange of information on the successes and failures of nations
in dealing with all matters of crime control.

CONTENTS

Acknowledgments   *ix*

Chapter One.   The United States   *1*
 1. International Concern in Light of the American Experience
 F. ADLER   *1*

Chapter Two.   Western Europe   *14*
 1. Female Criminality in the Netherlands   G. J. N. BRUINSMA,
 C. I. DESSAUR, AND R. W. J. V. VAN HEZEWIJK   *14*
 2. Female Criminality in Finland—What Do the Statistics
 Show?   I. ANTTILA   *64*
 3. Norwegian Women in Court   A. JENSEN   *84*
 4. Female Crime in England and Wales   T. C. N. GIBBENS   *102*
 5. Changing Patterns of Female Criminality in Germany
 W. MIDDENDORFF AND D. MIDDENDORFF   *122*

Chapter Three.   Socialist Countries   *134*
 1. The Criminality of Women in Poland   D. PLENSKA   *134*
 2. Crimes Against Life Committed by Women in Hungary
 G. RASKO   *145*

Chapter Four.   Africa   *158*
 1. A Preliminary Study of Female Criminality in Nigeria
 O. OLORUNTIMEHIN   *158*
 2. Female Criminality in Egypt   A. W. EL ASHMAWI   *176*

Chapter Five.   Latin America   *188*
 1. Argentine Statistics on Female Criminality   J. N. KENT   *188*
 2. Venezuelan Female Criminality: The Ideology of Diversity
 and Marginality   L. ANIYAR DE CASTRO   *215*

Chapter Six.   Asian and Pacific Region   228
   1. Criminality Amongst Women in India: A Study of Female
Offenders and Female Convicts   M. L. BHANOT AND SURAT MISRA   228
   2. Emancipation of Women and Crime in Japan   K. S. SATO   258

Index   273

ACKNOWLEDGMENTS

The credit for this volume goes to many workers in the field of crime prevention and control and to many professionals in the art of dissemination of information and of policy making. Above all, I wish to express my appreciation to those of my colleagues around the world who joined in contributing chapters to this book. Indeed, the book would not have been possible except as a co-operative venture, since no one scholar possessed the insight and experience to write about the situation regarding female criminality in all parts of the world. The scholars who did participate, deserve special commendation since they had to base their work on imperfect statistics, on imperfect governmental policies and on very preliminary analyses. Yet, these imperfections make for the strength of this volume: this is the incipient charting of an uncharted sea. Consequently, I also wish to thank our publisher, New York University Press, for taking the risk of publishing the *first* book on this topic. Lastly, my gratitude is extended to Miss Susan Holmberg, my industrious graduate assistant, for having faithfully assisted me in guiding this volume from the beginning to its appearance in print.

Freda Adler

*The Incidence of Female Criminality
in the Contemporary World*

CHAPTER ONE

THE UNITED STATES

1. International Concern in Light of the American Experience

FREDA ADLER

Freda Adler is Professor of Criminal Justice at Rutgers, the State University of New Jersey, Graduate School of Criminal Justice. Her primary interest in the field is in theoretical criminology, female criminality, and drug and alcohol abuse. She is consultant on female criminality to the United Nations, a faculty member of the National Judicial College, Vice-President of the Institute for the Continuous Study of Man, consultant to several international and national agencies, foreign and domestic, and criminology editor of various journals. Her publications include: *Sisters in Crime* (New York: McGraw-Hill, 1975); (coauthor) *The Criminology of Deviant Women* (Boston: Houghton Mifflin, 1979); (coauthor) *A Systems Approach to Drug Treatment* (Philadelphia: Dorrance and Co., 1974); (coauthor) *Medical Lollipop* (Philadelphia: Dorrance and Co., 1974); and numerous articles in professional journals.

The Contemporary American Scene

Five years ago *Sisters in Crime,* a study which indicated that female criminality in the United States had been on the rise for some time, especially in the area of property offenses was published. It was hypothesized that the increasing opportunities, temptations, challenges, stresses, and strains to which women were subjected in recent years caused them to act or react in a manner not previously experienced to the same extent among women, yet, strikingly, more in the manner in which men had reacted to the very same stimuli.

It is five years since that study. Still, female criminality is increasing in the United States and, indeed, women are even more involved in committing the types of offense that were formerly perpetrated primarily by men. In fact, although males still account for the greater number of absolute offenses, the female rate of increase between 1969 and 1978 surpasses the male rate for almost every crime listed in the Federal Bureau of Investigation's Uniform Crime Reports.[1] There are four exceptions: murder, prostitution and commercialized vice, sex offenses (except forcible rape and prostitution), and drug abuse violations. For all offense categories there was a total increase of 39 percent for women and 6 percent for men.

During the ten-year period 1969–78, the number of women arrested for robbery increased 62 percent while the male figure rose 32 percent. Similar differences are found in aggravated assaults (up 58 percent for women, 48 percent for men), other assaults (up 41 percent for women, 17 percent for men); burglary (up 92 percent for women, 32 percent for men); larceny (up 95 percent for women, 47 percent for men); arson (up 109 percent for women, 21 percent for men); fraud (up 219 percent for women, 63 percent for men); and weapons offenses (up 55 percent for women, 23 percent for men). It should be noted that the number of car thefts, embezzlements, and disorderly conduct offenses went down for men but continued to increase for women. Moreover, for those offenses showing a decrease for both sexes—drunkenness, gambling, and vagrancy—the rate of decrease was greater for males.

Whereas the adult arrest rate provides information about the present crime situation, the statistics for persons under eighteen years old predict a protracted association between women and crime. Girls continue to participate in all offenses except three—embezzlement, prostitution and commercialized vice, and drug abuse violations—at a rate of increase greater than that for boys. During the years between 1969 and 1978 the number of girls arrested for robbery went up 49 percent while the male figure rose 33 percent. Similar differences are found in aggravated assault (up 106 percent for girls, 60 percent for boys); other assaults (up 55 percent for girls, 40 percent for boys); larceny (up 59 percent for girls, 23 percent for boys); arson (up 50 percent for girls, 18 percent for boys); forgery (up 121 percent for girls, 49 percent for boys); fraud (up 148 percent for girls, 95 percent for boys); vandalism (up 48 percent for girls, 22 percent for boys); weapons offenses (up 54 percent for girls, 17 percent for boys); and driving while intoxicated (up 843 percent for girls, 265 percent for boys). The number of gambling offenses increased (54 percent) for girls while decreasing (−0.9 percent) for boys. For those crimes which decreased for both sexes—drunkenness, disorderly conduct, curfew violations, runaway—the rate of decrease for boys was greater than for girls. The number of auto thefts (similar to the adult figures) rose for girls (41 percent); it decreased for boys (−27 percent). For all offense categories combined there was an 18 percent increase for girls and a corresponding 10 percent increase for boys.

In addition to the national arrest statistics, preliminary studies indicate that young women are continuing their involvement in gang activity, either as partners in male groups or as rivals in their own all-girl gangs. At the present time investigators are actively engaged in both survey and participant observation of these groups.[2]

In 1975 I noted that the subject of women and crime had received little attention from the scientific community and the mass media, both tending to view female deviants as misguided children who had strayed from the appointed ways. This situation, however, has been considerably transformed by both the researchers and the researched. Now that women are continuing to move into the mainstream, both legitimate and illegitimate, the subject of changing deviant roles is becoming a recognized area of concern in the increasing body of research dealing with contemporary problems. Scientists are reviewing current female criminality in relation to historical stereotypes,[3] to the present criminal justice system,[4] and to future patterns of behavior.[5] The debate on whether or not females are innately more or less capable of committing crimes[6] has given way to investigations of the socialization process, or change thereof, which might be affecting the crime rate. Questions such as whether female criminals are more "malelike" than female noncriminals[7] and whether delinquent girls are exhibiting more "masculine attitudes" than nondelinquents[8] are presently under study. Women as terrorists,[9] armed robbers,[10] and white-collar offenders[11] have become the subjects of scientific inquiry.

We are also currently witnessing a return to the turn-of-the-century economic determinism which guided social reformers like William A. Bonger[12] and August Bebel in their explanations of the reasons for the *low* rate of female crime.

As a result of our social conditions, vice, excess, and wrong, crimes of all sorts are bred. All society is kept in a state of unrest. Under such a state of things woman is the chief sufferer. Numerous women realize this and seek redress. They demand, first of all, economic self-support and independence; they demand that women be admitted, as well as men, to all pursuits that her physical and mental powers and faculties qualify her for; they demand, especially admission to the occupations that are designated with the term "liberal professions."[13]

Radical criminologists of the present day are using some of these arguments in their probe of the contemporary *increase* in female crime. They suggest that future investigations break with former assumptions and start with a new feminist perspective, one in which sexist oppression is advanced as the crucial determinant of women's involvement in crime.[14] They call for contemporary studies which deal with the politics of the criminal justice system, on the one hand, and the realities of women's economic position in American society, on the other.[15]

Along with the current theoretical and empirical studies of the deviant *actions* of women, there is also ongoing research concentrated on the *reactions* of the police, courts, and corrections to female deviants. The historical perception of women as more dependent and emotional than men and less aggressive and defiant of authority has carried over to the criminal justice system, where the functionaries have chivalrously treated women more protectively than men. This paternalism is now being questioned.[16] By example, several attacks have been made on courts for upholding longer sentences for females on the grounds that women constitute a reasonable class for discrimination.[17] Their rationale has been that women, by virtue of their unique physiopsychological makeup, are more amenable than males to treatment and, therefore, could be confined until "cured" even if it meant that they would be institutionalized for greater lengths of time than their male counterparts. In other words, longer sentences for females had been defended on therapeutic, not legal grounds. Recently, the existence of these indeterminate sentencing statutes has been questioned under the equal protection clause of the Constitution.[18]

The processing of female juvenile delinquents has also come under scrutiny. In its exercise of *patria potestas,* the juvenile court has tried to reinforce familial requirements for conformity to traditional mores. It has, therefore, frequently upheld the double standard by maintaining sex-differentiated expectations—chastity and dependence for girls, self-reliance for boys—and their attendant sex-differentiated sanctions for noncompliance. Researchers are now testing whether this paternalism, which defends the social status quo, results in longer "protective" institutionalization of young girls for the status offenses of promiscuity, incorrigibility, and running away.[19]

Yet another population, women in prison, are slowly becoming the subjects of scientific inquiry. Traditionally small in numbers, committed for crimes which did not materially threaten the social order (e.g., prostitution), and exhibiting rather docile behavior when incarcerated, female prisoners evoked little scrutiny. Consequently, programs designed for, and appropriate to, women have been sparse and defective.[20] With the increasing numbers of women committing serious offenses, and the attendant rise in the institutionalized population, scientists are becoming more interested in studying the disparity in treatment between male and female inmates, with special emphasis on vocational and educational opportunities.[21]

Erosion of legal equality is harmful primarily because it leads to a system of justice which leans heavily on personal considerations. The social movement which has been promoting equal rights for women has also been arguing against special treatment, positive or negative, for female clients of the criminal justice system. Although more data are needed in order to test the many "discrimination" hypotheses, social researchers have, at the very least, drawn attention to an area that had heretofore been neglected.

It is clear from the growing emphasis of the scientific community on the topic of women and crime that female offenders are no longer an insignificant subset of the criminal population, nor are they merely an appendage to a system devised for processing and confining men. Hypotheses abound, proposals are being developed, universities are offering courses in the area, and conferences are being held—all with a direct focus on the etiology, societal reaction to, and processing of, female criminals. Original data are being collected in order for scientists with opposing approaches to demonstrate the empirical validity of their positions. It is hoped that these scientific demonstrations will be as free from ideological considerations as humanly possible.

The Concern of the International Community

In the concern about female criminality, the year 1975 was an important one. In that year, after decades of neglect, in an era when criminology had been a science devoted primarily to the study of male aspects of criminality, scholarly[22] as well as political attention suddenly focused on female criminality and noted that certain changes were taking place. Both the World Conference of the International Women's Year, at Mexico City,[23] and the Fifth United Nations Congress on the Prevention of Crime and the Treatment of Offenders, at Geneva, Switzerland,[24] helped direct the attention of all governments to the phenomenon. The World Plan of Action, adopted together with related resolutions by the World Conference on the International Women's Year, made specific reference to the prevention of crime and the treatment of offenders and called for national action regarding female criminality, a problem which was noted to be increasing in some parts of the world, and the rehabilitation of female offenders, including juvenile delinquents and recidivists. Research in this field, it was resolved, should include the study of the relationship between female criminality and other social problems brought about by rapid social change.

The situation pertaining to female criminality in many countries had been documented in the report of the Secretary General prepared under item 9 of the provisional agenda of the World Conference of the International Women's Year, entitled "Current trends and changes in the status and roles of women and major obstacles to be overcome in the achievement of equal rights, opportunities and responsibilities"[25] and in the working paper prepared by the Secretariat for the Fifth United Nations Congress on the Prevention of Crime and the Treatment of Offenders, entitled "Changes in forms and dimensions of criminality—transnational and national."[26]

The Fifth United Nations Congress on the Prevention of Crime and the Treatment of Offenders agreed that in order to remove the issue of female criminality from the realm of guesswork and to engage in successful social defense planning, all states should be invited to inform the United Nations of developments pertaining to female criminality and of the success or failure of their countermeasures. In addition, it called for controlled scientific studies to be undertaken on the interrelationship among socioeconomic development, the integration of women into national economic life, and female criminality. Such studies were to focus on comparisons of countries with different experiences and trends in female criminality, the causes and extent of differential treatment of women by the criminal justice system, and experiences in dealing with predelinquent and delinquent behavior of women and children outside the criminal justice system.[27]

Subsequently, in 1976 the Committee on Crime Prevention and Control agreed on the topic of *the incidence of female criminality, including prostitution and the traffic in women, and equal participation of women in the criminal justice system* as one of the items to be included in the Medium Term Plan of the Crime Prevention and Criminal Justice Branch for the period 1978–81, subject to the availability of extrabudgetary funds.[28] In addition, the General Assembly invited member states to inform the Secretary General of the situation concerning crime prevention and control in their respective countries, so that a final report, based on such information, could be submitted to the General Assembly at its thirty-first session.[29]

The Secretariat endeavored to fulfill this mandate by means of a questionnaire survey among member states. Some of the questions pertained to sex-differentiated criminality. Responses were received from sixty-eight nations, and a report, based on these responses, was submitted to the General Assembly at its thirty-second session.[30] The General Assembly received and discussed this report, noting it "with satisfaction." The report of the Secretary General on *Crime Prevention and Control* noted that "on the basis of the information received on crime rates measured by the number of offenders, it is possible to conclude that the over-all rate for the years 1970–1975 was approximately 900 offenders per 100,000 population annually and that the offender rate increased steadily by approximately 2 percent annually. For the period considered, the total increase has thus been about 15 percent. . . . The overwhelming proportion of the adult offenders were males, with a rate 10 times that for females. For juvenile offenders, the male rate was five times greater than that for females."[31]

In developing countries "the over-all rate of criminal offenders for the period 1970–1975 was approximately 800 per 100,000 population. The number of offenders increased at an annual rate of approximately 2.5 percent. The rate of increase for females was 30 percent higher than that for males. . . . the overwhelming proportion of adult offenders were males, with a rate 12 times that of females. For juvenile offenders, the rate for males was eight times greater than for females."[32]

In developed countries "the over-all rate of criminal offenders for the period 1970–1975 was approximately 1,000 per 100,000 population. The number of offenders has increased steadily at an annual rate of 1 percent. The rate of female offenders has increased 50 percent more rapidly than that of males . . . ; the overwhelming proportion of adult offenders were males, with a rate eight times that for females. For juvenile offenders, the rate for males was five times greater than that for females."[33]

Table 1 gives the overall composition of criminality by region, differentiated on the basis of sex. The following countries are included in the above analysis:

Table 1. Regional distribution of crime rates per 100,000 population, 1970–1975.[34]

	Countries of North Africa and the Middle East	Countries of Asia	Countries of Eastern Europe	Countries of Latin America	Countries of the Caribbean	Countries of Western Europe, Oceania, and North America
Offenders:						
Male adult	624.0	537.4	427.2	121.1	1,498.6	1,051.3
Female	45.2	48.1	68.0	16.6	181.9	128.5
Male juvenile	7.4	32.6	53.3	7.8	116.6	154.6
Female juvenile	1.0	2.2	3.7	2.2	15.6	33.6

North Africa and the Middle East: Algeria, Bahrain, Cyprus, Egypt, Iran, Iraq, Kuwait, Morocco, Oman, Qatar, and Syrian Arab Republic

Asia: Indonesia, Japan, Malaysia, Maldives, Pakistan, and Singapore

Eastern Europe: Poland and Yugoslavia

Latin America: Argentina, Chile, Costa Rica, Ecuador, El Salvador, and Peru

Caribbean: Bahamas, Barbados, Guyana, Jamaica, and Trinidad and Tobago

Western Europe, Oceania, and North America: Australia, Austria, Canada, Denmark, Finland, France, Federal Republic of Germany, Greece, Ireland, Italy, New Zealand, Norway, San Marino, Spain, Switzerland, United Kingdom of Great Britain and Northern Ireland, and United States of America

It is clear from these data that males make up by far the greatest proportion of the world's offender population. It is also clear that the rate of female criminality for both developing and developed countries is increasing faster than the male rate. A preliminary regional overview of data indicates that adult offender rates are extremely high for both Western European countries as well as the Caribbean region, with rates more than double those of other regions. This applies to both male and female adult offenders and to juvenile offenders.[35]

The countries of North Africa and the Middle East generally reported a "low rate of criminality," which was attributed mainly to a combination of social stability and economic advancement and a social structure based on closely knit interrelationships, strongly underpinned by Islamic legislation and moral values. Among these countries, Algeria reported a decrease in female criminality.[36]

For Asia a definite increase in most types of crime was reported for some countries. For Japan, a growth in the proportion of female criminality was deemed associated with increasing participation of women in community life, including working wives. In other Asian countries the situation was reported as stable, or the trend as pointing downward.[37]

Although the answers to the questionnaire have indicated changing crime trends, and some hypotheses regarding these have been put forth, it is not possible to present a more precise and detailed overview of sex-differentiated crime trend figures until funds are available for worldwide studies with a greater assurance of comparability. Such studies could also investigate certain correlations between male-female crime rates and socioeconomic development indicators. It might also extend to questions of prostitution and traffic in women, as well as to the question of equal participation of women in the criminal justice system.

In the past, scientists studying women in crime had related female criminality to biological and/or psychological sources, with scant attention to such structural functional considerations as the state of the economy, occupational and educational status, division of labor based on sex roles, and differential association. Formulation and implementation of social policy, however, require that all relevant factors be taken into account. Too often costly mistakes are made (sometimes irreversibly) because policy has not been developed with the benefit of specific knowledge gleaned from well-grounded research.

It should be clearly stated that statistical analyses present difficulties for a variety of reasons, especially because of the major problems of differential levels of sophistication of national data sources (indeed, some countries are only now beginning to compile basic census items creating categories for comparison). In the case of women, national statistics have even greater weaknesses. One of the most obvious has been termed the "invisibility" factor, that is, many of their jobs are located in the home. In addition, many women employed in rural areas are listed as either "farmers" or "unpaid family workers." In the industrial sector many women (especially in the Third World) are employed in "in-home" industries, and still others work "occasionally" and are not listed at all.

Nevertheless, given the weakness of the data, it is possible to document social changes (e.g., crime) to correlate these changes with other factors and to use these associations for planning and policymaking. With existing data it would be possible to undertake an investigation using patterns of criminal behavior and social control as dependent variables, and such indices as proportions of women in the labor force, mean levels of education, age of marriage, number of children, legal norms to divorce and abortion, right of women to hold property, proportion of population living in urban areas, and prevalence of preschool day care centers, as independent variables. Statistics on these socioeconomic indicators can be gleaned from data which have already been gathered for other purposes, frequently by specialized agencies of the United Nations system.

Since much of the international community is experiencing slowly changing patterns of participation of women in the economic life of their nations, it seems likely that for maximum effectiveness in the areas of crime prevention and control there is some immediacy for undertaking such analyses. The requisite analysis, however, is both expensive and time consuming. It is, above all, politically sensitive. It has not yet taken place. But concern about female criminality persists as its significance in the context of socio-economic development is becoming more widely known.

The Present Study

The American experience with respect to female criminality does not occur in isolation.[38] More than ever before the nations and cultures of the world are interdependent, economically, culturally, and socially. Many nations have reached the same stage of development; others are approaching it at an ever accelerating pace. Indeed, no society is stagnant. It therefore became important to view the American developments in a worldwide setting or, in other words, to study the issue of female criminality cross-culturally, worldwide, and in the context of socioeconomic development. This called for a comparative analysis of data on the question of whether women's increasing opportunities, temptations, challenges, stresses, and strains bear a relationship to the incidence of female criminality.

No one should be surprised that there are no accurate and uniform worldwide crime reports providing ready answers. Indeed, during my travels and inquiries around the world I discovered that, especially among developing countries, crime as such had an extremely low priority among national concerns, that crime statistics and criminological research ranked even lower, and that concern for female criminality was practically nonexistent.

Yet, the Fifth United Nations Congress on the Prevention of Crime and the Treatment of Offenders had already called for data and information "in order to remove the issue of female criminality from the realm of guesswork."[39] Here is a mandate, and a start had to be made to seek for elusive answers. Women should not have to wait for policymakers to assign higher priority ratings to crime statistics or to female criminality, nor should women be forced to postpone their inquisitiveness about female criminality to the day when methodologists will have devised a system of foolproof international data assembly and comparison in crime prevention and criminal justice.

The present study, then, cannot be viewed as the final "answer" to the mandate of the Fifth Congress, but it is an earnest effort to provide data and information on the issue for as big a part of the world as can be reached at this point.

Hardest to tell is the story of the African experience. Most of the countries of this continent emerged from colonial domination only a few years ago, and Africans are preoccupied with tasks of nation building, food production, education, and the eradication of diseases, so that problems of establishing crime statistics or of fighting crime take second billing. The African experience, therefore, cannot be related on the basis of statistics; other sources—including the mass media—must be consulted. Although the experiences of African nations are not identical, they are comparable to the extent that the African nations are experiencing similar developmental processes.

As regards the Latin American experience, the Venezuelan and Argentinian studies may well have applicability, in certain respects, for the continent as a whole, since Latin American women share the same socialization process which has, so far, provided them with unequal opportunities for participating in development. Where the restraining influence of family control continues, female criminality remains at a low level.

The experiences of the European socialist countries contained in this volume are undoubtedly representative of the experiences of other European socialist countries. Of future interest will be their political applicability to Western societies if certain social changes in the condition of women as participants in the economic process were to occur.

For the Western European countries we find in our studies an amazing amount of agreement regarding developments, and the reasons for these. While for adult females the statistics show no or only minor increases in criminality, the criminality of younger females increases more rapidly than that of their male counterparts. Although much of that criminality is in the petty offense category (e.g., shoplifting, drunken driving), increases are also noted for offenses of violence. Relations between female criminality and drug and alcohol use are noted. That female arrest and conviction rates (especially in the adult category) are not higher is attributed to the chivalry or courtesy factors, that is, hesitancy on the part of a predominantly male officialdom to apply the rigors of the law to women. Possibly, then, the dark figure of female criminality is higher than the male dark figure. Not surprisingly, all European contributors refer to the opportunity or differential association theories in explaining the current situation respecting female criminality. Simple correlationship between female employment and female criminality cannot be found; one has to look at the reality of forms and degrees of emancipation and of sharing in social, economic, and political responsibilities. In this respect, the European theoretical contributions differ little, if at all, from the African.

The experience of Arab states is, according to its authors, mirrored in the Egyptian contribution—the very first study on this issue for any of the Arab countries. The life conditions of women in the Arab world in general, and Egypt in particular, are comparable and fall into three categories: the modern city woman, the village woman, and the bedouin woman, with differing contributions to criminality, demonstrating the powerful impact of religious social control.

In that sense, the Japanese experience runs parallel. With intact familial and other social controls, crime rates in general have remained extremely low, although in the process of overall industrialization and participation of women in the economic life of the nation, the female portion of the arrest rate increased from 7.6 percent in 1946 to 19 percent in 1977.

These introductory comments are in no way to be deemed a statement of the philosophy of this book or of any of its individual chapters. They are, however, an identification of the recurrent theme, namely that of the socio-economic and political-cultural determinants of female criminality. With this finding, criminology does indeed become holistic, since, to a very large extent, male criminality had likewise long been regarded as the product of socioeconomic and political determinants.

Notes

1. Uniform Crime Reports, United States Department of Justice (Washington, D.C.: U.S. Government Printing Office, 1978), p. 189.

2. Dr. Anne Campbell, ongoing research supported by the Harkness Foundation.

3. Dorie Klein, "The Etiology of Female Crime: A Review of the Literature," *Issues in Criminology* (1973), 8 (2):3–30

4. Lois Frankel, "Sex Discrimination in the Criminal Law: The Effect of the Equal Rights Amendment," *American Criminal Law Review* (Winter 1973):469–473.

5. Rita Simon, *The Contemporary Woman and Crime* (Washington, D.C.: National Institute of Mental Health, 1975), pp. 84–88.

6. Otto Pollak, *The Criminality of Women* (Philadelphia: University of Pennsylvania Press, 1950).

7. Francis T. Cullen, Kathryn M. Golden, and John B. Cullen, "Sex and Delinquency," *Criminology* (November 1979), 17:301–310; G. F. Jensen and R. Eve, "Sex Differences in Delinquency: An Examination of Popular Sociological Explanations;" *Criminology* (1976), 13:427–448; S. Norland and N. Shover, "Gender, Roles and Female Criminality: Some Critical Comments," *Criminology* (1977) 15:87–104.

8. C. Giordano and S. A. Cernkovich, "On Complicating the Relationship between Liberation and Delinquency," *Social Problems* (April 1979), 26:467–481.

9. H. H. A. Cooper, "Woman as Terrorist," in Freda Adler and Rita Simon, eds., *The Criminology of Deviant Women* (Boston: Houghton Mifflin, 1979).

10. E. P. Spears, M. Vega, and I. J. Silverman, "The Female Robber," paper presented at the 1977 Annual Meeting of the American Society of Criminology, Atlanta, Georgia.

11. Richard F. Sparks, " 'Crime as Business' and the Female Offender," Freda Adler and Rita Simon, eds., *The Criminology of Deviant Women* (Boston: Houghton Mifflin, 1979).

12. William A. Bonger, *Criminality and Economic Conditions* (Boston: Little, Brown and Co., 1916).

13. August Bebel, *Women Under Socialism* (New York: New York Labor Co., 1904) [First edition in German, 1883].

14. Dorie Klein and June Kress, "Any Woman's Blues: A Critical Overview of Women, Crime, and the Criminal Justice System," *Crime and Social Justice* (Spring–Summer 1976), 5:34–49.

15. Joseph Weiss, "Liberation and Crime: The Invention of the New Female Criminal," *Crime and Social Justice* (Fall–Winter 1976), 6:17–27.

16. Stuart S. Nagel and Lenore J. Weitzman, "Women as Litigants," *Hastings Law Journal* (November 1971), 23:171–181.

17. Carolyn Engel Temen, "Discriminatory Sentencing of Women: The Argument for ERA in a Nutshell," *American Criminal Law Review* (Winter 1973): 358–372.

18. Leo Kanowitz, *Women and the Law* (Albuquerque: University of New Mexico Press, 1969).

19. Yona Cohn, "Criteria for the Probation Officer's Recommendations to the Juvenile Court," in Peter G. Garabedian and Don C. Gibbens, eds., *Becoming Delinquent* (Chicago: Aldine Press, 1970); Robert M. Terry, "Discrimination in the Handling of Juvenile Offenders by Social Control Agencies," *Journal of Research in Crime and Delinquency* (1967), 4:218–230.

20. R. R. Ardite, F. Goldberg, Jr., M. M. Hartle, H. H. Peters, and W. R. Phelps, "The Sexual Segregation of American Prisons," *Yale Law Journal* (May 1973): 1253–1268.

21. Linda R. Singer, "Women in the Correctional Process," *American Criminal Law Review* (Winter 1973): 300–308.

22. Freda Adler, *Sisters in Crime* (New York: McGraw-Hill, 1975); Rita Simon, *op. cit.*

23. U.N. Document E/CONF. 66/3, Add. 1 paras. 82–94.

24. U.N. Document A/CONF. 56/3,.paras. 95–109.

25. *Op. cit.*, n. 23.

26. *Op. cit.*, n. 24.

27. *Ibid.*, 56/10, paras. 18–19.

28. U.N. Document E/CN. 5/536, para. 69D.

29. General Assembly Resolution 3021 (XXXII), para. 4 of 19 December 1972.

30. Report of the Secretary General on Crime Prevention and Control A/32/199.

31. *Ibid.*

32. *Ibid.*

33. *Ibid.*

34. *Ibid.*

35. *Ibid.*

36. *Ibid.*

37. *Ibid.*

38. Freda Adler, "The Interaction between Women's Emancipation and Female Criminality: A Cross-Cultural Perspective," *International Journal of Criminology and Penology* (1977), 5:101–112.

39. *Op. cit.*, n. 24.

CHAPTER TWO

WESTERN EUROPE

1. Female Criminality in the Netherlands

G. J. N. BRUINSMA, C. I. DESSAUR, AND R.
W. J. V. VAN HEZEWIJK

Gerben Jan Nicolass Bruinsma is Lecturer and Research Associate at the Institute of Criminology, Nijmegen University. His primary interest in the field is theory formation in sociology and criminology. He is preparing a doctoral thesis on "Deviant Socialization" in which a general theory of the development of deviant behavior is tested. His publications include: (with R. van Hezewijk), "Criminologists, Officers and Decisions" (in Dutch), *Delikt en Delinkwent* (1978), 8, 10; (with M. A. Zwaneburg), "Applied Research Analyses" (in Dutch), *Delikt en Delinkwent* (1977), 7, 1. He presented the following papers: *Discretionary Justice in the Netherlands,* presented at the Annual Meeting of the American Society of Criminology, 1978; (with J. Fiselier) *The Poverty of Victimology,* presented at the Third International Symposium on Victimology, Munster, Federal Republic of Germany, 1979; *Explaining Women's Crime,* presented at the conference on Cross Cultural Research organized by the Research Committee for the Sociology of Deviance and Social Control of the International Sociological Association, the Hague, 1979.

Catharina Irma Dessaur is Professor and Director of the Institute of Criminology, Nijmegen University. Her primary interest in the field is the history of ideas with regard to the social sciences. She is a novelist and essayist under the pseudonym of Andreas Burnier. Her publications include: *Foundations of The-*

ory Formation in Criminology: A Methodological Analysis (s'-Gravenhage: Mouton, 1971); *Science between Culture and Counter-Culture,* commemoration speech, October 19, 1973 (Nijmegen: Dekker & Van de Vegt, 1973). "Towards a Macrosocial Conflict Model in Criminology," *Criminology between the Rule of Law and the Outlaws* (Deventer: Kluwer, 1976); *Women Education and Culture,* expert report for the Standing Conference of European Ministers of Education, Strasbourg, 1979. "Rape: The Last Resort of Patriarchy," *Abstracts on Criminology and Penology* (Leiden, 1979). She presented the following paper: *Criminology's Inhuman Humanism,* presented at the 8th International Congress on Criminology, Lisbon, 1978.

René Wilhelmus Jacobus Vincentius van Hezewijk is Lecturer and Research Associate at the Institute of Criminology, Nijmegen University. His primary interest in the field is theory formation and theory appraisal in criminology. He is preparing a doctoral thesis on the role of (implicit) metaphysics in some criminological and sociological theories. His publications include: (with G. Bruinsma), "Women's Crime: The Achilles' Heel of Criminology" (in Dutch), *Tijdschrift voor Criminologie* (1979), 21, 5; "The Selected Company of Suspects and Convicts" (in Dutch), *Kultuurleven* (1979), 46, 3; (with R. de Vries), "Systems Theory and the Philosophy of Science," *Annals of Systems Research* (1978), 7 (with G. Bruinsma), "On Decisions in the Penal Process" (in Dutch), *Delikt en Delinkwent* (1978), 8, 6.

1. Introduction

The feminist movement, which had its first heyday at the start of this century, showed a revival in the 1960s and is now a worldwide phenomenon. Owing to this "second feminist wave," the social sciences developed a new kind of interest in the social position of women and their sex-specific behavior and commenced a search for possible theoretical explanations. In criminology, in which women were either the ignored sex, as in all human sciences (history, economics, politicology, and large areas of sociology), or the sex whose behavior was interpreted on the basis of masculinist projections (Freudian psychodynamics), there were also signs of revived interest in women and of a critical reevaluation in criminological theory concerning them.[1]

A reconsideration of female criminality requires above all an inventory of the available data. For the Netherlands and for the period 1962–76,[2] we analyzed the figures with respect to registered criminality.[3] We also refer to three Dutch studies of self-reported crime in which women were questioned as well.

First, inventories of crime figures will be presented in sections 2, 3 and 4. Section 5 presents the discussion and interpretation of these findings. Three questions must be formulated which served as the basic problem statement of our study, analogous to the findings of sections 2, 3, and 4:

1. How can the quantitative and qualitative differences between female and male criminality be explained?[4]
2. Can the quantitative and qualitative differences in criminal behavior between categories of women be explained on the basis of the figures presented here?
3. To which extent are female and male offenders treated differently by officials at the various levels of the criminal justice system?[5]

A fourth question relates to what we shall call the "emancipation hypothesis" (Adler, 1976), according to which the increasing emancipation of women will lead to an increase of their relative contribution to the total criminality, to a wider variation of the offenses committed by them, or to an increased female recidivism.[6] We shall attempt to interpret the emancipation concept insofar as it is related to criminal behavior.

2. Differences in Criminality between Men and Women

The first problem mentioned in the introduction concerned the inventory and explanation of the qualitative and quantitative differences in criminality between men and women. This section focuses on the inventory of these differences for which we chiefly use the (official) figures on registered crime. Arrest rates and conviction figures are considered in this context. Section 2.2 presents a few results of self-reported crime studies. A possible explanation of the differences found is discussed in section 5.

2.1 *Arrest Rates.* An indication of the crime trend is found in the surveys (published annually in the Netherlands) of offenses and suspects known to the police. These annual surveys give the absolute figures, arranged by sex, by type of offense, and by suspect age (adults and minors). (Note: unless otherwise indicated, the absolute numbers have not been corrected for population structure.) Figure 1 presents a survey of the trend in female criminality. In recent years the percentage of female suspects of offenses known to the police has generally shown a slight decline (this percentage is made up of figures for minors as well as adults). The contribution of women to adult criminality is shown to diminish, whereas the contribution of girls to juvenile criminality is on the increase.

Figure 1. Percentage of female suspects (divided into adults and minors up to age 18) of the total number of suspects of offenses known to the police over the period 1962–76.

Source: Central Bureau of Statistics, *Maandstatistiek voor Politie,* 1964–77.)

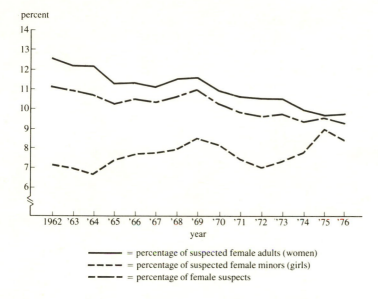

————— = percentage of suspected female adults (women)
– – – – = percentage of suspected female minors (girls)
— – — – = percentage of female suspects

Despite a decrease in clearance rates, the total number of suspects known to the police has doubled during this period. Table 1 gives an impression of this situation. Tentatively it can be concluded that the number of female suspects increased in the period 1962–76 but that the number of male suspects increased slightly more. Dividing the suspects in minors and adults, we observe a stronger increase for girls than for women in their contribution

Table 1.   Number of Reported Offenses, Clearance Rates, and Number of Suspects Known to Police, by Age and Sex.

	Absolute Number of Offenses Reported	Clearance Rates	Number of Suspects Known to Police	Adults		Minors	
				Male	Female	Male	Female
2	142,131	75,134 (52.8%)	79,365	51,126 (100%)	7,307 (100%)	19,449 (100%)	1,483 (100%)
6	519,490	168,161 (32%)	162,400	113,142 (221%)	11,918 (163%)	34,212 (176%)	3,128 (210%)

rce: Adapted from Central Bureau of Statistics, *Maandstatistiek voor Politie,* 1964–77.

to the total amount of crime. In section 3 we will pay more specific attention to minor and adult *female* suspects. In the next subsections we shall review the quantitative and qualitative differences between men and women (subsection 2.1.1.) and between boys and girls (subsection 2.1.2.).

2.1.1. *Men and women.* The first question is whether there are specific offenses for which women are more often known to the police than men. This is not the case. Figure 2 shows that the proportion of women in the total number of adult suspects has slightly decreased. The number of female suspects of offenses against life and the person also decreases, not only proportionally to men, but also in absolute figures (Table 2a).

The percentage of females suspected of offenses against public order and authority remained constant. The percentage of females suspected of of-

Figure 2. Percentage of *adult* female suspects (>18) of the total number of adult suspects, for offense categories known to the police over the period 1962–76.
(**Source:** Central Bureau of Statistics. *Maandstatistiek voor Politie.* 1964–77.)

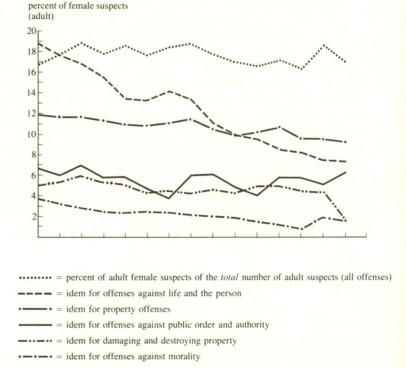

percent of female suspects
(adult)

········ = percent of adult female suspects of the *total* number of adult suspects (all offenses)

▬ ▬ ▬ ▬ = idem for offenses against life and the person

·▬▬▬· = idem for property offenses

▬▬▬▬ = idem for offenses against public order and authority

▬··▬·· = idem for damaging and destroying property

·▬·▬·▬· = idem for offenses against morality

Table 2a. Absolute Number of Adult Females Suspected of Offenses Known to the Police, by Offense Categories. In Parentheses the Percentage of the Total Number of (Male and Female) Suspects Known to the Police.

	Property Offenses	Damaging and Destroying Property Offenses	Offenses Against Life and the Person	Offenses against Public Order and Authority	Offenses against Morality	Total of All Offenses *	Of which Shoplifting †
1962	4,066	166	2,125	179	154	7,307	1,960
	(17.5)	(6.2)	(19.1)	(6.9)	(3.8)	(12.5)	(73.8)
1963	4,345	146	1,926	160	130	7,281	2,309
	(17.9)	(5.5)	(17.9)	(6.2)	(3.2)	(12.2)	(72.9)
1964	4,887	175	1,910	199	113	7,751	2,982
	(19.2)	(6.0)	(17.1)	(7.0)	(2.8)	(12.2)	(76.6)
1965	4,672	168	1,729	184	98	7,739	2,937
	(18.2)	(5.4)	(16.1)	(5.9)	(2.3)	(11.7)	(74.2)
1966	5,146	178	1,422	198	90	7,748	3,420
	(18.5)	(5.2)	(13.4)	(5.9)	(2.3)	(11.3)	(76.2)
1967	5,340	158	1,447	153	103	8,000	3,426
	(18.0)	(4.5)	(13.4)	(4.6)	(2.4)	(11.1)	(75.0)
1968	5,910	160	1,508	169	108	8,696	3,678
	(18.6)	(4.5)	(14.1)	(3.8)	(2.5)	(11.3)	(72.5)
1969	6,499	167	1,450	256	91	9,268	4,351
	(19.1)	(4.4)	(13.4)	(6.0)	(2.2)	(11.4)	(70.9)
1970	6,604	180	1,138	252	74	9,134	4,492
	(17.9)	(4.6)	(11.0)	(6.0)	(2.0)	(10.8)	(67.4)
1971	7,068	179	1,015	193	55	9,482	4,789
	(17.0)	(4.4)	(10.1)	(4.8)	(1.6)	(10.5)	(62.2)
1972	7,411	211	992	232	49	9,935	5,090
	(16.7)	(4.9)	(9.6)	(5.1)	(1.5)	(10.4)	(62.6)
1973	7,699	245	937	286	35	10,223	5,270
	(17.2)	(5.1)	(8.7)	(5.6)	(1.1)	(10.4)	(63.0)
1974	7,242	235	824	281	21	9,703	4,989
	(16.2)	(4.6)	(8.3)	(6.0)	(0.8)	(9.8)	(58.5)
1975	8,091	261	778	267	51	10,832	5,533
	(17.1)	(4.5)	(7.6)	(5.1)	(1.8)	(9.7)	(57.1)
1976	8,732	272	840	380	42	11,918	5,893
	(17.3)	(4.2)	(7.5)	(6.2)	(1.5)	(9.5)	(53.6)

Source: Central Bureau of Statistics, *Maandstatistiek voor Politie,* 1964–77.

*Total for adult females suspected of offenses reported to the police; not the total of the row.
†The shoplifting figure is included in the figure for property offenses.

fenses against morality and damaging and destroying property offenses showed a slight decline.

The greatest contribution by adult females was made to *property offenses*. The constant percentage of female suspects in this category averaged 17 percent from 1963 on. The absolute number of females suspected of property offenses doubled during this period, as did the absolute number of male suspects. Separate consideration of shoplifting in the category of property offenses reveals that the total number of shoplifting suspects showed a four-fold increase, from 2660 in 1962 to 4015 in 1976. The number of male suspects was 700 in 1962 and 5121 in 1976 (7.3 times as many); the number of female suspects was 1960 in the year 1962 and 5894 in 1976 (3 times as many). Table 2a presents, among other things, a survey of absolute numbers and percentages of shoplifters.

As pointed out, the absolute number of female suspects is increasing, the relative number is decreasing, and the distribution over the various types of offense is different. The above is well illustrated in a classical criminological research subject: shoplifting by women. Figure 3 and Table 2a clearly show that the absolute number of shopliftings committed by women is steadily increasing. The *relative number* of women among the suspects, however, is decreasing from 1967 on.

If *opportunity* is considered an important factor, then the above data suggest a marked increase in shopping by men.[7] Since about 1966 (Provo movement), men have apparently become less ashamed of shopping. Shopping has become a less typical activity of women (housewives). An additional factor is the fairly general introduction of the five-day working week in 1961. Men had an opportunity to go shopping on Saturdays. A purely economic explanation (greater affluence, more supermarkets, more temptation) is untenable, for male and female crime figures would keep abreast if this were a valid argument.

2.1.2. *Boys and Girls*. Table 2b presents the corresponding figures for females under age 18. Because of the smaller contribution of minors in the population, the percentages fluctuate more than the adult percentages. The relative contribution of girls to property offenses shows a slight increase; but that to destroying or damaging property offenses, offenses against life and the person, against public order and authority, and against morality shows some decrease. A striking feature is the increasing contribution of girls to shoplifting: from 20.5 percent in 1962 to 32.1 percent in 1976.

An even more striking fact, however, is that the women's contribution to adult shoplifting greatly exceeds the girls' contribution to juvenile shoplifting, yet diminishes over the years. We are probably dealing here with a not

Figure 3. Absolute number of shoplifting cases with female suspects, and percentages adult female suspects of total number of known suspects of shoplifting, 1962–76.
Source: Central Bureau of Statistics, *Maandstatistiek voor Politie*, 1964–77.)

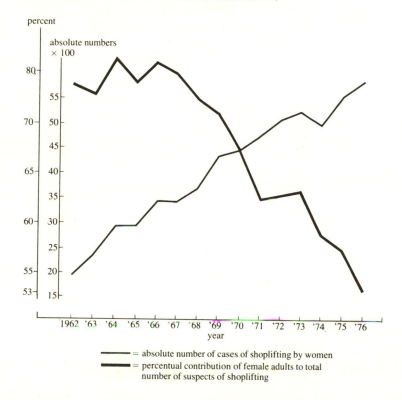

——— = absolute number of cases of shoplifting by women
━━━ = percentual contribution of female adults to total
number of suspects of shoplifting

readily explainable phenomenon that could be described by the term "equality tendency." This tendency perhaps originates from changing views on what a person (of a given sex) *can* or *cannot* do. Particularly in the instance of shoplifting, it is remarkable that men are more involved in shoplifting *when* shopping by men is more readily accepted as "normal." Apparently, it is also more normal for girls nowadays to do their *own* shopping instead of leaving it up to mother. The greater freedom and increased buying power of teenagers is perhaps somewhat more pronounced during this period in girls than in boys (overtaking effect).

The contrast between the adults (Table 2a) and the minors (Table 2b) is also conspicuous for other offense categories. Although the difference is less marked than in shoplifting, the relative contribution of girls to the total of

Table 2b. Absolute Number of Female *Minors* Suspected of Offenses Known to the Police, by Offense Categories. In Parentheses the Percentages of Female Minors of the Total Number of Juvenile Suspects (Boys and Girls) Known to the Police.

	Property Offenses	Damaging and Destroying Property Offenses	Offenses Against Life and the Person	Offenses against Public Order and Authority	Offenses against Morality	Total of All Offenses *	Of which Shoplifting †
1962	1,232 (8.0)	58 (4.5)	75 (10.2)	17 (3.6)	12 (1.5)	1,483 (8.3)	533 (20.5)
1963	1,181 (7.9)	23 (1.5)	66 (9.1)	29 (7.7)	24 (2.4)	1,422 (7.0)	517 (18.0)
1964	1,273 (7.8)	20 (1.4)	92 (10.4)	20 (4.3)	20 (1.4)	1,445 (6.6)	603 (18.7)
1965	1,398 (7.7)	40 (2.6)	81 (9.1)	30 (4.3)	8 (0.9)	1,620 (7.4)	675 (20.8)
1966	1,441, (8.9)	43 (2.5)	51 (6.0)	24 (3.3)	6 (0.7)	1,624 (7.6)	743 (23.7)
1967	1,478 (8.9)	28 (1.8)	81 (10.8)	22 (3.2)	13 (1.5)	1,716 (7.7)	712 (24.7)
1968	1,686 (6.3)	34 (2.2)	61 (7.7)	24 (3.1)	7 (0.7)	1,914 (7.8)	940 (26.6)
1969	1,873 (9.9)	23 (1.4)	68 (7.8)	23 (2.7)	9 (1.1)	2,129 (8.4)	1,041 (27.7)
1970	1,797 (9.3)	38 (2.2)	49 (5.7)	35 (3.5)	6 (0.9)	2,077 (8.1)	1,036 (28.1)
1971	1,828 (8.5)	32 (1.9)	46 (4.8)	45 (3.8)	5 (0.8)	2,074 (7.3)	1,023 (30.6)
1972	1,914 (7.8)	25 (1.4)	57 (5.9)	25 (2.4)	14 (2.4)	2,124 (6.9)	1,096 (28.6)
1973	2,114 (8.2)	32 (0.7)	35 (3.3)	49 (4.5)	5 (0.9)	2,318 (7.1)	1,225 (29.7)
1974	2,208 (8.6)	54 (2.2)	48 (4.8)	54 (4.8)	5 (0.9)	2,460 (7.5)	1,321 (29.5)
1975	2,522 (10.2)	59 (2.1)	56 (6.0)	52 (4.4)	3 (0.6)	2,763 (8.8)	1,567 (30.9)
1976	2,827 (9.8)	77 (2.2)	75 (5.8)	44 (3.0)	7 (1.3)	3,128 (8.4)	1,736 (32.1)

Source: Adapted from Central Bureau of Statistics, *Maandstatistiek voor Politie*, 1964–77.

*Total of female suspects (up to age 18) of offenses known to constabulary and municipal police. *Not* the total of the row.

†The figure for shoplifting is included in the figure for property offenses.

juvenile suspects of property offenses is still only half as great as the relative contribution of women to the total of adult suspects of property offenses.

Destroying or damaging property offenses[8] are committed more frequently by adult women than by girls; and the same applies to offenses against life and the person, against public order and authority, and against morality. Are women more "criminal" than girls? Or are boys more "criminal" than men? A simple comparison of the relative crime figures for girls and women, and for boys and men, respectively (Table 3), reveals that the girl to woman ratio changes, whereas the boy to man ratio remains relatively constant.

Table 3. Girl to Woman Ratio and Boy to Man Ratio of Crime Figures for the Period 1962–76.

	Girl : Woman	Boy : Man		Girl : Woman	Boy : Man
1962	1 : 4.9	1 : 3.1	1972	1 : 4.7	1 : 2.9
—	—	—	1973	1 : 4.4	1 : 2.9
1965	1 : 4.8	1 : 3.1	1974	1 : 3.9	1 : 2.9
—	—	—	1975	1 : 3.9	1 : 3.5
1971	1 : 4.6	1 : 3.4	1976	1 : 3.8	1 : 3.3

Source: Adapted from Central Bureau of Statistics, *Maandstatistiek voor Politie*, 1964–77.

2.2. *Convictions and Dismissals*. Generally speaking, the third and the fourth phase to be considered in a study of female criminality comprises the phase in which the public prosecutor and the judge deal with the offenses brought to the notice of the police. It is on this phase that most data are available. In the Netherlands an additional factor is of importance in this respect: dismissal of cases by the public prosecutor.[9]

Before comparing the dismissal figures and convictions of males and females for a number of years, it seems advisable to tabulate the figures for men and women per 100,000 inhabitants. Table 4 shows that the number of convicted males per 100,000 population decreased by 50 percent from 1947 to 1973. The number of convicted females in 1973 was only one third of the number in 1947. The number of convicted females in the population decreased relatively more than the number of convicted males. As already pointed out in section 2.1.2., however, these data do not warrant the conclusion that *crime* is declining. A number of factors cause a decline in the official figures for certain offense types. These factors are, briefly, a change in views on the seriousness of offenses (offenses against morality, and against life and person insofar as insult and such categories are concerned), an increased willingness of public prosecutors to dismiss cases, a lower clearance rate, and an increased incidence of less serious property offenses

Table 4. Number of Convicted Persons Per 100,000 Inhabitants, by Sex, for the Period 1947–73.

	1947	1948	1949	1950	1951	1952	1953	1954	1955
M	856	855	741	728	788	811	678	425	514
F	151	157	138	129	121	136	117	97	90

	1956	1957	1958	1959	1960	1961	1962	1963	1964
M	499	500	503	481	500	482	454	457	485
F	86	85	82	79	83	82	78	81	89

	1965	1966	1967	1968	1969	1970	1971	1972	1973
M	470	504	524	530	503	485	475	488	475
F	85	87	93	92	82	74	64	60	54

Source: Central Bureau of Statistics, *Criminele Statistiek*, 1949–75.

with consequently relatively more frequent dismissals. Some of these factors can be further considered on the basis of official figures. Table 1 has already shown the diminishing clearance rate. It is difficult to trace the influence of changing views on the seriousness of crimes, but two facts support a possible influence on the decreased absolute number of insult offenses reported to the police (from 2892 in 1962 to 1002 in 1976), and the only slight increase in the number of reported bicycle thefts (one of the most underreported crimes in the Netherlands; cf. Fiselier, 1978).

The number of dismissals, and the difference between men and women in this respect, will be discussed in further detail. A large number of offenses reported to the police, with known suspects, never reaches the courts. The discretionary power of the prosecutor may lead to a systematic *bias* in the selection of offenses to be dismissed. It may be that cases involving female suspects are dismissed more readily (for appropriate or inappropriate reasons), or that some types of offense involving women are more, and others less frequently dismissed than corresponding offense types involving men.

Table 5 presents a review of the ratio between convictions and dismissals, and the proportion of female convicts and dismissals. These figures also show that the total number of dismissals increased significantly during the period 1956–73, both absolutely and in relation to the number of convictions. While in 1956 the number of convictions was nearly twice that of dismissals, in 1973 the numbers were virtually equal. (Note: the two figures are not entirely comparable; we only mean to give an impression of the relative increase in the numbers.)

Table 5. Convicts and Persons Whose Case Was Dismissed by Sex, for the Period 1956-73.

Year	Convicts [1]					Persons Whose Case Was Dismissed [2]				
	M	%[3]	F	%[4]		M	%[5]	F	%[6]	
1956	28,849	(66.8)	3,788	(55.0)	32,637	14,322	(33.2)	3,105	(45.0)	17,427
1957	28,983	(66.0)	3,812	(54.7)	32,795	14,934	(34.0)	3,162	(45.3)	18,096
1958	29,687	(66.0)	3,756	(53.3)	33,443	15,324	(34.0)	3,297	(46.7)	18,621
1959	28,907	(64.1)	3,678	(52.0)	32,585	16,217	(35.9)	3,401	(48.0)	19,618
1960	30,635	(65.0)	3,937	(54.8)	34,572	16,518	(35.0)	3,242	(45.2)	19,760
1961	30,477	(59.8)	3,957	(53.7)	34,424	20,562	(40.2)	3,413	(46.3)	23,975
1962	29,893	(59.4)	3,838	(54.6)	33,731	20,430	(40.6)	3,190	(45.4)	23,620
1963	30,504	(60.0)	4,067	(56.7)	34,571	20,310	(40.0)	3,106	(43.3)	23,416
1964	33,279	(60.9)	4,507	(38.1)	37,786	21,337	(39.1)	3,251	(41.9)	24,588
1965	33,436	(60.7)	4,408	(59.3)	37,844	21,621	(39.3)	3,031	(40.7)	24,652
1966	34,607	(38.6)	4,395	(58.2)	39,002	24,433	(41.4)	3,157	(41.8)	24,590
1967	36,197	(60.1)	4,820	(57.7)	41,017	24,036	(39.9)	3,527	(42.3)	27,563
1968	37,948	(60.5)	4,921	(57.0)	42,869	24,763	(39.5)	3,706	(43.0)	28,469
1969	37,605	(56.3)	4,517	(47.4)	42,122	29,194	(43.7)	5,007	(52.6)	34,201
1970	37,833	(55.4)	4,160	(43.6)	41,993	30,510	(44.6)	5,372	(56.4)	35,882
1971	39,987	(55.2)	3,737	(39.0)	42,724	35,201	(46.8)	5,851	(61.0)	41,052
1972	40,230	(52.4)	3,628	(36.5)	43,858	36,581	(47.6)	6,304	(63.5)	42,885
1973	40,576	(52.1)	3,409	(35.0)	43,985	37,327	(47.9)	6,339	(65.0)	43,666

Source: Adapted from Central Bureau of Statistics, *Criminele Statistiek,* 1956-73.

[1] Including persons pronounced guilty, including offenses against laws other than the penal code, e.g., against Traffic Act, Narcotics Act, Copyright Act, Economic Offenses Act, etc. Figures pertain to convicted persons, not to number convictions, from Table 1 of *Criminele Statistiek* 1952-73.

[2] Figures pertain to number of dismissals, not to number of persons dismissed, for all offenses (see note 1, above).

[3] Percentual male contribution to total number of cases.

[4] Percentual female contribution to total number of cases.

[5] Percentual male contribution to total number of cases dismissed.

[6] Percentual female contribution to total number of cases dismissed.

The relative number of dismissals of the total number of cases involving female suspects increased from 45.0 to 65.0 percent. The percentage of dismissals of cases involving male suspects showed a smaller increase. This might indicate that cases involving women were more readily dismissed, especially from 1969 on. It is possible that female suspects have had relatively more benefit from a humanization of the prosecutorial policy with regard to dismissal. Perhaps the "courtesy hypothesis" applies in this context: officials of the criminal justice system take a more "courteous" attitude towards female suspects, at least so far as "typically" female offenses are concerned.

The question arises whether the increase of dismissals and the decrease of convictions applies to all offense types. Data from the U.S.A., for example, show that the number of female property crimes is increasing more rapidly than the number of female offenses against life and the person (L. Crites, 1976, p. 34). For a number of years (in order to insure overview), Appendix 1 lists the number of convictions and dismissals for men and women, and the female percentage of this total, for a number of offense categories in the Netherlands (cf. columns 1 and 2).

This confirms the conclusions reached on the basis of the police figures: female offenses against life and the person are diminishing. Women may have become more emancipated, but they have not become more aggressive. The police figures and the conviction rates indicate that offenses against life and person show both an absolute and a percentual decrease. There is an increase (by about 1100) of the number of dismissals of cases of offenses against life and person from 1956 to 1973. However, the number of dismissals of cases involving male suspects is significantly larger.

The number of property offenses committed by women is increasing. Both the absolute number of convictions and the absolute number of dismissals increased from 1956 to 1973. But the relative contribution of women has shown only a partial increase. The percentual police figures remain more or less constant, yet the percentages of convictions are diminishing after an increase (cf. 1960 and 1965 in Appendix 1). So there were relatively less female convicts in 1973 than in 1956, and relatively more dismissals for female suspects. To sum up: the number of females who show criminal behavior is increasing less rapidly than the corresponding number of males. Women, however, seem to obtain dismissal of their cases more readily, for reasons which cannot be easily established. The decision is up to the public prosecutor (nearly always a man). This greatly limits the number of possible explanations. One practical reason might be the limited availability of adequate penitentiaries (in which case the number of fines imposed on women should be larger). There are no data on the severity of sentencing.

An explanation of the diminishing (at least not increasing) contribution of women to criminality will be discussed later (cf. section 5).

2.3. *Self-report Studies*. Official figures on crime trends are known to have several disadvantages. An optimal impression of the trends could be gained if the *real* male and female criminality could be measured over, say, the last twenty-five years. But it is impossible to do this. An even partly reliable estimate of male and female delinquency is not available; not even for the period since 1970. A number of recent *dark number studies*, however, affords a general impression of male and female criminality in the recent past.

In their report on a *dark number study* among female university students,

R. Jongman and G. Smale (1972) present a comparison with the criminal behavior of male students. Female students commit evidently less crimes. In the questionnaires, 401 female students reported 1649 offenses, whereas 335 male students reported 4977 offenses. A female offender commits an average of 4.1 crimes, versus an average of 13.8 crimes per male offender, that is, a ratio of 1 : 3.4.

Both the number of offenses per person and the number of persons who committed one or several offenses was smaller for female than for male students. Of the female students, 64.6 percent had committed at least one of the 20 offenses listed in the questionnaire; for the male students this was 94.1 percent. There were fewer multiple offenders among the female than among the male students: the female multiple offenders averaged 6.4 offenses (modal category between 1 and 5), while the males averaged 14.7 offenses (modal category between 11 and 20).

The arrest risk (ratio between officially reported and self-reported offenses) did not differ much between the sexes: it was 3.0/1000 offenses for the female and 3.6/1000 offenses for the male students.

As already pointed out, men commit more offenses than women. The distribution over the various offense types also differs. Women commit relatively more thefts, particularly shoplifting, than men. Men on the other hand commit more offenses such as fraud or joyriding. Otherwise, few differences were observed.

L. Veendrick's study (1976), on a much larger scale, also shows that more men than women occasionally commit an offense, the male to female ratio being about 60 : 40 (for officially reported criminality, however, the ratio is 90 : 10). Moreover, men commit more diverse offenses than women. Women more often commit theft; men more often drive while under the influence and more often destroy property. In nearly every separate category, however, the number of male offenders exceeds that of female offenders.

Veendrick also studied the relation between age and sex on the one hand and the type of offense on the other. He found for both sexes that criminality increases up to age 17 and then decreases. For driving under the influence, however, Veendrick found the highest figure for females between 27 and 34 years, while for males the maximum was at age 50–64.

These are the only two Dutch studies in which *dark numbers* of relevance to our first problem were published. A remarkable feature in these studies is the difference between *dark numbers* and offenses known to the police. Men generally commit more offenses than women, but the difference is much smaller than the police figures suggest. A distinction should be made between persons who committed offenses (regardless of the number of offenses) and the average (or modal) number of offenses committed by an offender of one sex or the other. Men prove to commit more offenses per individual than women. The relatively large contribution of property offenses to female criminality can in part be explained by the smaller number of offenses committed on average by women (cf. Table 6). For property offenses, and especially the milder forms such as larceny and shoplifting, we find that women are more constant offenders throughout life than men. Figure 4 indicates that the percentage of offenders in the inquiry diminishes with increasing age, but that this trend is stronger for men than for women. We will return to this point in section 5.

Table 6.   Percentual Contribution of Theft to Total Number of Offenses in the Age Category Concerned.

	Theft		N (Total Number of Offenders per Age Category)	
Age	M	F	M	F
15–17	16%	25%	71	31
18–20	13%	21%	97	59
21–23	23%	15%	121	69
24–26	14%	10%	81	54
27–34	11%	15%	116	78
35–49	5%	7%	98	62
50–64	8%	3%	46	35

Source: L. Veendrick, Figures 5.4 and 5.7, pp. 35 and 38.

3. Differences in Criminality between Female Categories

The previous section discussed the qualitative and quantitative differences between female and male criminality in the Netherlands. So far, this has been the problem which criminologists paid attention to if they were interested in female criminal behavior. Attempts to explain these qualitative and quantitative differences have been guided mainly by monocausal theories of a biological or macrosociological nature. The implicit postulate was that women form a single group and that all women are identical. Variables considered important in explaining male criminal behavior were ignored or hardly considered in these attempts.

This fact is the more remarkable because criminologists have usually tried to explain crime in several ways, as *sophisticated* as possible. Subtle shades

Figure 4. Percentage of persons who committed an offense (specified in the question-naire), by age and sex.
(Source: L. Veendrick, 1976, Fig. 5.3, p. 34.)

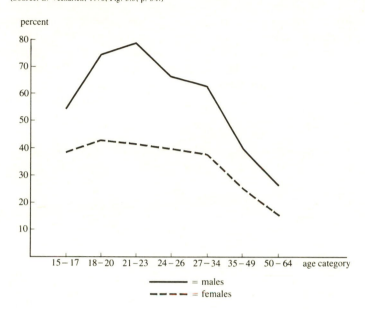

percent

15−17 18−20 21−23 24−26 27−34 35−49 50−64   age category

————— = males
− − − − = females

of difference, it was maintained, can be extremely important in an attempt to explain the various types of criminal behavior in different groups of offenders. Why these variables were ignored in the attempt to explain female criminal behavior, is a question that should be answered by the sociologists of knowledge.

The above-mentioned research practice has brought about little progress in our knowledge of female criminal behavior. In the Netherlands in particular, little empirical research has been done and, perhaps even more important, no or hardly any work has been done in theory formation. This means that anyone who wants to explain why one woman (or group of women) shows criminal behavior while the other woman (or group of women) does not or considerably less so, in fact stands empty-handed. The sole remaining source of inspiration is common sense.

Section 3.1. will first consider the question whether data on a number of characteristics of "criminal" women can be traced with the aid of official crime figures. Section 3.2. considers the results of the (sparse) *self-report studies*. Section 5, finally, briefly examines the extent to which data (if any) are pertinent to existing criminological theories or general theories of behavior and formulates an approach to an explanation of the absence of the initial conditions for criminal behavior in certain groups of women.

3.1. *Official Crime Figures.* It is presumably known that much male criminality is related to age. Younger males are generally more disposed to criminal behavior than older males. In a large proportion of the male population, criminal behavior seems to be dominant only during a particular period of life (adolescence). Only for a limited group of males does criminal behavior show a more persistent character. For women, the contrary would seem to be true: female criminality is less characteristic of a given period of life.

Table 7.   Females Suspected of Offenses, by Age (1955–76).

	1955	*1960*	*1963*	*1968*	*1970*
Adults	8,694	8,690	7,325	8,719	9,160
Minors	1,398	1,771	1,425	1,916	2,080
Total	10,092	10,461	8,750	10,635	11,240
Percentual contribution of minors to total	13.85	16.93	16.29	18.01	18.50

	1971	*1972*	*1974*	*1975*	*1976*
Adults	9,523	10,010	9,761	10,873	11,983
Minors	2,077	1,398	2,467	2,764	3,139
Total	11,600	12,136	12,228	13,637	15,122
Percentual contribution of minors to total	17.90	17.51	20.17	20.26	20.75

Source: Adapted from Central Bureau of Statistics, *Statistisch Jaarboek,* 1962–77.

Table 7 shows that, from 1962 on, the contribution of girls (<19 years) to the total female criminality is less than might be expected on the basis of their contribution to the total female population (which ranges between 20 and 21 percent). We do find that the contribution of girls to the total number of female suspects increased significantly from 1955 to 1977 (from 13.85 to 20.75 percent). This increase is a constant one, apart from some slight dips in 1963 and 1972. These data would seem to warrant the conclusion that the group of girls is making up for arrears in criminality; it was not until 1976 that this group reached a crime level which corresponded with its contribution to the total female population.

However, the above-mentioned increase is not found reflected in the figures on females convicted for offenses. In fact, we observe that the number of convicted girls diminishes. Since the figures on female suspects approximate reality more closely than those on female convictions, this decrease is more likely to be due to a more lenient policy of the criminal justice system than to the fact that criminality among girls did not increase.

Table 8 presents more detailed information on the relation between age and frequency of criminal behavior. We find that in 1962 the highest frequency of convictions lay in age category 21–24; followed by category 40–44; and in equal measures, categories 18–20, 25–29, and 30–34. Girls up to age 18 and the group over age 50 are underrepresented among the convictions. In 1973 we find that the age of categories over 34 show a marked decrease in the number of convictions per 100,000. In this year, crime is mainly concentrated in age group 18–20, followed by age category 30–34. In the course of time, however, all age categories have shown a decline in the number of convictions, from 78 per 100,000 to 54 per 100,-000. The girls (up to age 18) show only a small decrease—less marked than the decrease in the other age categories of convicted women.

Neither the relative decrease in the number of female suspects in relation to male suspects observed in the previous chapter nor the decrease in the number of convicted females can lead to the conclusion that female criminality is declining. While the relative decrease in female suspects was to be ascribed mainly to the marked increase in male suspects, the decrease in the number of convicted females can perhaps be explained by a more lenient attitude of the first-line officials of the criminal justice system: the police and the public prosecutor's office. That these decreases are not "true" decreases is clearly demonstrated in Figures 5 and 6 (and in Appendices 2 and 3).

In Figures 5 and 6, the number of juvenile and adult female suspects in 1962 is assigned the value 100. With the aid of this index figure, the extent to which quantitative changes have occurred in the separate offense categories in the past fifteen years, can be established. During this period the total number of female suspects for all types of offense increased. For girls the figure increased more rapidly than for women (211 vs. 163). This finding is consistent with the hypothesis (advanced in the preceding section) that girls are making up for arrears in their contribution to female criminality.

Focusing on the separate offense categories, we find that property offenses have likewise shown a marked increase, which was slightly quicker among girls than among women (229 vs. 215). While the rise in property offenses can be described as fairly constant, the situation with destroying and damaging property offenses is more complex. For the group of adult

Table 8. Women Pronounced Guilty, by Age, per 100,000 Population of Corresponding Age (Not Including Traffic Act).

Year	12–14 Year	15–17 Year	18–20 Year	21–24 Year	25–29 Year	30–34 Year	35–39 Year	40–44 Year	45–49 Year	50–54 Year	55–59 Year	60–64 Year	65–69 Year	70 and Over	Total
1962	14	65	106	126	106	106	103	114	102	85	77	53	36	8	78
1963	14	61	118	123	111	110	116	129	110	83	76	50	37	12	81
1964	8	61	105	139	124	125	126	124	116	113	77	63	55	17	89
1965	11	63	102	130	117	114	118	118	118	94	90	66	38	18	89
1966	20	64	100	133	110	111	110	120	105	101	77	65	42	15	87
1967	15	71	117	146	127	128	118	117	108	101	86	62	46	14	93
1968	27	89	129	127	133	122	118	123	98	95	75	59	32	12	92
1969	25	76	127	112	120	103	106	102	88	97	65	49	29	8	82
1970	18	52	127	118	123	98	93	90	79	69	50	38	26	7	74
1971	14	65	105	86	98	89	86	78	71	60	43	37	17	4	64
1972	12	44	102	104	93	99	79	69	60	51	36	26	14	3	60
1973	10	43	100	93	84	95	78	58	49	43	32	20	10	2	54

Source: Central Bureau of Statistics, *Criminele Statistiek*, 1963–75.

Figure 5. Index figures for the number of *adult* female suspects, by offense categories, over the period 1962–76 (1962 = 100).
(**Source:** Central Bureau of Statistics, *Maandstatistiek voor Politie*, 1964–76.)

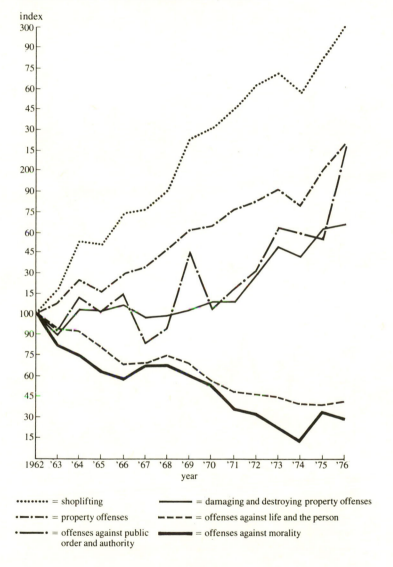

```
•••••••• = shoplifting                          = damaging and destroying property offenses

•—•—•• = property offenses           – – – – = offenses against life and the person

•——• = offenses against public   ━━━ = offenses against morality
        order and authority
```

Figure 6. Index figures for the number of suspected female *minors*, by offense categories, over the period 1962–76 (1962=100).
(**Source:** Central Bureau of Statistics, *Maandstatistiek voor Politie,* 1964–76)

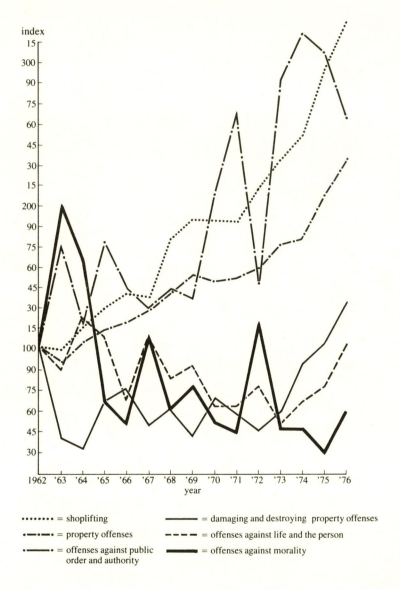

•••••••• = shoplifting   ———————— = damaging and destroying property offenses

•—•—•—• = property offenses   — — — — = offenses against life and the person

•————• = offenses against public   ▬▬▬▬▬ = offenses against morality
order and authority

female suspects, the number of destroying and damaging property offenses remains fairly constant from 1962 to 1972 (about 100); a marked increase is observed after 1972 (from 108 to 164). For the group of girls, the number of destroying and damaging property offenses shows fairly marked variations but remains below 70 until 1973. Only during the last three years of the period covered did the number of offenses in this category increase rapidly (from 55 to 133); it is to be noted that the absolute number on which these index figures are based is fairly small (166), so that minor changes are very conspicuous.

In the category offenses against life and the person, we find a fairly constant decrease for adult women (from 100 to 40); this can largely be explained on the basis of diminished prosecution in insult cases. The group of girls is less steady, and it is more difficult to detect a particular trend–even though the index figure remains below the 1962 level (except in 1964 and 1965).

Both female groups show an increase in offenses against public order and authority, but this cannot be described as constant. The peak values in 1969 and 1970 are largely explained by the marked social unrest in the Netherlands during this period. This was the time when demonstrations by a wide variety of social groups (students, trade unions) were the order of the day. At this time there are no discernible events which could explain other pronounced dips or peaks in the graph.

The number of offenses against morality committed by women shows a constant decline. Girls show a decline, too, but a less constant one. (The variable character of the decline of offenses against morality committed by female minors can be largely explained by the fact that this index figure is based on a very small number of suspects.)

The offense most frequently committed by females in the Netherlands is shoplifting. Both girls and women show a very marked increase in the incidence of this specific offense. For women the increase is evenly distributed from 100 in 1962 to 300 in 1976; for girls it extends from 100 in 1962 to 326 in 1976. An explanation will be discussed in a separate section.

The contribution of each type of offense to total female criminality is shown in Tables 9 and 10. A striking feature is the large number of both minors and adults suspected of property offenses. In 1976 property offenses accounted for about 90 percent of all offenses committed by girls and 73 percent of all crimes by women. In the group of girls the relative contribution of property offenses has slightly increased in the past fifteen years, from 83.07 to 90.37 percent. In the adult group, this percentage rises rapidly during the 1960s, and then becomes stabilized.

Table 9. Percentages of Suspected *Women*, by Offense Categories, Over the Period 1962–76.

	Property Offenses	Damaging and Destroying Property Offenses	Offenses Against Life and the Person	Offenses Against Public Order and Authority	Offenses Against Morality	Other Offenses	Total	Of which Shoplifting
1962	55.64	2.27	29.08	2.45	2.11	8.49	100%	26.82
1963	59.68	2.00	26.45	2.20	1.79	7.88	100%	31.71
1964	63.05	2.26	24.64	2.56	1.46	6.03	100%	38.47
1965	60.37	2.17	22.34	2.38	1.27	11.47	100%	37.95*
1966	66.42	2.30	18.35	2.56	1.16	9.21	100%	44.14
1967	66.75	1.98	18.09	1.91	1.29	9.98	100%	42.83
1968	67.96	1.84	17.30	1.94	1.24	9.72	100%	43.30
1969	70.12	1.80	15.64	2.76	0.98	8.70	100%	46.95
1970	72.30	1.97	12.46	2.75	0.81	9.71	100%	49.18
1971	74.54	1.89	10.70	2.03	0.58	9.26	100%	50.50
1972	74.59	2.12	9.98	2.33	0.49	10.49	100%	51.23
1973	75.31	2.40	9.16	2.80	0.34	9.99	100%	51.55
1974	76.69	2.42	8.49	2.89	0.22	9.29	100%	51.41
1975	74.69	2.41	7.18	2.46	0.47	12.79	100%	51.08
1976	73.26	2.28	7.04	3.19	0.35	13.88	100%	49.45

Source: Adapted from Central Bureau of Statistics, *Maandstatistiek voor Politie,* 1964–77.

Both in the adult and in the juvenile group, the relative contribution of the other offenses remains fairly constant, with the exception of offenses against life and the person committed by adult women, which diminishes from 29 percent in 1962 to 7 percent in 1976. As already pointed out, this can be explained by the fact that insult offenses are hardly reported and prosecuted any longer.

Tables 9 and 10 also indicate the relative contribution of shoplifting; this accounts for half the total of all offenses committed by female offenders (49 percent for women; 55 percent for girls). Both groups show the sharpest rise from 1962 to 1968–69, whereupon women show a degree of stabilization while girls show a slower increase.

The data from the official statistics would seem to warrant the following conclusions:

1. Total female criminality is increasing, the increase being marked in property offenses, and especially shoplifting.
2. Female criminal behavior chiefly involves property offenses.

Table 10. Percentages of Suspected Girls, by Offense Categories, Over the Period 1962–75.

	Property Offenses	Damaging and Destroying Property Offenses	Offenses Against Life and the Person	Offenses Against Public Order and Authority	Offenses Against Morality	Other Offenses	Total	Of which Shoplifting
1962	83.07	3.91	5.05	1.15	0.81	6.01	100%	35.94
1963	83.05	1.61	4.64	2.04	1.69	6.97	100%	36.36
1964	88.09	1.38	6.37	1.38	1.38	1.40	100%	41.73
1965	86.30	2.47	5.00	1.85	0.49	3.89	100%	41.67
1966	88.98	2.65	3.14	1.48	0.37	3.38	100%	45.75
1967	86.13	1.63	4.72	1.28	0.75	5.49	100%	41.49
1968	88.08	1.78	3.19	1.25	0.37	5.33	100%	49.11
1969	87.98	1.08	3.19	1.08	0.42	6.25	100%	48.90
1970	86.52	1.83	2.36	1.69	0.29	7.31	100%	49.88
1971	88.14	1.54	2.22	2.17	0.24	5.69	100%	49.32
1972	90.11	1.18	2.68	1.18	0.66	4.19	100%	51.60
1973	91.19	1.38	1.51	2.11	0.22	3.59	100%	52.85
1974	89.76	2.20	1.95	2.20	0.20	3.69	100%	53.70
1975	91.28	2.14	2.03	1.88	0.11	2.56	100%	56.71
1976	90.37	2.46	2.40	1.41	0.22	3.14	100%	55.50

Source: Adapted from Central Bureau of Statistics, *Maandstatistiek voor Politie*, 1964–76.

3. Criminality among girls shows a decrease which indicates an overtaking effect.
4. Female criminal behavior is concentrated mostly in age group 18–24.
5. Some 50 percent of all female suspects had committed shoplifting.

In the next section we consider the question whether the more reliable *self-report studies* confirm these results and whether these studies yield additional relevant data on female criminality.

It is difficult to reach unequivocal conclusions about the relation between employment and criminal behavior. For younger women, it seems to matter little whether they are employed or still receiving training. For the older women, however, employment outside the home does seem to exert some influence. Housewives are the evidently least criminal group. This relation between employment and criminality has also been studied on a macrosociological level. In her book *Women and Crime,* R. Simon (1975) tested several hypotheses on this subject with the aid of demographic and other statistical data collected in the U.S.A. Her hypotheses can be summarized as follows:

1. With increased participation of women in the labor process, they have increased opportunities to commit certain offense types; for example, theft, fraud, swindling and other *white-collar offenses*.
2. With increased participation, destroying and damaging property offenses are bound to diminish while property offenses increase.

Like Simon, we have resorted to (imperfect) statistics in order to test these hypotheses.

Table 11 shows that, relative to the increase in population in the Netherlands, the total female employed population has shown no spectacular increase. Considering this small increase on the basis of the degree of participation as yardstick, we find that in 1960, 21 percent of *all* women aged 14 and over were employed or practiced a profession, whereas in 1973 this was 22 percent.

Table 11. Number of Employed Women, by Marital Status, for the Years 1947, 1960, 1971, and 1973.

| | Employed Women × 1000 | | | |
	1947	1960	1971	1973
Married	198	173	466	658
Unmarried (Including Divorced and Widowed)	748	755	773	750
Total	944	928	1,239	1,308

Source: A. C. Boelmans-Kleinjan, 1976, p. 1.

According to the first hypothesis, there should be no discernible increase in female property crimes if participation remains unchanged. In the Netherlands, however, the index figure for property crimes rose from 100 to 215.

The above implies that this hypothesis (at least for the Netherlands) is refuted. According to the second hypothesis, aggressive offenses should remain constant or increase in the Netherlands. This is in fact true for aggressive offenses (the index figure rose from 100 in 1962 to 164 in 1976). But offenses against life and the person and against property showed a decrease, even though this is mostly due to reduced prosecution of insult.

Offenses against order and authority show a more marked increase than destroying or damaging property crimes (from an index figure of 100 in

1962 to 212 in 1976). For the time being, the second hypothesis is not refuted for the Netherlands.

3.2. *Self-report Studies*. In their dark number study among female university students, Jongman and Smale (1972) established that the A students (humanities) committed significantly more offenses than the B students (sciences). They also established that A students who commit offenses average a larger number of offenses than B students (15.5 vs. 13 offenses). In both groups of students, property offenses accounted for most of the criminality; and shoplifting was relatively the most frequent property offense.

A students also differed from B students in that they showed a higher incidence of sexual offenses [10] and drug offenses, whereas B students were more inclined to commit aggressive offenses. Jongman and Smale assumed that the greater social engagement of the A students caused more dissatisfaction with social norms, which in turn led to a higher crime rate in this group.

More information can be obtained from Veendrick's study (1976). He found a significant decrease in percentage of female offenders per age group with increasing age. Criminality was highest in the female age group 18–20, followed by the group 15–17, while self-reported crime showed a fairly pronounced decline from age 27 on. Not only did criminality decrease, but the variation in the pattern of offenses also diminished with increasing age.

Of the older women (over 27), 25 percent reported having committed at least one offense; for the younger group, this percentage was significantly larger (43 percent). The younger group mostly committed swindling, vandalism, fencing, and theft.

Female offenders differ not only in age, but day-to-day activities also correlate with the quality and quantity of criminal behavior. Employed women average the largest number of offenses and are least confined to one type of offense. Housewives are the least "criminal," and if they commit an offense, they largely confine themselves to a single type of offense.

For the group of older women (over 27) we find about twice as many offenders (37 percent) among employed women as among housewives (19 percent). Veendrick also established that employed women more readily admit having committed an offense when they are employed at a higher level. However, there is no statistical correlation between type of work and quality of the offense (the latter also applies to younger women). There is no correlation between criminal behavior among housewives and the husbands' professions, nor between criminality among younger women and their level of formal education (in this respect, they differ from young males).

Table 12.   Number of Crimes per Offender for Three Categories of Women Aged 15–26.

	Women in Training (N = 105)		Employed Women (N = 103)		Housewives (N = 19)	
One offense type	58	55.2%	47	45.7%	14	73.7%
2–3 offense types	35	33.3%	41	39.8%	4	21.1%
4 or more offense types	12	11.5%	15	14.6%	1	5.3%
Average number of different crimes per offender	1.90		2.12		1.50	

Source: Adapted from L. Veendrick, *Verborgen en geregistreerde criminaliteit in Groningen*, Institute of Criminology at Groningen, 1976, p. 48.

The most recent dark number study of female criminality is made by Hauber and Kingmans-Schreuder (1978). They found that criminality in younger women (16–25 years) correlates negligibly with employed or domestic work. In the group of older women (>25 years) however, employed women were relatively more criminal than housewives. Housewives were found to commit offenses mostly in relation to family and household (shoplifting); employed women commit more offenses which relate to their work (fraudulent expense accounts, fraudulent use of public transport).

In his study on shoplifting in department stores, Fiselier (1974) found that the arrest rate was highest for girls aged 10–14. The arrest rate subsequently decreases per age category, to remain stable from age 30 on. On the basis of these figures he rejected the stereotyped view that shoplifting is a typical offense of women in the climacterium or of pregnant women. Of the arrested shoplifters age 19 and over, 26 percent were unmarried, 47 percent married, 15 percent divorced, and 12 percent widowed. Fiselier explained the relative overrepresentation of the last two groups with the hypothesis that divorce or loss of the partner is a considerable financial setback for women.

Fiselier found that the majority of arrested female offenders were schoolchildren and students. This is not surprising in view of the large number of juvenile female offenders arrested. Some 25 percent of the arrested female shoplifters were employed women, while only 10 percent were housewives. Shoplifters were evenly distributed over the social strata. Fiselier also found that adult female shoplifters (over age 18) stole more articles than girls (median 2 and 1.3., respectively). Girls preferably stole perfumery articles and costume jewelry, while women preferably stole clothes, foods, and household articles. A striking fact was that the type of article stolen accentuated the role of women in a given phase of life: female shoplifting is typically *sex-role linked*.

To sum up, Dutch criminology is ill informed about female criminality. Empirical or theoretical information is scanty. The few data from different sources (official and self-report figures) nevertheless reveal a constant situation, apart from the important variable age. Self-report studies show a greater contribution of females under age 18 than the official statistics. The most conspicuous feature of female criminality is the dominant position of shoplifting in the offense pattern: about 50 percent of female offenders are shoplifters. These findings are confirmed to some extent by the self-report studies and cannot be explained solely with the hypothesis that officials of the criminal justice system focus selective attention on this offense when women are concerned.

4. Differential Treatment of Women

A question to be considered separately is whether women are treated differently from men in the criminal justice system. There is little information on this question.

In the Netherlands there are considerably more prisons for male than for female offenders. If only for this reason, placement of male offenders in the most "suitable" penitentiary is much simpler than that of female offenders. There are only two prisons for female offenders, whereas for male offenders there are about twenty-four houses of detention, six institutions for juvenile delinquents, ten closed prisons, several open prisons and a labor colony.

The number of female prisoners is small. The average for 1970, for example, was only 38, including 19 women in pretrial detention. (There were 2,568 male prisoners in 1970.) The small number of female prisoners does not enhance ministerial attention for this category.

Unlike the preceding stages in the criminal justice system, imprisonment is an exclusively female situation, with an all-female prison staff and personnel.

According to Hutte (1972), a relatively large number of female prisoners are serving long sentences. In Rotterdam, for example, 5 of the 13 convicted women in 1970 were imprisoned for serious offenses (murder, manslaughter, complicity in murder, provocation of murder, and theft leading to homicide); their sentences totalled forty-two years.

These facts warrant the conclusion that in the most serious offense cate-

Table 13. Percentages of Unconditional and Conditional CGC of the Total Number of Convicts, by Sex.

	Number of Convicts		Unconditional CGC		Conditional CGC	
	M	F	M	F	M	F
1952	27,188	4,687	0.75%	0.28%	1.19%	0.60%
1953	22,890	4,069	0.94	0.27	1.35	0.74
1954	20,811	3,999	1.05	0.35	1.95	0.48
1955	20,695	3,769	1.19	0.45	1.61	0.50
1956	20,910	3,694	1.25	0.38	1.86	0.62
1957	21,352	3,719	0.94	0.22	1.85	0.67
1958	21,917	3,647	1.00	0.30	1.94	0.69
1959	21,318	3,549	0.65	0.08	1.63	0.25
1960	22,462	3,808	0.58	0.18	1.28	0.29
1961	21,932	3,811	0.53	0.16	0.97	0.24
1962	21,017	3,674	0.44	0.14	0.94	0.08
1963	21,453	3,890	0.45	0.05	0.86	0.15
1964	23,117	4,287	0.43	0.21	0.79	0.26
1965	22,724	4,157	0.56	0.05	0.90	0.02
1966	23,602	4,129	0.47	0.15	1.04	0.10
1967	24,847	4,489	0.40	0.02	0.77	0.09
1968	25,434	4,492	0.46	0.04	0.85	0.13
1969	24,472	4,060	0.34	0.02	0.82	0.30
1970	23,967	3,707	0.37	0.05	0.71	0.03
1971	23,841	3,232	0.48	0.03	0.51	0.03
1972	24,806	3,081	0.34	0.10	0.44	0.03
1973	24,477	2,836	0.29	0.04	0.28	0.00

Source: Adapted from Central Bureau of Statistics, *Criminele Statistiek*, 1952–73.

gories the difference in severity of punishment between men and women is less large than that in categories of "average" seriousness.

A sentence imposed relatively few times in the Netherlands is commitment to government care (CGC), a measure (not a punishment) taken in order to have suspects considered not (entirely) legally responsible undergo "compulsory treatment with therapeutic possibilities, for the protection of the society." Generally, CGC is imposed in combination with a short prison sentence. The judge(s) can choose between conditional and unconditional CGC. Every two years the judge has to decide on an extension of CGC, and in this decision the medical advice supplied by the director of the institution as well as the seriousness of the offense are taken into account. In any case, however, the duration of CGC is uncertain for a convicted person sentenced to CGC, and it is nearly always longer than a prison sentence. This explains why suspects regard the uncertainty of CGC as abhorrent and prefer a prison sentence.

A comparison of conditional as well as unconditional CGC imposed on men and on women discloses a larger percentage of male convicts than of female convicts given CGC. The percentages have always been small (never exceeding 2 percent for men and 0.74 percent for women), and have further diminished since 1956. (This is partly explained by an increase in relatively minor property offenses since 1956. Judges seldom impose CGC and relatively often a fine for minor property offenses.)

In the literature it is sometimes suggested that deviant women are more readily regarded as "abnormal" than deviant men. If this were true, then the CGC percentages for women should be much larger than those for men. But they are not. It may be that deviant women are more readily pronounced insane, but we had no opportunity to test this hypothesis. Be this as it may, certificates of insanity are relatively independent of criminal behavior: having committed an offense, a legally insane woman (or partly insane woman) would be committed to government care and consequently included in the figures discussed here. (Note: there are very few certificates of complete lack of criminal responsibility which warrant CGC without a prison sentence. In 1973, CGC without a prison sentence was imposed on 8 persons, CGC with placement in a mental hospital was imposed on 11, and 14 persons were placed in a mental hospital without further legal proceedings. The corresponding figures in 1960 were 22, 6, and 15, respectively; the number of women involved is unknown to us [Central Bureau of Statistics, *Criminele Statistiek,* 1973].)

5. Discussion

In this final section an attempt will be made to answer the questions posed in the introduction. We hope to offer an explanation of the qualitative and quantitative differences in criminal behavior between males and females. Space does not permit a more detailed explanation of the differences between female categories; nor can the differential treatment of women by the criminal justice system be discussed in detail. However, a few lines will be devoted to the relation between female crime and the emancipation of women.

The available quantitative data outline the following pattern:

- Both the official figures on registered crime in the Netherlands and the data from self-report studies warrant the conclusion that, considering their contribution to the total population, women commit significantly fewer offenses than men. In this respect, the Netherlands are no exception to the rule.

- ''Criminal'' women commit a lower average number of offenses than ''criminal'' men.
- The relative contribution of women to the total reported criminality decreased during the period 1962–75.
- Both sexes show the same age peak for offenses: 18–24 years.
- Both sexes show a decrease in official crime rates with increasing age; but the decrease is less pronounced in women than in men.
- Men and women show a slightly different distribution over the various offense types; women are more confined to a single offense type than men.
- Both for men and for women, *property offenses* account for most of the total criminality.
- During the period 1962–75, the absolute number of females suspected of *property offenses* doubled; since the same applies to the males, the relative contribution of the females remained virtually constant.
- *Shoplifting* is still the most characteristic offense of females. The absolute number of females suspected of shoplifting has shown a fourfold increase, but the relative female contribution diminished. The absolute number of males suspected showed a sevenfold increase.
- For females, the number of *offenses against life and the person, offenses against morality* and *damaging and destroying property offenses* have diminished.
- The number of *offenses against public order and authority* by females remained constant.
- If the group of female suspects are divided into women and girls, the latter show an ''overtaking effect.''
- Data supplied by the public prosecutor's office indicate that cases involving female suspects are more readily dismissed than those involving male suspects. An analysis of the exercise of discretion at the various stages of the criminal justice system shows that women are favored at all levels.[11]
- Correctional programs are less differentiated and less liberal for women than for men. However, the number of women serving (usually long) prison sentences is minimal.
- Commitment to government care—a measure experienced as very disagreeable by offenders—is less often imposed on women than on men and has diminished for both groups since 1958.

Attempts to explain the sex-linked differences in criminal behavior may be made on a biological, a psychological, or a sociological level.

For the testing of theories the difference between men and women in most offense types provides an ideal situation for empirical-theoretical science. Assuming that men and women do not essentially differ in characteristics which lead to criminal behavior (or prompt such behavior in a voluntaristic sense), explanations of (types of) criminal behavior should demonstrate why female criminality is lower than male criminality. For example, if factors A and B are sufficient and necessary conditions for criminal behavior Y, then Y_f should equal Y_m unless it is demonstrated that A and/or B are not the same in men and in women, or unless there is a factor X which also exerts an influence on the criminal behavior of the members of one of these sexes. In the last mentioned case, theory $(A \wedge b) \rightarrow Y_{f+m}$ is wrong and should be altered to read $(A \wedge b \wedge X) \rightarrow Y_{f+m}$.

Of course the weak spot in this argumentation is the question whether men and women are really equal, and in which respect. Biologically, there are obvious differences. But is there a difference in gender? To answer this question we need a theory which indicates—in terms of gender—what differences are important, *if there are differences*. However, the emphasis must remain on the theoretical aspects, on the validity of theories to explain criminal behavior in general and/or sex related. What should be avoided is a moral rejection of authors who, however injustly, accept an essential difference between men and women. In principle, biological and psychological explanations are not untrue because they are morally objectionable.[12] They have to be evaluated on the basis of their scientific merit. In that case, too, they may prove to be untenable; but this has nothing to do with their moral value.

The preceding sections have clearly demonstrated that there are differences in criminal behavior between men and women. The figures on unrecorded crime, those on offenses reported to the police, and those on convictions and case dismissals, clearly show that the male contribution to criminality in the Netherlands far exceeds the female contribution. Moreover, the male contribution is generally on the increase.

Apart from one single type of offense, F. Adler's conclusion with regard to the U.S.A. does not apply in the Netherlands. She reported that *"dramatic differences in arrest rates"* had developed between men and women (F. Adler, 1975, pp. 16–20). The contrary would seem to be true in the Netherlands. It can be deduced from Table 1 that, in general, the figure for known suspects rose between 1962 and 1976 by 121 percent for men, by 76 percent for boys, by 63 percent for women, and by 110 percent for girls. For adults, we therefore see a significant difference to the disadvantage (or to the advantage, if one likes) of women. Among girls, however, a dramatic increase can be observed.

Only two types of explanation need be considered: either an explanation which postulates a difference in character between men and women (leaving aside the question whether this is nature, nurture, or a combination of these); or an explanation based on an effort to establish, in existing criminological theories, precisely those differences in initial conditions that cause women to commit less criminal behavior than men. Inevitably, such theories should also explain why the differences between different categories of women are so marked.

Next, we will present brief arguments which eliminate a number of possible interpretations of the figures presented. Subsequently, a brief discussion will be devoted to several approaches made in the past in order to achieve an explanation. Finally, we intend to give an example of an explanation of property offenses, indicating a "spurious relation" with what is generally known as "emancipation."

To begin with, the increase in criminal behavior proves not to be strictly parallel with the increase in population. Some types of offense are declining, but most of them are on the increase. For men, the increase is as a rule greater than for women. Briefly, the figures do not keep abreast of the increase in the number of potential offenders: *people*. This fact indicates that an explanation solely based on the postulate "it is in man's nature" is improbable.

Men differ from women biologically, but this difference is not sufficient to explain the fluctuations in the various types of crimes. While both the appearance and the biological constitution of men and women may prompt a difference in people's reaction to man or woman, the effect of the reaction is no longer biological but psychological and sociological. It is in the latter fields that an explanation of male and female criminality is more likely to be found. With respect to the *reaction* to human behavior, we may think of differential categorization (placement of a person in a psychological category) and of differential attribution (the attribution of several other characteristics on the basis of a single characteristic). As a rule, nothing is more readily perceived than the difference in external appearance between men and women. Categorization is simple, quick, and polar. Once categorization has taken place, attribution of stereotyped characteristics will follow readily.

The more the person(s) whose behavior is evaluated differs in category from the evaluator, and the more behavior is regarded as wrong (*they are* wrong; *we* are right), the more that person will be held responsible for his or her mistake, and the sooner his or her behavior will be considered criminal. The courtesy hypothesis comes under this heading (*"she* was at fault, but women are more sensitive and weaker, and therefore *I* am so courteous as not to imprison her").

Not all differences in criminal behavior, however, can be explained from the reactions of criminal justice officials and citizens. The causes/motives of criminal behavior must be regarded as partly independent of these reactions. Criminal behavior is an *act,* with a cause that is not to be sought exclusively in the effects of the behavior. To explain the reactions to (criminal) behavior is one scientific problem; to explain the (criminal) behavior is another.

Explanations in the biological school of thought seem to be based on the postulate: "There is a biological difference between man and woman, and this leads to a difference in criminality." C. Lombroso, J. Cowie, V. Courie, and E. Slater are among the authors who accept this reasoning as a basis to explain the difference in criminal behavior between men and women.

An important recent biological hypothesis maintains, in summary, that the male hormones, such as testosterone, are responsible for what is known as aggressive behavior (cf. Hutt, 1972). If aggressive behavior is considered in its widest sense, including enterprising behavior focused on the outside world, much criminal behavior can be regarded as aggressive behavior. In that case, aggressive criminal behavior should consist not only of the traditional offenses (aggressive offenses, offenses against life and the person, sexual aggression, armed robbery, etc.) but also of any type of behavior which attempts, regardless of the law, to cause drastic improvement of a person's economic position (swindling, fraud, theft, etc.).

From the biological point of view, the fact that female testosterone production is considerably less than male testosterone production could be an explanation of their surprisingly small contribution to criminality. Bearing in mind that testosterone production in women is relatively higher before puberty and after the climacterium than during the fertile years, one might expect increased "aggressive" behavior precisely during these two periods.

Even if "aggressive" behavior is interpreted in this wider sense, however, there is no question of a positive correlation between testosterone production and criminal behavior. On the contrary: female criminality is lowest during these two periods. A psychological or sociological explanation would therefore seem to be more plausible.

The psychological tradition is less extreme. Psychological research programs are characterized by the postulate that men and women differ in psychological terms. The female psyche so differs from the male psyche that it prompts a quantitative and qualitative difference in criminality. S. Freud is of course the great protagonist of this approach, but similar explanations can also be deduced from the theories of A. Adler and C. G. Jung.

W. I. Thomas and G. Konopka can be accepted as protagonists of the sociopsychological school, although W. I. Thomas is a "borderline case." He maintains that the psychological difference between man and woman results in a dualism (catabolism versus anabolism) [13] which has social aspects. In this respect, Thomas is as interesting as the more sociologically oriented authors.

The sociological school of thought is very extensive. In this tradition, structural functionalistic theories (the function of prostitution for the societal structure); role theories (women play a role which differs from that of men, and women therefore have a different pattern of behavior); class theories (women belong to lower classes because they have less power; whether or not this leads to more or less criminality remains obscure); and (sub)cultural theories (courtesy, other types of contact, other expectations with respect to women) have their place.

Finally, mention should be made of the "ideological" school. This would include the fairly strong contemporary tendency of usually female authors to take a critical view on the position of women, as theoretical object, in the theories usually formulated by men. However important and interesting this ideology-critical work may be, not much scientific research (in the traditional sense of the words) has so far been done in this context and on the basis of these premises.

It seems advisable, in explaining the differences in criminal behavior between the sexes, to proceed from a general theory which does *not* account for the sexes in advance. That is a theory which might explain any type of criminal behavior, and in which the difference in the crime figures for the two sexes results from one or several differences in the initial conditions, which can differ according to place and time.

If next a distinction is made by *types* of criminal behavior (there is no such thing as criminality in general), it might be possible to find a plausible explanation. It seems *possible,* though by no means absolutely necessary, that differences in the initial conditions of criminal behavior are caused by different types of factors. In one case (e.g., aggressive offenses), the (biological) disposition to the formation and establishment of a status hierarchy in the group, differs between men and women. This could be the "cause" of the differences in figures (Van Dijk, 1977). In the field of property offenses, for example, sociological factors might cause women to fulfill the initial conditions for criminological theories to a lesser degree than men (differential association and differential opportunity). The differences between the sexes in numbers of offenses against public order and authority and against morality would be explained better by theories of the sociology of law than by etiological theories of deviance.

A differentiated approach may on the one hand have less theoretical content (fewer *general* predictions can be made), but on the other hand it has the advantage of a better linkage with general theories on sociocultural developments and psychological influences on behavior.

An example may illustrate this: the possible explanation of differences in the numbers of property offenses. The cause of the rapid increase in property offenses committed by females up to age 18, particularly in larceny (Table 2b), can be simple. In the years since about 1965, an economically important market has swiftly developed in response to the new "teenager culture." Teenagers were rather suddenly discovered as an economically interesting group. The availability of (pocket) money for clothes, makeup, phonograph records, and disco-bar visits created a market which soon started to create new "needs" and supported the demand for more pocket money. This applies to girls as much as to boys, so that the relative contribution to criminality increased. Needs, after all, create relative deprivation, and relative deprivation can lead to simple theft (shoplifting). Moreover, the teenager group has expanded. The development began with the 18–20-year-olds, but the 16-year-old rapidly also developed increased buying power (mopeds); so did the 14-year-old; and today even the 12-year-old represents a large market, specifically for phonograph records (Grease!).

Why it is that—apart from shoplifting—female criminality shows a slightly less marked increase than the corresponding figure for men is less simply explained. On the basis of the figures, an explanation with the aid of the emancipation hypothesis seems excluded (the emancipation theory would read: "when women emancipate, their qualitative and quantitative criminality will come to resemble that of males more closely"; a definition of "emancipation" will be considered below). At best, the markedly increased shoplifting by males might be explained by emancipation of *men*, but for the other types of offense emancipation does not (yet) seem to play a role. The growth curve shows no abrupt deflection anywhere. Both the percentage and the absolute number of female offenses against life and the person diminish, probably as a result of the increase in abortions and divorces. The number of female offenses against morality was small to begin with and is decreasing further. And even the female contribution to crime rate is diminishing. Only female offenses against public order and authority are increasing in number, but remain proportionally constant.

A more plausible explanation of the difference in number of property offenses between males and females is suggested by the differential association theory in a reformulated version. K-D. Opp specified and modified Sutherland's theory in five "if . . . then . . ." statements.[14]

1a   The more frequently a person contacts with deviant behavior patterns,

p   the stronger will be the preponderance of positive definitions of deviant behavior, and

q   the more frequent there will be communications about techniques which are relevant to the performance of deviant behavior.

2a   The higher the priority of deviant contacts,

b   the stronger the preponderance of positive definitions of deviant behavior,

c   the higher the degree of identification with the source of deviant contacts,

p   the higher will be the intensity of norms regulating deviance.

3a   The more frequently a person receives communications about techniques which are relevant to the performance of deviant behavior,

p   the more effective will be this person's techniques of performing deviant behavior.

4a   The more intensive a person's needs,

b   the more intensive this person's norms regulating deviance

c   the more effective his/her techniques for performing deviant behavior, and

d   the greater the possibilities to perform deviant behavior,

p   the more frequently this person will be engaged in deviant activities for which the deviant norms are relatively intensive and for which the techniques are relatively effective and the possibilities relatively great.

5a   The more frequently persons behave deviantly,

p   the more frequent are their contacts with deviant behavior patterns.

A person will show criminal behavior when conditions 1a, 2a–c, 3a, and 4a–d are fulfilled. Especially for property offenses, it is not inconceivable that fewer women than men fulfill all the conditions.

The theory could also be used to explain the difference in figures for other types of offense. It is to be borne in mind, however, that in comparison with property offenses *other* conditions of this theory have to be more (or less) fulfilled. For example, it is possible that the increase in "political" offenses will apply to feminists also, and will lead to an increase in female offenses against public order and authority and against life and the person. No pertinent figures are yet available. Such figures need not necessarily show this trend: the official reactions to feministic political activism can be very lenient for political tactical reasons.

The changing sense of morality causes some sexual offenses to be more often regarded as such, and other offenses less. Rape is likely to be more frequently reported, but the total figures on offenses against morality are bound to show slight changes when legislation on abortion is adjusted. The number of female offenses against morality will therefore show a greater decrease than the corresponding figures for men. This does indicate some changes in views on the degree of autonomy of women.

Space does not permit us to evolve similar explanations for all types of offense. It seems more advisable to give a more detailed account of one of the most striking findings of our analyses: the dominant position of shoplifting in the total female criminality. Not only do suspects of shoplifting account for nearly 50 percent of all females suspected of an offense, but this offense also shows an increase. This impression of female criminality may be a distortion of reality. For example, the dark number of shoplifting is known to be very large; it is typically an offense which enters the record only if the offender is caught in the act. This means that a possible discretionary handling by policemen and shop security officers is strongly reflected in the official figures on known offenders. However, the scanty self-report studies made among women do not alter the impression given by the official statistics. It is therefore justifiable to raise the question: Why do women confine themselves largely to shoplifting?

With the aid of the general theory of K-D. Opp, it is possible to find an answer to the question why women largely confine themselves to shoplifting, and why they do this to an increasing extent. Opp's theory states that a person perceives techniques relevant to deviant behavior as being more effective the more frequently he or she communicates about these techniques. In a Western society, boys and girls are socialized in different ways. Boys are expected to tinker, while girls are expected to play with dolls. Boys are expected to show initiative, while girls are expected to adopt an expectant attitude. Consequently, boys are better taught how to handle certain things than girls. Boys learn technical skills in the first phase of social-ization in the primary group, chiefly from the father. Girls communicate much less with the father about these subjects.

The differential socialization process is continued at school, where boys mainly prefer the technical subjects, while the girls choose the nontechnical subjects. This sex-role-linked socialization process causes the effectiveness of technical skills to be lower in girls than in boys. As a consequence of this difference in perception, certain types of criminal behavior are regarded as impossible by girls because they believe that they lack the technical skill required (e.g., burglary and auto theft).

Shoplifting is one of the types of offense which requires minimal techni-cal skill. It is therefore plausible that a woman who fulfills the other initial conditions of the theory opts in favor of the simplest (criminal) activity—shoplifting—in view of her limited technical skill and knowledge.

The increase in shoplifting can be explained by the enhanced opportuni-ties to commit this offense. The number of supermarkets rapidly increased in the Netherlands in the 1960s. This type of store contributed to the disap-pearance, for economic reasons, of small neighborhood shops and door-to-door delivery services (e.g., bakers). The competition battle led to a situa-tion in which people became dependent on shopping centers situated farther from their homes. On the other hand, the increased floor space in supermar-kets and department stores also enhanced opportunities to remove articles without paying for them. For example, Fiselier (1975) found an almost lin-ear correlation between the increase in floor space in supermarkets and the increase in shoplifting.

In view of the above, it is a plausible postulate that shoplifting opportun-ities increased. According to the theory, this increase of opportunities should be accompanied by an increase in criminal behavior. The increased figures for female shoplifting are explained by the increased opportunities for crim-inal behavior, together with a relative lack of technical skills required for other types of crime.

The second item in our problem statement concerned an explanation of the qualitative and quantitative differences in criminality among different female categories. In the Netherlands, however, even less information is available on differences between female categories than on differences be-tween men and women in this respect. The theory used to solve the first problem (K-D. Opp's theory), however, strikes us as suitable also for an attempt to explain why one woman does, and the other woman does not, show criminal behavior. Space does not permit us to present the argumen-tations used to explain why some women do fulfill the initial conditions outlined in this theory while other women do not. Nor does space permit a detailed discussion of the established[15] differential treatment of women in the criminal justice system. In this respect, of course, K-D. Opp's theory cannot be effectively used.[16] The so-called courtesy hypothesis plays a role in the area of this sociopsychological theory.

A few notes should finally be made on the relation between criminal behavior and emancipation. With regard to the hypotheses on the relation between social learning processes, opportunity, and social reactions, it is undoubtedly true that women as a rule find themselves in a social situation which inhibits their criminality. As their "emancipation" progresses, the differences in criminal behavior between the sexes should diminish. During the period studied, however, no such diminution occurred in the Netherlands. This would seem to warrant the conclusion that either the social variables of any theory provide no sufficient conditions to explain criminal behavior in general or that women in the Netherlands have not emancipated (in a sense yet to be defined) in the Netherlands, or both.

In view of the traditional sociological and sociopsychological theories on criminal behavior, it makes sense to distinguish four different aspects of what is generally described as "emancipation."

One aspect concerns the proportional participation of groups in public life (e.g., women and ethnic minorities). This is true only if positions in the socioeconomic, judiciary, political, governmental, and cultural fields are occupied by a proportional number of (in this case) women. The degree to which proportional participation has been achieved could be denominated *the material level of emancipation.*

A prerequisite for this level of emancipation is the extent to which formal possibilities for participation in a society are available. This second aspect could be denominated *the formal level of emancipation.*[17]

The third aspect concerns *the autonomy of women.* We would reserve this term for the degree to which the individual woman makes independent decisions, is responsible for these decisions, and makes use of the available social "space" and the right of self-determination instead of allowing her behavior to be dictated by male wishes and projections.

The fourth aspect is the *"liberation"* on the group level, that is, the increasing consciousness of women as a group, the strivings of women as a group to attain the right of self-determination (e.g., alteration of the female role in marriage; other views on abortion). What is involved here is a collective change of women's attitudes toward women as a group—a process analogous to the redefinition process among Negroes (*"black is beautiful"*).

These four aspects of emancipation cannot be regarded as a single independent entity. There is partial interdependence, which is to say that, for example, a high level of material emancipation does not always imply a high level of autonomy. On the other hand, women with a high degree of autonomy can live in a society with a low level of material emancipation.

Acceptance of these different aspects implies that criminology, when studying the relation between female emancipation and criminal behavior, cannot proceed from a simple relation between employment and crime rate. If we apply the four aspects to the situation in the Netherlands, we find that the level of material emancipation is low (lowest among EEC members). Formal emancipation is more advanced but is not yet completed.[18]

On the other two aspects (autonomy and liberation), no data are available. On the basis of personal observations, however, we can contend that these aspects are becoming more and more apparent, particularly in young women.

In our opinion, the conventional types of criminality can hardly be regarded as autonomous behavior, either in men or in women. Nor can liberation be simply related to crimes, although an increase in political (i.e., feministic) offenses by women can be expected: more or less aggressive demonstrations; more self-defense against male assaults, attempts at rape, and maltreatment. So far, however, Dutch crime figures have shown little or no indication of this.

In recent criminological literature we observe a tendency to relate female crime to emancipation of women. One tries to prove that: (1) emancipated women will show more *male* criminal behavior; and (2) higher crime rates and a more various range of criminal behaviors are indicators of emancipation and/or liberation and/or autonomy. These hypotheses are not supported in our research. For reasons of principle we also disagree with the second hypothesis. Criminal behavior can never be an indicator of autonomous behavior. It would be better to reverse this hypothesis and state that a decrease in their crime rate is an indicator of the emancipation of *men*.

Notes

*We thank J. Fiselier and L. Gunther Moor for their comments on an earlier draft of this paper.

1. See F. Adler, 1975; R. Simon, 1975; C. Smart, 1976.

2. The period 1962–76 was chosen because during this period the principal crime figures were collected in a uniform way, and can therefore be compared without undue problems.

3. We point out that Dutch law distinguishes only between *lesser offenses* (roughly comparable to misdemeanors) and *serious offenses* (roughly comparable to indictable offenses or

felonies). The former are minor violations, e.g., violations of the Traffic Act and possession of up to 30 g of soft drugs; the latter are the more serious offenses defined in the penal code, ranging from insult and simple theft to murder or specific offenses.

4. The following classification of offense types is used in this study:

Offenses Against Public Order and Authority:

- against the security of the state and against royal dignity (sections 92–114)
- against public order (sections 131–51)
- offenses constituting a public danger (sections 157–58)
- against public authority (sections 177–206)

Offenses Against Morality:

- sexual offenses (sections 239 and 242–49, including *abortus provocatus*;
- other offenses against morality (sections 240, 241, and 250–54)

Offenses Against Life and the Person:

- insult (sections 261–71)
- against life (sections 287–299)
- maltreatment (sections 300–306)
- manslaughter and grievous bodily harm (sections 307–9)

Note: this category does include the relatively less serious insults but not the offense of *abortus provocatus,* which is included among the offenses against morality.

Property Offenses:

- counterfeit (sections 208–15)
- other forgeries (sections 216–35)
- simple theft (section 310)
- burglary (section 311, sub 5)
- other aggravated thefts (sections 311 and 312, excluding category n 1)
- poaching (sections 314 and 315)
- embezzlement (sections 321–23)
- fraud/swindling (sections 326–39)
- receiving of stolen property (sections 416–17 bis)

Destroying or Damaging Property Offenses:

- malicious damage (sections 350–54)

5. See G. Bruinsma, 1978.

6. This hypothesis is not new in criminology. For a long time criminologists have done research on this hypothesis. For instance, C. Lombroso in 1894, C. Wichman in 1914, Hudig in 1939, Kempe in 1965.

7. It might be interesting to study the question whether there is not only an increase in male visits to stores but also a decrease in female visits.

8. See n. 4.

9. The public prosecution is the only prosecuting body the Dutch law knows. Despite this monopoly, the public prosecutor is not obliged to initiate proceedings. Even if there is sufficient evidence to prove that someone has committed an offense, the public prosecutor may still

decide not to prosecute on grounds derived from the common interest (the so-called principle of expedience laid down in articles 167 and 242 C.P.). This right extends to all offenses. The public prosecutor is free not to prosecute even if the victim of an offense requests a prosecution.

10. This category does not include prostitution, because this way of earning wages is not regarded as an offense in the Netherlands.

11. See G. Bruinsma, 1978. In this paper the author evaluates the most recent studies in the decision-making process at the various levels of the criminal justice system. He finds that at all levels men run a higher conviction risk than women.

12. If there are any criteria for assessing the truth of a theory, morality will certainly not be one of them.

13. Animal drives which are destructive of energy and creative, respectively energy storing and passive. It is noticeable that Thomas used biological concepts to indicate these (supposed?) male and female attitudes. Testosterone is, for example, a so-called anabolic steroid; it stimulates the synthesis of proteins from fats and amino acids and promotes muscle growth and recovering. Athletes use the androgenic substances in order to increase their physical powers.

Estrogens and progesterone have a catabolic effect: they encourage the breakdown of proteins and control fat depositions and retention of water. Beef cattle are treated with estrogens in order to increase in weight.

14. K-D. Opp, 1974, p. 177.

15. See n. 11.

16. See, for example, J. Eiser and W. Stroebe, 1972.

17. A very special form of emancipation is involved when a group (of women, in this case) not only has access to positions or privileges defined by the dominant group but can create new positions and privileges which are accepted to a comparable extent (J. S. Mill, *On Liberty*). An example is the women's bar.

18. There are a number of legal obstacles which impede the acquisition of certain positions by women. For example, a career in the Netherlands' armed forces is not attainable for women. The positions of postman and priest are likewise unattainable.

References

Adler, F. *Sisters in Crime*. New York: McGraw-Hill, 1975.

Boelmans-Kleinjan, A. C. "De werkende vrouw in Nederland." *Intermediair*. Vol. 12, no. 20, May 14, 1976, pp. 1–7.

Bruinsma, G. J. N. "Discretionary Justice in the Netherlands." Paper presented at the Annual Meeting of the American Society of Criminology, Dallas, Texas, November 8–12, 1978.

Centraal Bureau voor de Statistiek. *Maandstatistiek van rechtswezen, politie en branden*. Vols. 8–10. Zeist: De Haan, 1964, 1965, 1966. May issues, and the annual surveys published therein.

Centraal Bureau voor de Statistiek. *Maandstatistiek Politie en Justitie*. Volo. 11–21. Zeist: De Haan, 1967; 's-Gravenhage: Staatsuitgeverij, 1968–1977. May issues and the annual surveys published therein.

Centraal Bureau voor de Statistiek. *Criminele Statistiek*. Zeist: De Haan, 1958–1966; 's-Gravenhage: Staatsuitgeverij, 1967–1976.

Crites, L. "Women Offenders: Myth versus Reality." In L. Crites, ed. *The Female Offender*. Lexington: D. C. Heath, 1976.

Eiser, J. R., and W. Stroebe. *Categorization and Social Judgement*. London: Academic Press, 1972.

Fiselier, J. P. S. *Winkeldiefstal in Warenhuizen*. Nijmegen: Dekker & Van de Vegt, 1974.

Fiselier, J. P. S. "Een opinieonderzoek over winkeldiefstal." *Nederlands Tijdschrift voor Criminologie*. Vol. 17, no. 2 (April 1975): 74–78.

Fiselier, J. P. S. *Slachtoffers van delicten; een onderzoek naar verborgen criminaliteit*. Utrecht: Ars Aequi Libri, 1978.

Hauber, A. R., and H. Kingmans-Schreuder. "Vrouwen in hun doen en laten." *Tijdschrift voor Criminologie*. Vol. 20, no. 1 (1978): 3–16.

Hudig, J. C. *De Criminaliteit der Vrouw*. Utrecht/Nijmegen: Dekker & Van de Vegt, 1939.

Hutt, C. *Males and Females*. Harmondsworth: Penguin, 1972.

Hutte, P. E. *Mensen in onvrijheid*. Alphen a/d Rijn: Samson, 1972.

Jongman, R. W., and G. J. A. Smale. "Ongeregistreerde criminaliteit onder vrouwelijke studenten." *Nederlands Tijdschrift voor Criminologie*. Vol. 14 (1972): 1–11.

Kempe, G. Th. "De vrouw, de man en de misdaad." *Maandblad voor Berechting en Reclassering*. Vol. 44 (October 1965): 210–241.

Lombroso, C., and G. Ferrero. *Das Weib als Verbrecherin und Prostituirte*. Hamburg: Königlich Schwedisch-Norwegische Hofverlagshandlung, 1894.

Mill, J. S. *On Liberty*. Harmondsworth: Penguin, 1974 [1859].

Opp, K-D. *Abweichendes Verhalten und Gesellschaftsstruktur*. Darmstadt und Neuwied: Luchterhand, 1974.

Simon, R. *Women and Crime*. Toronto and Boston: Lexington Books, 1975.

Smart, C. *Women, Crime and Criminology: A Feminist Critique*. London: Routledge & Kegan Paul., 1976.

Van Dijk, J. J. M. *Dominantiegedrag en geweld; een multidisciplinaire visie op de veroorzaking van geweldmisdrijven*. Nijmegen: Dekker & Van de Vegt, 1977.

Veendrick, L. *Verborgen en geregistreerde kriminaliteit in Groningen*. Groningen: Kriminologisch Instituut, 1976.

Wichman, C. "De criminaliteit der Vrouw." In *Het Encyclopedisch Handboek: De vrouw, de vrouwenbeweging en het vrouwenvraagstuk*. Deel I. Amsterdam: Elsevier, 1914. Pp. 662–690.

Appendix 1. Total Number of Convictions and Case Dismissals (m + f), Percentual Female Contribution to These Totals, and Female : Male Ratio Per Age Group, by Offense Types, for 1956, 1960, 1965, 1970 and 1973.

1956

	Conviction for (Offenses Against):						Dismissals for (Offenses Against):					
	Public Order and Authority	Morality (including Abortion)	Life and the Person	Property Offenses	Damaging and Destroying Property Offenses	Total	Public Order and Authority	Morality (including Abortion)	Life and the Person	Property Offenses	Damaging and Destroying Property Offenses	Total
Absolute total *	1,516	2,604	5,443	13,288	1,499	24,350	664	1,166	3,847	6,907	1,286	13,870
% of women	9.76	6.76	23.15	14.52	8.74	15.51	18.50	6.60	31.30	16.10	13.20	19.40
18 years	1 : 17.5	1 : 18.4	1 : 4.7	1 : 10.5	1 : 20.1	1 : 10.7	1 : 13.0	1 : 12.4	1 : 3.0	1 : 8.9	1 : 15.1	1 : 7.9
18–21 years	1 : 16.3	1 : 8.5	1 : 6.6	1 : 6.3	1 : 24.0	1 : 15.5	1 : 4.8	1 : 10.8	1 : 3.1	1 : 5.8	1 : 22.7	1 : 5.9
21–25 years	1 : 11.6	1 : 16.0	1 : 7.5	1 : 6.8	1 : 14.9	1 : 8.1	1 : 6.5	1 : 18.2	1 : 3.4	1 : 5.1	1 : 11.4	1 : 8.9
25–30 years	1 : 8.6	1 : 16.9	1 : 3.7	1 : 4.3	1 : 9.9	1 : 6.7	1 : 3.0	1 : 22.0	1 : 2.2	1 : 5.8	1 : 7.8	1 : 4.1
30–40 years	1 : 8.1	1 : 12.7	1 : 2.8	1 : 6.0	1 : 10.9	1 : 5.2	1 : 4.4	1 : 12.4	1 : 1.8	1 : 4.2	1 : 3.1	1 : 2.8
40–50 years	1 : 7.9	1 : 12.3	1 : 2.7	1 : 4.2	1 : 6.3	1 : 4.2	1 : 4.8	1 : 10.9	1 : 2.2	1 : 3.7	1 : 4.1	1 : 3.2
50–60 years	1 : 6.0	1 : 10.5	1 : 2.6	1 : 3.6	1 : 5.1	1 : 3.8	1 : 3.7	1 : 18.2	1 : 1.8	1 : 3.1	1 : 3.2	1 : 3.0
60–70 years	1 : 5.4	1 : 26.4	1 : 2.6	1 : 2.6	1 : 3.0	1 : 7.8	1 : 3.5	1 : 15.0	1 : 2.7	1 : 3.2	1 : 9.2	1 : 3.6
70 years	1 : 3.0	1 : 29.0	1 : 2.7	1 : 5.5	1 : 6.0	1 : 6.1	1 : 2.0	1 : 52.0	1 : 2.4	1 : 2.9	1 : 3.1	1 : 3.7

female : male ratio

1960

	Absolute total*	% of women
	1,762	7.03
	2,703	4.70
	5,949	18.60
	13,977	16.40
	1,652	7.20
	26,043	14.47
	977	16.27
	1,833	4.09
	4,441	27.13
	7,836	18.70
	1,334	9.67
	16,421	18.47

female : male ratio

Age	1,762	2,703	5,949	13,977	1,652	26,043	977	1,833	4,441	7,836	1,334	16,421
18 years	1 : 26.7	1 : 184.0	1 : 11.5	1 : 12.9	1 : 43.3	1 : 15.4	1 : 17.1	1 : 68.1	1 : 4.9	1 : 1.8	1 : 36.1	1 : 4.2
18–21 years	1 : 18.0	1 : 25.7	1 : 8.8	1 : 7.7	1 : 20.4	1 : 9.3	1 : 5.4	1 : 16.4	1 : 4.7	1 : 3.9	1 : 20.2	1 : 4.1
21–25 years	1 : 20.5	1 : 33.2	1 : 9.2	1 : 6.9	1 : 22.8	1 : 9.2	1 : 4.4	1 : 21.8	1 : 4.5	1 : 4.9	1 : 13.2	1 : 6.1
25–30 years	1 : 15.7	1 : 37.0	1 : 6.2	1 : 6.7	1 : 12.6	1 : 8.0	1 : 5.5	1 : 32.3	1 : 3.1	1 : 4.1	1 : 9.2	1 : 4.6
30–40 years	1 : 10.7	1 : 16.6	1 : 3.5	1 : 4.4	1 : 8.4	1 : 4.9	1 : 4.7	1 : 20.1	1 : 2.1	1 : 3.6	1 : 5.6	1 : 3.3
40–50 years	1 : 8.2	1 : 11.2	1 : 3.2	1 : 2.9	1 : 7.9	1 : 3.7	1 : 3.9	1 : 12.9	1 : 2.2	1 : 3.2	1 : 6.0	1 : 3.1
50–60 years	1 : 6.9	1 : 14.5	1 : 2.6	1 : 2.0	1 : 9.3	1 : 3.0	1 : 3.1	1 : 14.1	1 : 2.0	1 : 2.3	1 : 3.6	1 : 2.7
60–70 years	1 : 11.5	1 : 19.0	1 : 3.4	1 : 1.7	1 : 20.0	1 : 3.2	1 : 5.9	1 : 14.3	1 : 2.6	1 : 2.2	1 : 6.7	1 : 3.3
70 years	1 : 3.0	1 : 53.0	1 : 7.3	1 : 2.0	1 : 18.0	1 : 5.6	1 : 12.0	1 : 76.0	1 : 5.2	1 : 1.1	1 : 3.5	1 : 4.3

1965

	Absolute total*	% of women
	1,798	5.45
	2,250	1.91
	4,364	13.80
	15,831	20.60
	1,960	4.30
	26,703	15.40
	976	13.80
	1,847	2.50
	3,819	20.60
	9,662	16.80
	1,631	8.80
	17,935	15.30

female : male ratio

Age	1,798	2,250	4,364	15,831	1,960	26,703	976	1,847	3,819	9,662	1,631	17,935
18 years	1 : 27.1	1 : 270.0	1 : 14.0	1 : 14.1	1 : 171.5	1 : 16.9	1 : 7.6	1 : 92.8	1 : 4.9	1 : 8.7	1 : 17.8	1 : 3.5
18–21 years	1 : 107.3	1 : 117.0	1 : 19.2	1 : 7.9	1 : 122.3	1 : 11.8	1 : 12.6	1 : 28.8	1 : 6.7	1 : 6.0	1 : 24.3	1 : 7.7
21–25 years	1 : 20.7	1 : 103.0	1 : 11.0	1 : 5.8	1 : 36.1	1 : 8.2	1 : 7.2	1 : 30.3	1 : 5.9	1 : 6.4	1 : 15.1	1 : 7.3
25–30 years	1 : 16.0	1 : 110.7	1 : 7.9	1 : 4.6	1 : 21.5	1 : 6.7	1 : 5.6	1 : 32.1	1 : 5.0	1 : 6.1	1 : 12.0	1 : 6.7
30–40 years	1 : 8.3	1 : 40.7	1 : 4.7	1 : 3.1	1 : 14.0	1 : 4.5	1 : 6.2	1 : 27.5	1 : 3.2	1 : 4.3	1 : 7.4	1 : 4.6
40–50 years	1 : 7.2	1 : 19.8	1 : 3.9	1 : 1.5	1 : 11.1	1 : 2.5	1 : 5.0	1 : 39.2	1 : 2.8	1 : 2.7	1 : 4.6	1 : 3.3
50–60 years	1 : 12.3	1 : 37.8	1 : 4.6	1 : 0.8	1 : 4.7	1 : 1.9	1 : 3.6	1 : 19.0	1 : 3.0	1 : 1.6	1 : 5.3	1 : 2.5
60–70 years	1 : 17.0	1 : 40.0	1 : 5.2	1 : 0.7	1 : 5.2	1 : 1.5	1 : 2.3	1 : 30.0	1 : 3.5	1 : 1.2	1 : 4.8	1 : 2.3
70 years	1 : 3.0	1 : 28.0	1 : 8.5	1 : 0.6	(0 : 18.0)	1 : 2.0	1 : 7.0	1 : 38.0	1 : 2.8	1 : 0.9	1 : 6.0	1 : 2.6

Appendix 1. (Cont.)

	Conviction for (Offenses Against): 1970						Dismissals for (Offenses Against):					
	Public Order and Authority	Morality (Including Abortion)	Life and the Person	Property Offenses	Damaging and Destroying Property Offenses	Total	Public Order and Authority	Morality (Including Abortion)	Life and the Person	Property Offenses	Damaging and Destroying Property Offenses	Total
Absolute total*	1,939	1,432	4,487	17,685	2,030	27,573	1,641	2,019	4,161	15,829	2,066	25,716
% of women	5.70	1.00	8.30	17.70	3.90	13.40	10.20	87.60	4.90	7.30	35.90	8.30
18 years	1 : 25.6	1 : 123.0	1 : 46.3	1 : 16.2	1 : 54.7	1 : 19.0	1 : 10.2	1 : 87.6	1 : 4.9	1 : 7.3	1 : 35.9	1 : 8.3
18–21 years	1 : 21.6	1 : 90.0	1 : 30.2	1 : 9.1	1 : 55.5	1 : 12.3	1 : 13.0	1 : 103.0	1 : 10.0	1 : 5.9	1 : 16.6	1 : 6.9
21–25 years	1 : 14.6	1 : 230.0	1 : 13.4	1 : 5.7	1 : 33.3	1 : 8.0	1 : 7.9	1 : 130.5	1 : 7.6	1 : 4.4	1 : 11.5	1 : 5.9
25–30 years	1 : 9.0	(0 : 230.0)	1 : 13.3	1 : 4.2	1 : 23.4	1 : 6.1	1 : 11.3	1 : 23.0	1 : 4.4	1 : 3.4	1 : 12.6	1 : 4.6
30–40 years	1 : 26.6	1 : 322.0	1 : 11.4	1 : 3.2	1 : 19.3	1 : 5.1	1 : 6.9	1 : 33.1	1 : 3.9	1 : 2.4	1 : 11.4	1 : 3.5
40–50 years	1 : 13.0	1 : 61.3	1 : 5.2	1 : 1.9	1 : 8.3	1 : 3.0	1 : 5.8	1 : 27.4	1 : 3.1	1 : 1.5	1 : 8.9	1 : 2.4
50–60 years	1 : 16.0	1 : 19.6	1 : 5.5	1 : 1.2	1 : 10.1	1 : 2.3	1 : 8.7	1 : 19.8	1 : 3.1	1 : 0.9	1 : 4.6	1 : 1.6
60–70 years	(0 : 7.0)	(0 : 39.0)	1 : 5.9	1 : 0.8	1 : 14.0	1 : 1.7	1 : 3.2	1 : 64.0	1 : 3.0	1 : 0.9	1 : 3.6	1 : 1.6
70 years	(0 : 1.0)	(0 : 12.0)	1 : 5.4	1 : 1.1	1 : 7.0	1 : 2.9	(0 : 3.0)	(0 : 43.0)	1 : 3.6	1 : 1.0	(0 : 12.0)	1 : 2.3

(Age rows: female : male ratio)

1973

	1,186	844	4,018	18,470	2,024	27,220	1,840	1,782	4,930	20,668	2,528	31,748
Absolute total*	7.20	1.70	5.60	13.10	3.30	10.30	9.90	1.20	15.10	21.70	7.60	17.70
% of women												
18 years	1 : 47.0	1 : 72.0	1 : 58.7	1 : 24.1	1 : 157.5	1 : 27.6	1 : 7.8	(0 : 277.0)	1 : 8.6	1 : 9.9	1 : 31.1	1 : 10.6
18–21 years	1 : 45.9	1 : 37.5	1 : 40.4	1 : 12.4	1 : 91.8	1 : 16.3	1 : 12.4	1 : 89.0	1 : 12.1	1 : 6.9	1 : 21.1	1 : 8.0
21–25 years	1 : 20.5	1 : 141.0	1 : 27.5	1 : 8.0	1 : 77.6	1 : 10.8	1 : 15.0	1 : 88.0	1 : 7.4	1 : 4.3	1 : 20.7	1 : 5.9
25–30 years	1 : 14.2	1 : 142.0	1 : 21.3	1 : 5.5	1 : 28.0	1 : 7.8	1 : 10.0	1 : 59.6	1 : 6.0	1 : 1.2	1 : 12.8	1 : 4.2
30–40 years	1 : 14.4	1 : 31.1	1 : 11.0	1 : 3.5	1 : 15.4	1 : 6.19	1 : 6.6	1 : 96.5	1 : 5.2	1 : 2.0	1 : 7.7	1 : 3.2
40–50 years	1 : 11.9	1 : 63.0	1 : 8.5	1 : 2.9	1 : 11.8	1 : 4.3	1 : 4.7	1 : 46.0	1 : 4.3	1 : 1.5	1 : 5.0	1 : 2.4
50–60 years	1 : 7.6	(0 : 40.0)	1 : 7.5	1 : 1.7	1 : 6.6	1 : 2.7	1 : 5.2	1 : 27.7	1 : 3.5	1 : 1.0	1 : 4.8	1 : 1.8
60–70 years	(0 : 8.0)	(0 : 12.0)	1 : 11.2	1 : 1.0	1 : 2.5	1 : 2.0	1 : 17.0	(0 : 66.0)	1 : 5.1	1 : 0.7	1 : 7.2	1 : 1.4
70 years	(0 : 0)	(0 : 4.0)	(0 : 13.0)	1 : 1.3	(0 : 7.0)	1 : 4.3	(0 : 2.0)	(0 : 25.0)	1 : 3.0	1 : 0.9	1 : 5.0	1 : 1.6

female : male ratio

Source: Adapted from Central Bureau of Statistics, *Criminele Statistiek*, 1956, 1960, 1965, 1970, and 1973.

*(m + f)

Appendix 2. Index Figures for the Number of Female *Adults*, by Offense Categories, Over the Period 1962–76 (1962 = 100).

	Property Offenses	Damaging and Destroying Property Offenses	Offenses Against Life and the Person	Offenses Against Public Order and Authority	Offenses Against Morality	Other Offenses	Total	Of which Shoplifting
1962	100	100	100	100	100	100	100	100
1963	107	88	91	89	84	93	100	118
1964	120	105	90	111	73	70	106	152
1965	115	101	81	102	64	144	106	150
1966	127	107	67	111	58	116	106	174
1967	131	95	68	85	67	129	109	175
1968	145	96	71	94	70	136	119	188
1969	160	101	68	143	59	130	127	222
1970	162	108	54	104	48	144	125	229
1971	174	108	48	108	36	158	130	244
1972	182	127	47	130	32	169	136	260
1973	189	147	44	160	23	165	140	269
1974	178	141	39	157	14	178	133	255
1975	199	157	37	149	33	224	148	282
1976	215	164	40	212	27	268	163	300

Source: Central Bureau of Statistics, *Maandstatistiek voor Politie,* 1964–77.

Appendix 3. Index Figures for the Number of Female *Minors*, by Offense Categories, Over the Period 1962–76 (1962 = 100).

	Property Offenses	Damaging and Destroying Property Offenses	Offenses Against Life and the Person	Offenses Against Public Order and Authority	Offenses Against Morality	Other Offenses	Total	Of which Shoplifting
1962	100	100	100	100	100	100	100	100
1963	96	40	88	171	200	142	96	97
1964	103	35	123	118	167	22	97	113
1965	113	69	108	176	67	71	109	127
1966	117	74	68	141	50	66	110	139
1967	120	48	108	129	108	106	116	134
1968	137	59	81	141	58	115	129	176
1969	152	40	91	135	75	149	144	195
1970	146	66	65	206	50	171	140	194
1971	148	55	61	265	42	133	140	192
1972	155	43	76	147	116	100	143	206
1973	172	55	47	288	42	82	156	230
1974	179	93	64	318	42	102	166	248
1975	205	102	75	306	25	75	186	294
1976	229	133	100	259	58	110	211	326

Source: Central Bureau of Statistics, *Maandstatistiek voor Politie*, 1964–77.

2. Female Criminality in Finland— What Do the Statistics Show?

I. ANTTILA

Inkeri S. Anttila is Professor of Criminal Law, and has been Director of the Research Institute of Legal Policy at the Ministry of Justice. Her primary interest in the field is the application of research to decision making within the criminal justice system. She has actively participated in crime policy planning, was Minister of Justice in the Finnish cabinet in 1975, served as President of the Fifth United Nations Congress on the Prevention of Crime and the Treatment of Offenders, Geneva, 1975, and as a member of the United Nations Committee on Crime Prevention and Control. Her publications include: eleven books and about one hundred articles on criminal law, criminology, and crime control.

As is the case in most countries, criminality in Finland today is, above all, male criminality. At least for the past century male criminality has been so much larger that in normal conversation, in public debate and even in the compilation of statistics and in criminological reports there is often no separate mention of female criminality or of female offenders.

Year	Total Accused	Females Accused N	%
1900	38,838	2,889	7
1910	44,167	3,398	8
1920	59,981	5,060	8
1930	145,192	7,872	5
1940	48,249	4,949	10
1950	143,513	9,614	7
1960	205,744	10,963	5
1970	216,236	15,027	6
1971	214,826	13,116	6
1972	227,455	—	—
1973	299,553	17,498	7
1974	324,225	22,304	7
1975	378,293	27,752	7
1976	304,689	23,574	8

The accompanying table presents the total number of women accused before courts of first instance and their proportion among those accused over the past seventy-five years.[1] The table shows that the total amount of female criminality has increased considerably since the beginning of the century. Even so, the increase is not as large as it is for male criminality. The statistics do not show any sudden changes. The relatively high proportion of female offenders in 1940 is simply explained by the fact that during the war most young male offenders were brought before special military courts, as they were members of the armed forces.

The statistics for "total criminality" cover a great number of different offenses, and thus variations in the total amount of criminality do not allow any far-reaching conclusions. This is especially true of variations in the long-term trend, as these may be due to legislative reforms, for example. Such is the case for countries such as Finland where the effect is heightened by the fact that the crime statistics cover all offenses, up to and including very slight ones such as traffic offenses. One example would be that the decriminalization of public drunkenness at the beginning of the 1970s removed some 70,000 offenses from the statistics. This offense, which would normally have led to a fine, was predominantly a male offense. Thus, even if a table giving the amount of total criminality may provide a rough idea of the behavior pattern of the different sexes, it is very poorly adaptable to international comparisons. In most other countries the crime statistics deal only with the more serious types of criminality.

Table 1. Offenders Sentenced to Imprisonment in Courts of First Instance, 1951–76.

Year	Total Sentenced N	Women Sentenced N	%	Year	Total Sentenced N	Women Sentenced N	%
1951	8,594	933	11	1964	13,650	821	6
1952	8,869	890	10	1965	13,291	671	5
1953	8,930	883	10	1966	14,014	764	5
1954	8,388	767	9	1967	14,994	802	5
1955	8,218	740	9	1968	14,898	751	5
1956	7,822	611	8	1969	14,913	699	5
1957	8,734	716	8	1970	15,428	682	4
1958	9,429	713	8	1971	20,364	847	4
1959	9,969	778	8	1972	20,233	830	4
1960	10,587	774	7	1973	22,517	766	3
1961	11,447	775	7	1974	25,664	999	4
1962	11,531	735	6	1975	29,074	1,063	4
1963	12,513	761	6	1976	29,707	1,111	4

Therefore, in order to obtain a better picture of the proportion of male and female criminality as well as their variations, we should turn to offenses which lead to imprisonment.

Table 1 gives the number of women sentenced to imprisonment from 1951 to 1976. It should be noted that these figures include both those sentenced to conditional imprisonment and those sentenced to unconditional imprisonment. Therefore, the table does not give the number of offenders entering prison during the year in question.

The figures in Table 1 show that there has been an increase in serious female criminality during the 1960s and 1970s. However, as an examination of Table 1 reveals, the increase in male criminality has been even greater.

Table 2 and Figure 1 illustrate the number of *female prisoners* over the years. We can first note that the daily female prison population has varied greatly since the beginning of the century. It increased steadily during the 1920s and rose to over 1,000 during the 1930s. During World War II, it rose again to the same heights. Since then, however, there has been sharp decrease in the female prison population. During part of the 1970s, it even fell to less than a tenth of what it was thirty years earlier. During the second half of the 1970s, the figure rose again, this time from 100 to over 130.*

Table 2. Size of the Prison Population and the Number of Female Prisoners, 1917–78.

Number of Prisoners at the End of the Year	Men N	Women N	Total N	Percentage of Women %
1917	4,022	383	4,405	9
1918	4,666	697	5,363	13
1919	5,581	731	6,315	12
1920	6,491	685	7,176	10
1921	5,667	600	6,267	10
1922	5,202	614	5,816	11
1923	5,460	553	6,013	9
1924	5,983	557	6,540	9
1925	6,600	738	7,338	10
1926	6,278	664	6,942	10
1927	6,700	628	7,328	9
1928	6,631	610	7,241	8
1929	8,062	663	7,825	8
1930	7,074	699	7,773	9

*The rapid and almost linear reduction of the number of female prisoners illustrated by the graph in Figure 1 alarmed prison authorities to the extent that in 1966 they decided to ask the Institute of Criminology for a forecast of the future number of female prisoners. This forecast would then be used to determine the size of the female wing in the new prison building project

Number of Prisoners at the End of the Year	Men N	Women N	Total N	Percentage of Women %
1931	7,273	803	8,076	10
1932	7,556	823	8,379	10
1933	8,129	1,052	9,181	11
1934	7,570	1,189	8,759	14
1935	7,263	1,104	8,367	13
1936	6,476	911	7,387	12
1937	5,544	807	6,351	13
1938	5,048	709	5,757	12
1939	3,516	422	3,938	11
1940	4,630	469	5,099	9
1941	7,768	645	8,413	8
1942	7,933	1,024	8,957	11
1943	7,083	1,383	9,466	15
1944	4,720	1,012	5,732	18
1945	8,281	1,181	9,452	12
1946	7,658	1,106	8,764	13
1947	7,842	1,049	8,891	12
1948	7,634	908	8,592	11
1949	7,534	851	8,385	10
1950	6,786	721	7,507	10
1951	5,756	528	6,284	8
1952	6,540	503	7,043	7
1953	6,860	505	7,365	7
1954	6,119	410	6,529	6
1955	5,608	358	5,966	6
1956	5,518	347	5,865	6
1957	6,115	317	6,432	5
1958	6,480	335	6,815	5
1959	6,794	374	7,168	5
1960	6,477	311	6,788	5
1961	6,332	283	6,615	4
1962	6,183	299	6,482	5
1963	6,615	274	6,889	4
1964	6,293	270	6,563	4
1965	6,843	222	7,065	3
1966	7,367	207	7,574	3
1967	5,664	124	5,788	2
1968	5,720	144	5,864	2
1969	5,090	112	5,202	2
1970	4,722	84	4,806	2
1971	4,892	107	4,999	2
1972	4,498	93	4,591	2
1973	4,615	91	4,706	2
1974	4,954	108	5,062	2
1975	5,575	131	5,706	2
1976	5,477	122	5,599	2
1977	5,258	147	5,405	3
1978	5,227	146	5,373	3

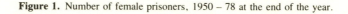

Figure 1. Number of female prisoners, 1950 – 78 at the end of the year.

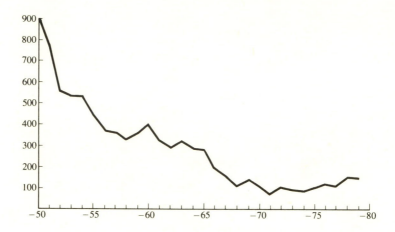

As there have also been large variations in the male prison population, it is interesting to examine the female proportion of the total prison population. For over twenty years, women have accounted for 2 to 3 percent of the prison population, and so there have not been any significant changes.

When analyzing female criminality, it is of course necessary to examine specific crime categories. Table 3 shows some of the offenses for which female offenders have been sentenced to imprisonment from 1957 to 1972 (no more recent data are available). Table 4 shows the relative number of male and female offenders who have been sentenced for various offenses in the years mentioned.

As *property offenses,* especially theft offenses, have accounted for a relatively large share of female criminality, separate data are provided on these. Table 5 shows the number of female offenders accused and sentenced for property offenses, while Table 6 illustrates the situation for theft offenses. The tables, which include offenders sentenced to both imprisonment and fines, show that while there have been some variations in the proportion of female criminality, during the postwar years this proportion has remained between 11 and 17 percent. Also, there has been no increase of note during recent times.

in Hämeenlinna. The forecast (dated March 13, 1967, reported in a Council of Europe working paper, Törnudd, 1971) suggested that the downward trend would soon turn upward and—if no allowance were made for certain proposed legislative reforms—would probably exceed the 150 level in 1975.

Table 3. Females Sentenced to Imprisonment in Courts of First Instance, by Crime Category, 1957–72.

Crime Category	1957 n	1958 n	1959 n	1960 n	1961 n	1962 n	1963 n	1964 n	1965 n	1966 n	1967 n	1968 n	1969 n	1970 n	1971 n	1972 n
Theft offenses	318	340	373	357	357	389	385	434	379	412	410	403	353	300	391	350
Embezzlement, fraud	88	72	88	68	70	60	57	68	61	52	60	53	48	56	60	53
Robbery, extortion	7	2	5	10	7	7	10	7	7	16	23	16	36	32	36	36
Other property offenses	30	36	26	34	26	16	27	36	22	36	39	37	36	31	42	53
Forgery of a document	45	70	74	55	77	61	75	79	62	65	83	78	89	91	134	127
Illegal sale or preparation of distilled beverages	61	48	53	76	68	54	63	68	36	44	38	32	18	10	13	11
Misleading authorities, perjury	32	37	41	51	43	32	43	24	32	36	33	31	23	38	43	28
Drunken driving	6	5	10	13	17	15	13	20	25	38	53	43	43	72	68	92
Violent offenses	13	10	14	8	22	12	13	17	8	17	13	13	11	15	22	39
Sexual offenses	14	18	17	9	19	12	13	4	7	7	8	5	1	1	2	1
Arson	6	4	6	5	7	7	1	3	2	1	3	1	1	2	–	1
Other penal code offenses	92	68	66	83	57	67	58	56	63	39	32	31	28	21	21	17
Other offenses	4	3	5	5	5	3	3	5	3	1	7	8	12	13	15	27

Table 4.   Offenders Sentenced in Courts of First Instance for Various Offenses.

| | Sentenced Persons Per 100,000 of the Same Sex | | | | | |
	1950	1955	1960	1965	1970	1975
Larceny offenses						
males	182	131	165	213	269	668
females	36	24	24	42	52	117
Assault offenses						
males	154	149	112	122	167	302
females	6	4	3	2	4	10
Drunken driving						
males	68	75	88	228	623	628
females	0	0	1	1	3	11
Perjury						
males	5	7	7	4	4	6
females	1	1	2	1	2	1

The share of women among *violent offenders* has remained quite small. Much historical data on this "traditional" offense are available for Finland. These data show that even in earlier times violent criminality has been predominantly male criminality. However, at times in the past the number of

Table 5.   Number of Females Accused Before Courts of First Instance for Certain Property Offenses and Their Proportion of the Total Number of Accused, 1935–76.

| | Theft Offenses | | Embezzle-ment | | Fraud | | Forgery of a Document | |
Year	N	%	N	%	N	%	N	%
1935	699	14	76	8	98	11	64	15
1940	682	16	58	9	60	11	40	15
1945	728	20	291	20	266	17	321	31
1950	876	18	222	15	209	14	118	22
1955	652	17	128	9	193	10	108	20
1960	603	13	88	10	203	13	128	18
1965	1,199	18	110	12	142	12	121	17
1970	1,626	18	102	16	164	11	172	18
1971	1,965	16	96	13	201	12	262	21
1972	—	—	—	—	—	—	—	—
1973	2,226	15	75	14	196	10	297	20
1974	2,389	15	316	12	—	—	244	16
1975	2,786	15	91	19	342	16	255	16
1976	2,612	14	346	11	—	—	257	17

Table 6. Number of Offenders Sentenced for Theft Offenses in Courts of First Instance, Number and Percentage of Female Offenders, 1910–70.

Year	Total Sentenced N	Females Sentenced N	%	Year	Total Sentenced N	Females Sentenced N	%
1910	2,066	245	12	1945	12,335	2,510	20
1915	2,349	268	11	1950	4,317	757	17
1920	3,251	551	17	1955	3,248	534	16
1925	2,181	331	15	1960	4,068	543	13
1930	2,760	387	14	1965	5,698	986	17
1935	4,065	591	14	1970	7,386	1,232	18
1940	3,287	571	17				

women guilty of the most aggravated form of violent crime, homicide, has been relatively greater than what it is today. Table 7 shows that as recently as thirty years ago, immediately after World War II, the relative number of homicides committed by women (when compared with the size of the female population) was over three times the present size. Also, these numbers do not include women sentenced for infanticide. If this were done, the difference would be even more marked. The 1882 court statistics, which for the first time include figures on the number of offenders sentenced to "imprisonment in the penitentiary," shows that at that time more women were sentenced for infanticide (46) than men for all other types of homicide (44)!

Table 7. Men and Women Sentenced for Violent Offenses Against the Person in Courts of First Instance and Courts-martial, Per 100,000 in Population, 1895–1975 (Not Including Infanticide). Figures Include Attempts and Complicity.

Year	Number of Men Sentenced/100,000 Male Population	Number of Women Sentenced/100,000 Female Population
1895	2.9	0.5
1905	7.1	0.4
1915	3.6	0.3
1925	18.2	0.5
1935	9.6	0.3
1945	11.3	0.7
1955	3.6	0.5
1965	3.2	0.1
1975	4.1	0.2

Source for 1895–1935 figures: Verkko, 1951.

The present situation is completely different. As shown by Table 8, the number of infanticide cases has consistently decreased. Today, only 1 to 4 women are sentenced for infanticide each year, which is only a fraction of the annual figures for previous decades.

Table 8.   Infanticide: Offenses Reported to the Police and Women Sentenced in Courts in First Instance, 1950–76.

Year	Offenses Reported to the Police N	Women Sentenced N	Year	Offenses Reported to the Police N	Women Sentenced N
1950	29	15	1964	11	5
1951	15	11	1965	14	9
1952	22	16	1966	11	6
1953	22	9	1967	9	6
1954	15	11	1968	3	1
1955	17	13	1969	7	4
1956	14	8	1970	8	1
1957	11	15	1971	3	3
1958	14	7	1972	8	4
1959	11	—	1973	8	2
1960	18	10	1974	3	2
1961	8	5	1975	3	1
1962	8	9	1976	6	4
1963	10	6			

Even so, attention may be drawn to the fact that there is an evident increase in the number of violent offenses committed by women during the 1970s. There is also a very clear increase in *drunken driving,* which with the exception of very rare cases, first surfaced as female criminality during the 1960s. According to the most recent statistics, drunken driving is as common among women as are violent offenses. This trend for both violent offenses and drunken driving appears to be connected with a cultural change, the fact that alcohol use among women has increased. A recent analysis of Finnish crime trends (Törnudd, 1978) notes:

Assault offences and drunken driving show a somewhat different pattern. The recent increase has been steeper among women. It would seem natural to connect this phenomenon with the changing attitudes towards alcohol among women. As in other countries where heavy drinking of strong spirits dominates the alcohol consumption pattern, Finnish alcohol attitudes have traditionally been polarized into drinkers and abstainers, the latter group being dominated by women. The recent years have seen a dramatic change: the idea of total abstinence is growing less and less popular—the increase in drinking, particularly heavy drinking, has been more rapid among women. (Mäkelä 1975, Simpura 1978, pp. 119–20)

Another way of illustrating the share and significance of female criminality is to rank various offenses according to the proportion committed by women. This is done in Table 10, which gives the situation in the Scandinavian countries in 1969. Table 9 compares the situation in 1964–66 with that in 1974–76.

Data on the trend in criminality show that in theft offenses, and specifically so-called ordinary (not aggravated) thefts, the female proportion has

Table 9. Offenders Accused of Various Offenses in the Courts of First Instance in 1975 and Proportion of Women.

Offense	All Offenders N	Women N	%
Infanticide	1	1	100
Defamation	138	39	28
Perjury	336	66	20
Embezzlement	481	91	19
Theft, petty theft	17,005	2,700	16
Forgery of a document	1,548	255	16
Illegal sale of alcohol	1,253	199	16
Dealing in stolen property	1,586	193	12
Homicide	18	2	11
Fraud	2,183	246	11
Breaking the peace	445	45	10
Sexual offenses (excl. rape)	252	25	10
Extortion	135	11	8
Negligent manslaughter	143	11	8
Manslaughter	56	4	7
Aggravated theft	1,806	86	5
Impeding an official	4,759	227	5
Unauthorized use of a motor vehicle	1,950	92	5
Causing a serious injury through negligence	239	11	5
Robbery	861	46	5
Petty assault	2,813	109	4
Aggravated assault	509	13	3
Assault	4,287	125	3
Drunken driving	14,257	259	2
Arson	106	1	1
Attempted homicide or manslaughter or aiding and abetting in same	30	—	—
Forcible rape	104	—	—

Table 10. Proportion of Females Sentenced Out of All Offenders Sentenced in Finland, Denmark, Norway, and Sweden, 1969.

	Total Sentenced N	Female %
FINLAND		
Embezzlement, fraud	849	25
Misleading an authority, perjury	757	20
Forgery	759	18
Theft offenses	7,374	14
Robbery, extortion	429	8
Assault offenses	4,297	2
Drunken driving	5,782	1
DENMARK		
Perjury	34	47
Forgery	929	19
Dealing in stolen property	71	14
Embezzlement, fraud, dishonesty toward a principal	1,050	12
Theft offenses	7,267	11
Robbery	103	9
Violence against an official	72	7
Unauthorized use	1,590	3
Assault offenses	976	2
NORWAY		
Perjury	86	21
Misleading an authority	34	15
Theft offenses	5,299	12
Dealing in stolen property, accessory after the fact	342	12
Forgery of a document	630	11
Fraud	198	10
Embezzlement	221	10
Robbery, extortion	68	6
Assault offenses	641	4
SWEDEN		
Perjury	501	18
Theft offenses	19,825	17
Fraud, embezzlement	5,788	15
Dealing in stolen property	2,209	13
Forgery	288	12
Robbery	248	3
Homicide, assault	4,254	3
Unauthorized use of a motor vehicle	3,350	2

generally exceeded 10 percent. Dealing in stolen property and embezzlement belong in the same category.

It may be surprising to note that the female proportion is also much higher with regard to two other offenses, document forgery and perjury (in court or before the police), although the absolute figures for these offenses are much lower than for theft. It is also interesting that the same situation is to be found in the other Scandinavian countries. In Denmark, Norway, and Sweden, perjury ranks highest; in Finland, it holds second place. One possible explanation for this is that the perjury is committed in order to aid a husband or friend accused of an offense; this is well suited to the woman's role as "background," this time for an offense. However, in the absence of research results, this cannot be verified.

Even though it has been noted above that there is reason to focus attention on offenses leading to imprisonment—in other words, the more serious offenses—in this connection there is one offense that should be mentioned, though it almost always leads to a fine only. As shown by Table 11, the proportion of women out of all offenders sentenced for *defamation* is surprisingly high. In the absence of studies on the subject, nothing more precise may be said of these cases. However, it is interesting to note that the number of both men and women accused of defamation has decreased, decade after decade. During recent years, the number of women accused for this offense has been around 25–53 per year. As this is an offense which typically can be brought to court only if the complainant so wishes, this decrease must be due to a change in attitudes. It is a question, not only of the

Table 11. **Total Number of Persons Accused of Defamation and Proportion of Women Accused, 1955–75.**

Year	All Offenders N	Women N	Women %	Year	All Offenders N	Women N	Women %
1955	443	184	41	1966	133	50	38
1956	370	155	42	1967	111	53	48
1957	380	164	42	1968	94	45	48
1958	383	146	38	1969	112	28	25
1959	—	—	—	1970	74	19	26
1960	262	140	53	1971	79	25	32
1961	193	71	37	1972	—	—	—
1962	106	32	30	1973	85	35	41
1963	170	74	43	1974	—	—	—
1964	145	69	48	1975	138	39	29
1965	143	47	33				

extent to which a person feels himself or herself "insulted," but also to what extent he believes that he can "regain his honor" through the courtroom ritual.

Statistics for Finland are available on the *age breakdown* of men and women sentenced to imprisonment. Table 12 shows the situation during the 1920s and the 1930s and presents the number of offenders sentenced for property offenses in relation to the total number of people in the same age group. Table 13 gives the age breakdown for theft offenses during the 1960s, and Table 14 shows the breakdown for all offenders sentenced to imprisonment in 1976. The tables reveal the well-known fact that, regardless of sex, criminality is above all typical of the younger age groups.

Table 12.   Male and Female Offenders Sentenced to Imprisonment in Courts of First Instance, By Age, Per 100,000 in the Same Age Group, 1924–38.

Age	Men All Offenses	Property Offenses	Women All Offenses	Property Offenses
15	283	235	37	29
16	379	289	50	39
17	529	348	82	61
18	765	430	104	67
19	973	467	109	69
20	1,417	526	116	65
21	1,592	485	123	61
22	1,292	497	125	60
23	1,143	472	109	53
24	1,039	450	96	40
25–29	835	364	91	39
30–34	566	255	73	27
35–39	355	168	65	23
40–44	245	122	58	19
45–49	177	89	45	14
50–54	124	65	39	13
55–59	81	42	19	7
60–64	50	23	11	3
65–	18	8	2.8	0.9
15–84	498	266	59.4	26.6

Source: Kaila, 1950.

Why Does Both Male and Female Criminality Increase?

As the statistics indicate that female criminality has not increased in Finland any more than male criminality, it is clear that there are common factors which explain the increase in both male and female criminality.

Table 13. Age of Offenders Sentenced for Theft Offenses in Courts of First Instance. (Comparable Figures for the 1970s Are Not Available.)

Year	Total Women N	15–17 %	18–20 %	21–24 %	25–29 %	30–39 %	40–49 %	50–59 %	60– %	Age Unknown %
1964	1,612	28	15	9	7	14	11	7	3	5
1965	1,643	25	18	10	8	11	12	6	3	7
1966	1,619	26	19	11	7	11	11	7	3	5
1967	1,849	24	18	11	7	13	12	8	4	3
1968	1,826	24	17	12	8	13	11	8	3	3
1969	2,123	22	16	13	8	13	12	7	3	5

Year	Total Women N	15–17 %	18–20 %	21–24 %	25–29 %	30–39 %	40–49 %	50–59 %	60– %	Age Unknown %
1964	10,670	26	15	12	11	17	9	5	1	5
1965	10,279	25	16	11	10	16	9	4	1	8
1966	10,374	23	18	13	11	16	9	4	1	4
1967	11,498	22	19	14	11	16	10	4	1	3
1968	12,589	21	19	17	11	15	10	4	1	3
1969	13,392	19	18	18	11	15	10	3	1	4

Table 14. Age of Offenders Sentenced to Imprisonment in Courts of First Instance, 1976.

	Total	Unconditionally Sentenced							
		15–17	18–20	21–24	25–29	30–39	40–49	50–59	60–
Men	28,596	738	2,129	3,493	3,790	3,198	1,667	554	137
Women	1,111	23	75	98	80	50	28	9	5
Both sexes	29,707	761	2,204	3,591	3,870	3,248	1,695	563	142

	Total	Conditionally Sentenced							
		15–17	18–20	21–24	25–29	30–39	40–49	50–59	60–
Men	12,890	1,959	2,704	2,265	1,947	1,978	1,227	539	271
Women	743	137	162	143	93	113	67	22	6
Both sexes	13,633	2,096	2,866	2,408	2,040	2,091	1,294	561	277

Today, both sexes are increasingly affected to the same degree by various legal norms. There has been a continuous migration from the countryside to the cities and other population centers, where the number of crime opportunities is considerably larger. The explosive increase in the supply of com-

modities has affected the increase in both male and female property offenses. Especially within the younger age groups, the easier availability of
attractive commodities is likely to increase pressures toward breaking the
law. In addition, alcohol consumption in Finland has consistently increased
during the past years; and both men and women have been increasingly
caught up by unemployment.

Why Is There Still So Little Female Criminality?

Possible Differences in the Official Crime Control System. As year after
year considerably fewer women than men are sentenced, there must be some
relatively permanent factors which explain this difference. One possible explanation would be that the official crime control system operates in a selective manner, so that men have a greater risk of being sentenced.

There are no differences inherent in *legislation* which would explain the
low level of female criminality. The only offense which by definition can be
committed only by a man is forcible rape. (However, a woman may be
guilty of aiding and abetting or of incitement.) The statistical significance of
this offense is very slight, as shown by the accompanying table.

Year	Men Accused of Rape N	Per 100,000 Males Over 15 Years of Age
1970	114	7
1971	92	5
1972	70	4
1973	88	5
1974	103	6
1975	104	6
1976	84	5

Infanticide, on the other hand, is an offense that can only be committed
by the mother of the child in question. As observed previously, only from
1 to 4 women are sentenced for this offense annually.

The differences between male and female criminality may also be due to
differences in the effectiveness of the official crime control system. In this
vein, it has often been suggested that a greater proportion of female criminality remains hidden. Indeed, it appears evident that there is a difference
in the *dark figure*. This is due, for example, to the fact that the offenses

most common among women are those for which the dark figure is also very large, such as property offenses. Mention should also be made of the observation, based on experience, that women often remain in the "background" as inciters or abettors and do not participate in the actual commission of the offense. Also, as more female than male criminality occurs within the family circle, this increases the dark figure for female criminality even further.

This explanation is used, for example, in a study on hidden criminality among schoolchildren published in Sweden (Elmhorn, 1969). The report begins by observing that the self-reported criminality of schoolgirls was about one-third that of schoolboys, and that the offenses committed by schoolgirls were more often of a trivial nature. But it is also observed that for every offense committed by a schoolgirl and reported to the police, 11 offenses committed by schoolboys were reported to the police. Doubtless this shows the greater possibility of girls' offenses remaining hidden. A shoplifter study carried out in Finland, which dealt not only with crimes reported to the police but with all actual apprehensions, showed that 57 percent of the cases of shoplifting ($N = 795$) were committed by women, and that of the adult shoplifters 78 percent were women (Aromaa et al., 1970).

The size of female hidden criminality, however, does not under any circumstances explain the low level of female criminality in general.

Another common hypothesis in criminological literature is that our official crime *control system favors women:* for example, there is a greater possibility that charges raised against women will be dropped for lack of evidence than is the case for men. The accompanying table gives the number of men and women accused before courts of first instance as well as the relative number of cases where the charges were dropped.

	Cases Where Charges Were Dropped, per 1,000 Accused of the Same Sex	
Year	Men	Women
1966	24	37
1967	20	34
1968	23	33
1969	25	30
1970	23	33
1971	23	37
1972	—	—
1973	54	38
1974	69	59
1975	78	55

In the absence of specific research, there is no reason to conclude any-thing on the basis of the differences in the proportion of charges dropped other than the fact that the small share of women among offenders commit-ting "manifest" offenses—for example, committed in public places (street fighting) or among those committing offenses which generally enter the sta-tistics only when there is ample proof (drunken driving, when detected by the police at a *razzia* roadblock)—may explain at least a large part of the difference.

There are extensive difficulties in trying to ascertain sentencing practices should we content ourselves with the aggregate figures to be found in the statistics. This is due to the fact that in individual cases the severity of the sentence is affected by, for example, the previous record of the offender and the circumstance of the offense. For instance, one Finnish study noted that there was a large difference in the granting of pardons to men and women convicted of homicide. On closer analysis, this difference could be ex-plained almost entirely by the simple fact that only 1 in 8 of the convicted women had been in prison before, while 1 in 3 of the men had a previous record of imprisonment (Anttila; Törnudd; Westling, 1969). Also the pattern in every court statistic, where women are given conditional imprisonment sentences relatively more often than men, is of little information value, as long as we do not have any more precise information on the nature of the cases. Studies on this matter are not available in Finland.

The belief that men and women are accorded different treatment in court is generally connected with the fact that most judges are male. At least in Finland, the trend is toward a more balanced situation in this respect. At the present, 40 percent of those entering the law faculties are women, and roughly the same figure holds true for those receiving their degree. As for the placement of female lawyers, it is known that fewer women than men follow a career on the bench, but doubtless the very fact that a large number of women graduate every year in law will lead to a greater influx of women in court.

A Finnish study on the general sense of justice noted that women have a stricter attitute toward so-called moral offenses but a more lenient attitude toward property offenses than men (Mäkelä, 1966). On the other hand, there are no studies that would reveal whether or not this also holds true for women who are trained for the bench. Sociological studies on court practice appear to show that the "severity" of each individual court's sentencing practice can be largely explained by the tradition that has been adopted by that court. At least as long as female judges are in the minority, it would appear probable that they would each adapt themselves to the court's tradi-tion, and thus there would not be any essential changes in sentencing practice. Should female judges form the majority, it could be that the sentencing practice would be stricter for domestic violence by men, forcible rape, and sexual offenses (Anttila, 1975). If it is true that women are treated more leniently than men in court, it would appear probable that a greater balance on the bench would lead to more equitable treatment of those before the bench.

Possible Differences Outside the Official Crime Control System. The principal reasons for the low amount of female criminality are doubtless to be found among factors outside the official crime control system. In Finland, one cannot accept the explanation that the official social position of men and women is very different. The legal equality of women is not a recent phenomenon. As is well known, woman suffrage in Europe was first granted in Finland in 1906. Since 1901 women have had the right to enter any faculty in the universities, and since the 1950s a majority of those entering the university have been women (the last official statistics are from 1974, when women accounted for 51 percent of the first-year students). For over fifty years women have been eligible for almost all government posts; at present, only military posts and the office of priest are exceptions to this. The share of women in the nonagricultural labor force has been consistently increasing decade after decade; it is very high when compared with the other Scandinavian countries (Figure 2). In Finland, marriage and childbirth no longer necessitate giving up work outside the home. According to the 1970 census, 66 percent of all women 25 to 59 years old were economically active. This percentage is the highest in Scandinavia (the corresponding figure in Sweden was 56 percent; in Denmark, 53 percent, and in Norway, 45 percent).

The role of women in society is certainly not dependent only on employment conditions. A naturally important factor is their *role in the family*. In this respect, the Finnish woman's position has not changed very much over the past decades. The general attitude is that the woman is still primarily responsible for housekeeping and especially for the raising of children. A woman's leisure time, and possibly especially the leisure time of women who work outside the home, is limited. It is true that modern Finnish culture grants women the right to work outside the home, but a woman with a family is expected to use most of her time taking care of her family. In this, the family has noticeable informal social control over women.

A factor often connected with male leisure time in Finland is the *use of alcohol*, and men continue to consume more alcohol more frequently than women; this is especially true of strong alcohol. The extensive violent criminality of men in Finland has traditionally been touched off by alcohol, and the use of alcohol affects many other types of criminality for men.

Surveys of public opinion in Finland, as in the other Scandinavian coun-

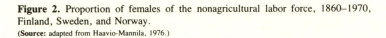

Figure 2. Proportion of females of the nonagricultural labor force, 1860–1970, Finland, Sweden, and Norway.
(**Source:** adapted from Haavio-Mannila, 1976.)

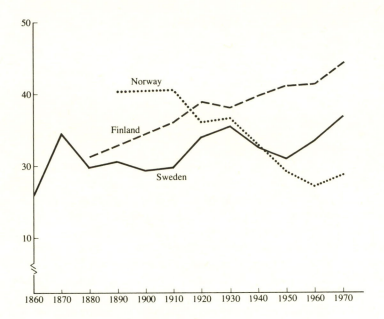

tries, show that *the role of the offender is often linked with a male role,* starting with the youngest age groups. Even in this respect there have scarcely been any essential changes recently.

In the light of the above, then, we may summarize our findings by noting that:

1. Criminality in Finland has risen steeply during the 1970s, and this has affected both male and female criminality. The increase in male criminality, however, has been greater than for female criminality, with the exception of drunken driving.
2. The more rapid increase of drunken driving among women can be explained by changes during the 1970s in alcohol consumption by women.
3. The fact that no dramatic changes can be found in female property criminality can be explained above all by the fact that the female proportion of the labor force outside the home has been large for

many decades, and in this respect there have been no radical changes since World War II.

4. The low level of female criminality when compared with male criminality can be explained primarily with reference to traditional role patterns and to the limited amount of leisure time accorded women.

It may be that reports and studies on female criminality have been given so little attention because of the low significance of female criminality when compared with male criminality. However, the very differences in the absolute amount of criminality is interesting even when this amount remains the same year after year, even decade after decade. The differences must be connected with the economic circumstances and cultural traditions in society, and they must reflect underlying differences in the position and role of men and women. The explanations found for the low amount of female criminality may tell us something about the more extensive criminality of men, and thus lead to the discovery and corroboration of regularities of criminality in general.

References

Anttila, Inkeri. "Women in the Criminal Justice System." Unpublished paper, 1975.

Anttila, Inkeri and Achilles Westling. "A Study in the Pardoning of and Recidivism among Criminals Sentenced to Life Imprisonment." *Scandinavian Studies in Criminology*. Vol. 1. Oslo, 1965.

Anttila, Inkeri and Patrik Törnudd. *Kriminologia*. Porvoo, 1970.

Anttila, Inkeri and Patrik Törnudd. *Kriminologi*. Stockholm, 1973.

Aromaa, Kauko, Patrik Törnudd and Kirsti Wartiovaara: *Department Store Shoplifters*. Institute of Criminology. Series M:6. Helsinki; 1970 (stencil).

Elmhorn, Kerstin. *Faktisk Brottslighet Bland Skolbarn*. Statens offentliga utredningar (1969):1. Stockholm, 1969.

Haavio-Mannila. "Elina: Economic and Family Roles of Men and Women in Northern Europe." Paper presented at the International Liaison Committee of National Council on Family Relations; New York, 1976 (stencil).

Kaikla, Martti. *Nuorisorikollisuus*. Porvoo, 1950.

Mäkinen, Tuija. *Kvinnobrottsligheten i Finland i skenet av statistiken*. Institute of Organization and industrial Sociology. Arbeijdsnote 76-1. Copenhagen, 1976 (stencil).

Pyrrö, Leena. *Henkirikokset Suomessa vuosina 1969–1972*. Institute of Criminology. Series M:23. Helsinki, 1973 (stencil).

Törnudd, Patrik. *Crime Trends in Finland 1950–1977*. Research Institute of Legal Policy 29. Helsinki, 1978.

Törnudd, Patrik. "Forecasting the Number of Female Prisoners in Finland." Paper presented at European Committee on Crime Problems. Council of Europe. Strasbourg, 1971 (stencil).

Verkko, Veli. *Henki- ja pahoinpitelyrikollisuuden kehityssuunnan ja tason määräämisestä I*. Helsinki, 1931.

Verkko, Veli. *Homicides and Suicides in Finland and Their Dependence on National Character*. Copenhagen, 1951.

Notes

1. Unless otherwise mentioned, the sources used in this paper are either the court statistics or the police statistics published by the Central Statistical Office of Finland.

3. Norwegian Women in Court

A. JENSEN

An-Magritt Jensen is Junior Executive Officer at the Central Bureau of Statistics. Her primary interest in the field is the connection between fertility and the working situation of females. Her publications include: "The Place of the Female Offender in the Penal System," *Structural Violence against Women* (1975), 22; "Female Criminality," *Nordic Journal of Criminal Science* (1978), 4; "Female Criminality in Three Latin Countries," San José, Costa Rica: "Ilanud" (in press). A summary appears in *Ilanud Al Dia* (1979), 5.

Of the 4 million inhabitants of Norway, approximately 10,000 persons yearly are being punished and the overwhelming part are men. Females constitute 7 percent of the offenders. As is the tendency in other countries, the difference in numbers between convicted women and men is very large and it seems to be a consistent feature. After some years of increase in the number of female offenders, at the end of the 1960s and the beginning of the 1970s, the latest years have shown a stabilizing or even decreasing tendency as regards female offenders. However, while females constitute a small part of the total number of offenders, they account for an even smaller proportion of those sentenced to imprisonment. Altogether, 3,065 persons were sentenced to unconditional imprisonment in 1976; of those, 84 (or less than 3 percent) were women.[1]

Few females are punished to start out with; their number gets smaller the more severe the punishment. To understand this, we have to consider two facts. First, females in Norway are charged with less severe offenses than men (e.g., simple vs. aggravated larceny). Second, male offenders are more often recidivists than females (two thirds of the men versus one third of the women). To a great extent it is possible to find an explanation of the different sentencing practices vis-a-vis men versus women in their respective crime patterns and criminal background.

In this study we shall concentrate on the following questions: who women offenders are; in what kind of life situation they committed their crimes; and what the sanctions were against them.

The study does not deal with an analysis of the total number of convicted women, nor with a random selection among them. The documents of penal cases in the city court of Oslo, 1977, are the starting point. These total 63 cases constitute the study population. If our purpose is to learn something about the female offender in general, this sample has its obvious weaknesses. First of all, the women in the study constitute less than 10 percent of the total number. This is due to the fact that even though most of the female offenders are living in Oslo, only a few of them have their cases submitted to the city court. Most of the women are referred to the court of examining and summary jurisdiction. The differences between the cases handled by the two courts generally include the seriousness of the crime and the criminal background of the offender. This means that the sample of women tried in the city court is unrepresentative in regard to those two factors. The ones tried in the city court have committed more severe offenses and have more criminal experience than the ordinary female offender in Norway.

The strong point of this sample, however, is that the documents of the city court (in contrast to those of the court of examining and summary jurisdiction) give detailed and systematic information of the background of the offender and the circumstances of the crime, and these data were needed in order to accomplish the goals of this study. While our findings do not, therefore, allow us to generalize to all female offenders in Norway, what we do learn is important.

We look first at the social background of the women, then at their law-breaking activities, and finally at the sanctions of society. Where data are available, we compare the official crime statistics of all female offenders to those of the city court sample.

Social Background

Let us first look at the overall age distribution of female offenders in Norway.[2] Diagram 1 shows that most of them are young. Eighty-four women are 16 years old. Thereafter the curve drops with rising age. However, it is difficult to say whether we are facing a steadily falling trend, since the criminal statistics do not specify the data for each age level above 24 years of age but, rather, use broader categories.

As we can see from Diagram 2, the city court women are older than the ordinary female offenders. The youngest was 16, the oldest was 49. The peak was at 22 years of age, with most women in the city court in that category. It is interesting to note that the number of female offenders did not consistently decrease with rising age. On the contrary, women in their

Diagram 1. Total number of female offenders and their age.

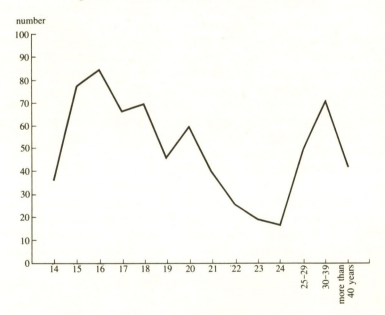

Diagram 2. Women in the City Court and their age.

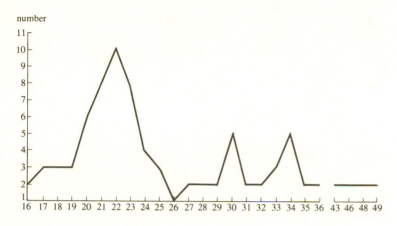

<arly thirties make up another peak in the curve. We do not know whether
his represents a general trend or not. But at least in this study we are con-
ronted with the following cycles: the age group of the early twenties fea-
ures a period of high criminal activity for women. This period coincides
with a time when they may have left their parents' home and do not yet
ave their own families. The middle of the twenties seems to be the age of
ope. Family life has just started, and the children are small. At the begin-
ing of the thirties, dreams are often ruined. Problems have emerged and
an no longer be solved in a legal way. For most of the women lawbreaking
t this age means the resuming of an activity abandoned years earlier. This
ccurs at a juncture when the nuclear family either is given up or is facing
 severe crisis.

Civil Status. Male criminals in Norway differ from the "normal popula-
ion" in the category of family status; they are usually single or divorced.
rom the court documents we find that the same tendency is valid for
women. Of the 63 women nearly 50 percent were unmarried. Twenty per-
ent were divorced; only 16 percent were married. Compared with other
women in Oslo at the same age level, these women were more often derived of having their own family than were the nonoffenders. In addition,
he married women frequently seemed to have serious marital problems. In
many cases this circumstance had a clear connection to their criminal acts.

One example is AA. She appeared in court charged with having falsely
eported the theft of a stereo recorder and a furcoat from her home. AA had
aken out home insurance some days earlier and was told by the insurance

company that the loss had to be reported to the police. The police became suspicious because half a year earlier this woman had reported another loss, and at that time she had received 6,000 Norwegian kroner (one U.S. dollar is approximately 5 Norwegian Kr) as compensation. The suspicion was strengthened by the fact that they could find no trace of housebreaking. The explanation the accused gave was that she feared her husband would leave her. Their relationship had been rather bad for a long time. She wanted to secure her personal property before he left. For this reason she sold her stereo recorder and furcoat. Afterward she was afraid of what he would say and invented the burglary story.

Another example is BB. She had a son from a prior marriage and was now married to CC. CC had alcohol problems. BB had a parttime job and opened a salary check account. During one month she withdrew more than 9,000 Kr in cash from this account. The net salary for the same month was around 1,000 Kr. Her husband was drinking heavily at the time and spent all his money on liquor. BB's son went to a private high school, and money was needed for tuition. The alimony from her first husband was very small. BB explained that the reason for her offense was the family's economic situation. She returned most of the money later.

Two features seem to be common for married women in terms of their lawbreaking activities. One is the situation when husband and wife conspire in breaking the law, as in the example of DD and EE. She stole the wallet from an unknown man while her husband was talking to him. The second common feature is that the offense is committed when the family is facing a severe crisis. Thus, there are two opposite tendencies. Either the offense is one in which the woman acts together with her man, or it is one in which such togetherness is lacking. The situation underlines the fact that a woman's activity has to be analyzed more than simply in its relationship to a male partner.

Employment Status. While 54 percent of all women in Oslo at this age level are employed, only 30 percent of the women in this study have jobs. This lesser connection with the labor market is even more marked when we look at the kind of work performed by the sample. For many the work seemed to have little stability; the jobs were "extras." Several were included in a special work program run by the aftercare and employment office. All of them had typical "female jobs." They were washing, cleaning canteens, knitting, working as assistants in offices, and so on. Both the salary and the social status of their jobs were low.

Accordingly, the women had, in general, a marginal connection with the labor market. Most of them had no employment, and the few who did were very poorly paid and had jobs which only lasted for a short period.

Living Area. Oslo is, like most cities, clearly divided into different areas for specified social groups. The general pattern of Oslo is that rich people live in the western parts of the city while poor people live in the eastern parts. A survey of living conditions shows that the population living in the western areas earn more money, have a higher education, and have more spacious dwellings than those in the eastern areas. In contrast, the population on the east side has a greater need for social services.

Altogether 75 percent of the female offenders appearing before the city court lived on the east side of Oslo (central and suburbs). Eleven of the women lived outside Oslo; consequently; they are not included here. West-side women were clearly underrepresented in the sample. Only 8 percent of these women were living in the most prominent westside suburbs. Compared with the general distribution of the population in Oslo as regards living area, the central parts of the eastside were dominant with respect to female offenders brought before the city court.

The conclusion drawn from these data on social variables (civil status, subsistence, and living area) clearly seems to indicate that the women sentenced in the Oslo city court belong to the least privileged strata of the population. According to the above indicators, the women showed similarities to other marginal groups in that they have a high divorce rate, lack integration into the labor market, and live in the poor districts of the city.

Lawbreaking Activity

Let us now take a brief look at the general picture of lawbreaking activities among women in Norway. Diagram 3 gives an overview of the development of the most important female offenses from 1958 until today.[3] We see that simple larcenies have been the dominant offense, reaching a peak in 1966 when 325 women were convicted of this crime. But we also see that after that year this kind of offense has decreased gradually, while at the same time other offenses have become more important. This development seems to represent a change in the character of female criminality from the more cautious minor thefts to the more daring aggravated ones.

In approaching this change we have to pay more attention to the year 1969. During that year, for the first time, offenses involving public danger (hereafter referred to as narcotics) were recorded as a significant female

Diagram 3. Total number of female offenders, 1958 – 76.

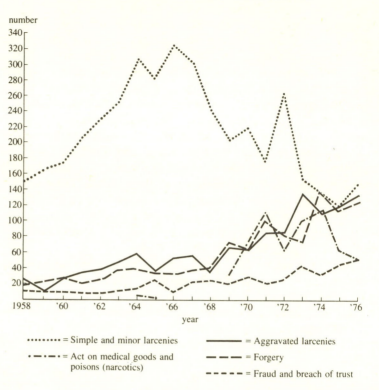

.... = Simple and minor larcenies ———— = Aggravated larcenies

• — • — • = Act on medical goods and — — — = Forgery
poisons (narcotics)

— - — - — = Fraud and breach of trust

criminal activity. During the same year there was an increase in forgery and
aggravated larcenies. We shall here submit the hypothesis that there exists
a close relationship between the increase of narcotics offenses, forgery, and
aggravated larcenies, and that these increases may be traced back to the
introduction of drugs to Norwegian youth, which took place in the late
1960s.

Females in the City Court. Female offenders in the city court of Oslo
seem to be fairly representative of the ordinary female offender in Norway
regarding the categories of crime. (However, as mentioned before, the act
within each crime category is probably more serious for the city court de-
fendant.)

We see that the sample shown in Table 1 is fairly underrepresented in
aggravated larcenies and overrepresented in narcotics and the receiving of
stolen goods. However, we have to be aware that this may be due to coin-

Table 1.   Female Offenses, Percent.[4]

	City Court	In Norway
Simple and minor larcenies	19.0	20.2
Forgery	19.0	17.2
Aggravated larcenies	12.7	19.0
Narcotics	12.7	7.4
Receiving stolen goods	12.7	6.4
Simple fraud	11.1	7.4
Violence against person	4.8	2.8
Embezzlement	3.2	2.9
Others	4.8	16.7
Total	100.0	100.0
	(N = 63)	(N = 702)

cidence because of the small number of women appearing in the city court. From this point, we go on to study the hypothesis of the relationship between various offenses and the use of alcohol and drugs.

Lawbreaking and the Use of Drugs or Alcohol. The first question is to what extent the court documents showed some evidence of the use of alcohol and drugs among the women. From Table 2, we see that more than 40 percent of the women had some connection with narcotics, and of these 31.7 percent were declared drug addicts in court. In addition, 19 percent either had severe alcohol problems or had committed their offenses while under the influence of alcohol. Altogether, 60 percent of the women were in one or the other way involved with drugs or alcohol. Most of them used drugs. Moreover, it should be noted that these figures indicate the minimum extent of involvement, since it may simply indicate that nothing was said in court about the use of drugs by the remaining subjects.

In order to grasp more firmly the change in character of female criminality at the end of the 1960s, we shall analyze the distribution of the relationship of the various crimes to drug and alcohol use. In Diagram 4 we find a clear connection between narcotics and the crimes of forgery, simple larcenies,

Table 2.   Female Offenses and the Use of Drugs or Alcohol, Percent.

Drug addicts	31.7
Connection to narcotics	11.1
Alcohol	19.0
None	38.1
Total	99.9
	(N = 63)

Diagram 4. Offenses and drug use, percent.

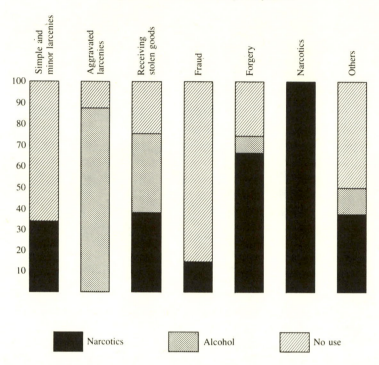

and receiving stolen goods.[5] This is especially marked for forgery, where 66 percent of the women accused of this offense had some association with narcotics. At the same time, there seems to be no link between aggravated larcenies and drugs. This may be due to the fact that in general, the rise in aggravated larcenies is found among the youngest females, 14–17, while the subjects of this study are mostly women over 22 years of age. It should be noted that in the cases where a woman was accused of more than one offense—most of the cases—only the most severe offense was codified in accordance with the practice of the Norwegian *Criminal Statistics*. The most "typical" offenses by the women in their mid-twenties and older (who are highly represented in this study) is forgery, which is considered a more severe offense than aggravated larceny. The problem might be clarified by an example.

The lawbreaking behavior of HH is typical. She was accused of falsely signing and cashing seven checks amounting to 3350 Kr. Furthermore, she cashed six checks which a boyfriend signed, 1750 Kr in all, and finally she signed and cashed another eleven checks, for a total amount of 3400 Kr. She had also stolen wallets in restaurants on four different occasions. She was accused of forgery and aggravated larceny. According to the court: "she has grown up under difficult circumstances. For many years she has been a drug addict and has been in many psychiatric institutions. The accused suffers from chronic inflammation of the liver." HH's offense was codified as forgery, but it is likely that her offenses financed her use of drugs.

Returning to Diagram 4 and the aggravated larcenies, we find that 7 of these 8 women had been under the influence of alcohol. However, there seem to be important differences in the pattern of offenses between those who were under the influence of alcohol and those who were under the influence of narcotics. It was typical that the lawbreaking activities of the women accused of forgery (narcotics) had been going on for a long time, often for one or more periods lasting from fourteen days to a month. The lawbreaking activity in this period was intense. On the other hand, the aggravated larcenies were more often a sudden inspiration under the influence of alcohol.

This was the case of II who on a particular occasion was in downtown Oslo at night. Passing by a jewelry store, she found that the pane had been smashed and repaired with tape. She was drunk. She met a man and they returned together to the store. The man removed the tape from the pane and stole some silver jewelry (valued at 1500 Kr) which he placed in her bag. They were caught while doing this.

Diagram 4 tells us that the use of narcotics and alcohol is not equally distributed among the various offenses. This supports the hypothesis that the change in female criminality at the end of the 1960s must be viewed in the light of the large-scale introduction of narcotics into Norway at the time. But we also see another tendency, that is, that some offenses seem to have no connection with either drugs or alcohol, as is the case with fraud. Embezzlement (which is included in the group of "others") is another example.

Three Groups

In analyzing the relationship between female criminality and drug and alcohol use, three groups of women emerge. The first group is composed of women using narcotics who were punished mostly for forgery, simple larceny, and drug offenses. The second is the one comprised of women in the "alcohol" group who were punished for aggravated larcenies. And finally there is the group of women with no connection with either drugs or alcohol and who were punished mainly for fraud. We will continue with a survey of the characteristics of the life situation of the women in each of these three groups.

Narcotics. Twenty-seven of the total number of women in this study had some connection to narcotics. Of those 20 were defined as drug addicts in court. They were accused of extensive criminality. The dominating offenses were against property. They found crime useful as a means of financing their daily use of drugs. Most of the women were young, from 20 to 23 years old. It was more common for the younger ones to be accused of offenses against the laws on narcotics, while the older ones were more often accused of forgery. The "narcotics" women often had a considerable criminal background. Only 3 out of 27 had not been punished previously. Very seldom had they established their own family. One was married and one was divorced. Nine of the women had children, and less than half of them lived together with a man. Most of the women lived in the poor sections of Oslo, but still, compared with the other two groups, women from the wealthiest parts of the city were overrepresented here. This was the case with regard to 7 of the 27 women in this group. Regarding class background, the latter differed from all of the rest. They were the "well-off" children who had gone astray. JJ was one of them.

She was in her early twenties. According to the court documents, she had been a drug addict for ten years and had been punished several times. This time she was accused of shoplifting. She concentrated on leather jackets. What she stole, she afterward sold for a trifle in order to finance her drug abuse. Regarding her background, the court documents say that JJ "is an adopted child and feels rejected by her father, a well-known physician. The first time she came in contact with drugs, in the beginning of her teens, her parents had her committed to a private psychiatric clinic for observation. From that time on she has been sent to different boarding schools until now when she has no contact with her parents."

Within the "narcotics" group there seem to be greater class differences than among the rest of the women in the study.

Alcohol. Twelve of the women in the sample had either committed their crime under the influence of alcohol, or the court documents emphasized an alcohol problem. More than half of them were accused of aggravated larcenies. In this group there were clear age differences. They were either quite young or rather old. Half of the women were between 30 and 35 years old.

LL was a representative of the young women. She was 17 and had been drinking all day long together with two boys. In the evening they wanted more to drink and broke into a supermarket where they stole beer and cigarettes. LL was keeping watch outside. They were caught while doing this.

The older women had been using alcohol over a long period. MM was a woman in her mid-thirties. She was with a man when she met NN, also a woman. MM was drunk and suggested a burglary. When NN refused, she was knocked down by MM. Later on MM and her male friend met a man unknown to them. Together they stole his wallet and watch. She was accused of aggravated larceny and violence.

Nine of the 12 women had been punished previously. Most of them had been dependent on alcohol for a long time, and many had received treatment. A few of them were married to husbands with the same kinds of problem. Including the divorced women in this group, most of the older women had marriage experience. All but one came from the least privileged parts of Oslo.

Nonusers. These women numbered 24. They were not necessarily nonusers of drugs or alcohol. The nonuser status may simply refer to the fact that the court documents said nothing about it. Even considering this defect in the material, this group differs from the two former ones in several ways. Their most frequent offenses were fraud, simple larcenies, and embezzlement. The urgent economic needs were striking. These women had committed their crimes in a situation of hopelessness and despair. An example of this is OO.

Her offense consisted of having opened a salary account in her name and overdrawing it by approximately 7000 Kr. Half a year earlier she had left her husband, who was unemployed and an alcoholic. She did not receive support for the children, and her husband refused to leave their apartment. Moreover, he did not pay the rent. In order not to lose that apartment she had to pay the rent both for the original apartment of the couple, to which she expected to return, and for her temporary one. In this situation, she explained to the court, she had to get money somehow.

The majority of the women lived on the east side of Oslo, and mostly in the newly established satellite towns. Many of the women were in their late twenties. Thirteen of the 24 women were between 24 and 48 years old; the rest were about 22 to 23 years old. As regards the pattern of offenses and earlier criminal experiences, those two subgroups differ. We will begin with those aged 24 years and older. The example of OO is representative of this subgroup.

The majority had been punished before, but a long time ago. They returned to the criminal activity which they had left years ago at a moment when they were experiencing a very difficult situation. Most of them were or had been married. According to the court documents, all of them had gone through profound crises in their marriage. Some of them explained their offenses as being a consequence of their marital problems.

Those under 24 years are the most confusing group to describe. They were accused of different kinds of criminality. They had relatively little experience with penal justice. Only one had been punished before. Few had established their own families. In this group there might have been use of drugs which was not being reported.

In Sum. The sample material of 63 women was divided into three groups according to their association with drugs and alcohol. It turned out that the groups differed from each other in the following respects: offense pattern, age distribution, former punishments, and family relationship. The common feature for the women was that they had committed some crime or other, but apart from that they were in completely different life situations.

Inside the Penal System

Criminality in itself does not reveal very much about the life situation of a person. Getting registered in the crime records may be an isolated event in a well-established existence. This was also the situation for some of the women.

One example is the high official who, after a pleasant evening in the restaurants of the capital, wished to buy an antique watch out in the street. The transaction was interrupted by the police. This woman came into the records by accident and most certainly will not return. But that was an exception. It seems that criminality follows rather fixed patterns. As we have seen already, for most of the women their entrance in the crime records was not accidental. Most of them were already well known in court. Of the 63 women, 43 had either been sentenced before or had had the charges withdrawn. The distribution of different kinds of punishment has to be considered against this background.

From Table 3, we see that the most common punishment was a conditional prison sentence, since almost 43 percent were punished in this way. We also see that 25 percent pay for their crime by serving time in prison. When we add those who served some of their punishment in prison (the combination of alternative), we end up with a rather high percentage of imprisoned women. Thus the fact is substantiated that, compared with all female offenders in Norway, these women had a long criminal career. Only 13 percent of the total number of female offenders in the country go to prison every year.

Table 3. Kind of Punishment, Percent.

Conditional prison sentence	42.9
Unconditional prison sentence	25.4
Combination of conditional and unconditional prison sentence	14.3
Suspended sentence	7.9
Fine	1.6
Acquittal	7.9
Total	100.0
	(N = 63)

Prison and Children. A common assumption about why fewer women are sentenced to severe punishment than men has been the relationship between women and their children. Twenty-two of the women in this study had children, most of them one child. As is shown in Table 3, around 8 percent of the total number of women got a suspended sentence. In none of these cases did this prove to be because of the relationship to a child. Rather, a characteristic feature for these women was that the offenses seemed to be an isolated instance in an otherwise well-structured life.

What kind of punishment did the women with children get? Of the 22 women, 10 had to serve all or part of their sentence in prison, while the rest received a conditional prison sentence. Moreover, in less than half of the latter cases the court's motivation included the relationship to a child. The child was the main argument against imprisonment in a couple of cases only:

The case is that the accused has a 6 year old child. It will be very difficult to find an appropriate place for the child if the mother is imprisoned.

In one of the cases the judge evaluated the total life situation of a woman. He found that she was going through a period of stabilization:

PP has had severe problems for years. This year she had a daughter. She states that she lives with the child's father and that she has submitted an application for social insurance (for unmarried mothers). Furthermore, she says that she ended her drug abuse at the start of pregnancy and that her life situation is becoming more stable. The court concludes that these are special reasons for giving another conditional prison sentence. The accused has established her own family and now has something to live for. She has the possibility of getting support from her fiancé and is now responsible for a child.

But being responsible for a child is not an argument in itself in favor of a conditional sentence. QQ had the same background as the woman just mentioned. She was also accused of extensive offenses against property. She had the responsibility for a child of 3 months and was living alone. In her court documents we can read that "a little child makes immediate serving of the sentence difficult." QQ got five months' imprisonment, to be served at a later date.

Ten women with children had to go to prison. We do not know the consequences.

Punishment and the Use of Drugs and Alcohol. Also with respect to punishment there are systematic differences between the women classified in the groups "narcotics," "alcohol," or "non-users." Clearly the women in the "narcotics" group received the most severe sentences. For that reason we shall discuss them separately; the two other categories are combined together into one group ("alcohol" and "non-users"). The number of women in each of these two main groups is 27 and 36 respectively.

In all, 25 women had to serve the whole or part of their sentence in prison; 60 percent of them belonged to the "narcotics" group. All of these women except one were defined in court as drug addicts. On the other hand, 60 percent of the women in the combined group ("alcohol" or "non-users") were sentenced to conditional imprisonment.

The difference between the two main groups is even more significant when we look at the duration of the prison sentence. It clearly turns out that "narcotics" women got longer prison terms (i.e., more than six months) with regard to both conditional and unconditional sentences.

Also regarding pretrial detention we find a difference between the two main groups. Of the total sample, 25 had been in pretrial custody. Seventeen of them were in the "narcotics" group. This means that while "narcotics" women constitute 43 percent of all the women in this study, they make up 68 percent of those being kept in pretrial detention. They also had to spend more time there than the rest of the women. The longest stay was that of a young woman in her early twenties who was a drug addict. She had to spend five months in pretrial custody, although not consecutively. We see that many of the "narcotics" women had to serve jail time which has to be regarded as more severe than ordinary unconditional prison sentences. One of the reasons is that these women are always uncertain of the final result of their case.

Does this practice mean that the judges want to use imprisonment as a starting point for further treatment of these women? There are few indicators of this. Twenty women were defined as drug addicts. Only in 9 cases did the court recommend treatment. The most striking feature is that the court used its opportunity to recommend expiation in a treatment institution to a very small extent. The difficulties created thereby are obvious. As early as 1969 we could read in the annual report of the only female prison in Norway, Bredtvedt:

> During the last years of the period concerned, the need for medical assistance has grown considerably. This is due to the fact that the number of prisoners with nervous difficulties has increased. A significant part of the women have had psychiatric problems, often combined with abuse of alcohol and narcotics. They have been difficult to deal with, and have been the cause of much unrest in the institution. The growing number of drug addicts detained in pre-trial custody has been one of the most important problems. Because of the complexity of these cases their terms in pre-trial custody have been extraordinarily long, and the court has forbidden them to receive visitors and letters. These circumstances have made the treatment even more difficult. The strain on the officers at Bredtvedt has often been considerable, and has resulted in a great amount of sick leaves.[6]

Today, ten years later, nothing seems to have changed. The officers' situation is obviously difficult. It is also evident that the situation for these women is unbearable. Two attempts at escape took place in April 1978. In both cases the women were drug addicts.

Summary

What we have learned about female criminality through this study concerns some, but not all, women brought into court. We have seen that in some respects the women tried in the Oslo city court were not representative of the "ordinary" female offender in Norway. First of all they were older and maybe as a consequence had a longer experience with the penal system than usual. This, of course, in turn influenced the kind of sentences they received. But still, what we have learned is important enough.

We have found that most of the women were in their early twenties, with a peak at 22 years of age. But we also found that the crime curve did not systematically decline for older women. We had another peak for the age group at the beginning of their thirties. For these women criminality seemed to be the way out of a situation strained by marital and economic problems. Most of the women were unmarried or divorced. Only a few made their own living by regular work. Compared with other women in the region of Oslo, the women in the study confronted particularly difficult problems as regards the labor market. Most of them were living in the poorest parts of Oslo.

Their crime pattern was dominated by property offenses. It seemed relevant to divide the women into three groups based on their relationship to the use of drugs and alcohol.

The women involved with drugs constituted a major group. Usually they were accused of forgery or simple larcenies, and of course, other offenses against the legislation on narcotics. They were in their early twenties, often unmarried. Many of them were responsible for a child, and some were living with the father of the child. The small number of women from the wealthiest parts of Oslo largely belonged to this group.

Most of the women in the "alcohol" group were accused of aggravated larcenies. A few of them were quite young, but mainly the group consisted of the older women in this study. The latter were either married to a man who also had alcohol problems, or they were divorced.

The last group, with no registered relationship to drugs or alcohol, was to a great extent accused of fraud or simple larcenies. They were mainly at the middle level in the age distribution. Their situation was characterized by acute or constant economic and marital crises.

Because a great number of the women had some association with narcotics, two groups (with or without a relationship to narcotics) formed the basis of our analysis of the sentences given by the court. We found clear differences between the two groups. In every sense the "narcotics" women got the most severe treatment in court. Frequently they received unconditional prison sentences, and theirs were also the longest ones. They often had to spend time in pretrial custody. Only seldom were they allowed to serve their term in a treatment institution.

Over a period of the last ten years female criminality in Norway has changed, not in volume, but in character. If we use the male criminal pattern as a norm, we find a general tendency toward more equality in the criminal patterns of the two sexes. At first glance this seems to support the hypothesis of a link between changes in female criminality and female liberation. But after going deeper into the problem, we find that the changes, to a great extent, are due to the expanding use of narcotics among young people in the last decade. The use of drugs started in Norway just as in other Western countries, as a wave of protest against the "establishment." Today little of this antimovement is left in Norway. A study of the development of the use of narcotics in Norway has shown the changes among the drug users regarding social background and personal resources.[7] The tendency has clearly been a "proletarization" of the users, and especially regarding those who are brought into court. They come mainly from the working class, have usually left school prematurely, and often have severe personal problems.

The young women among them are the carriers of the changes in female criminality. Thus, it is difficult to make a connection with female liberation.

As an explanation for the small number of convicted females, as compared with males, we often hear that there exists a kind of "gentlemen's agreement" against punishing a woman. This may be true for some female offenders, although according to this study not for female drug addicts. As we saw, the judges in the city court gave drug addicts more severe sentences than other females; and, of course, here lies a potential change in the sex distribution of the prison population. Perhaps the gentlemen's agreement is valid for some, as in the case of the well-established woman from the western part of Oslo. She had put a leather jacket in her bag during a shopping trip in town. Her husband had a high income, and the couple had two children. For some weeks she had had nervous problems and had been taking tranquilizers. According to a doctor's statement, a consequence of this medication was that she felt withdrawn and weary. According to her, she had no intention of stealing the leather jacket. The judge believed her, and she was acquitted. But she was not a typical representative of the women appearing in court. She was one among the few—she was lucky. And of course, the judge was right. Why should she steal?

Notes

1. *Criminal Statistics*. Sanctions 1976. Table 16.
2. *Criminal Statistics*. Sanctions 1976. Table 3.
3. *Data Archives of Norwegian Criminality*. File 10.
4. *Criminal Statistics*. Sanctions 1976. Table 9. The figures are from different years: 1977 for the court figures and 1976 for those of *Criminal Statistics*. Others are: 1 robbery, 1 false accusation, 1 false evidence.
5. Others are: 1 robbery, 1 false accusation, 1 false evidence, 2 embezzlement, and 3 violence. Altogether 8.
6. *The Yearbook of the Prison Board 1950–1969*. Pp. 180–181.
7. *Narkotikakonflikten*. Britt Bergersen Lind: Glydendal Norwegian Publishers, 1974.

4. Female Crime in England and Wales

T. C. N. GIBBENS

Trevor Charles Noel Gibbens is Emeritus Professor at the Institute of Psychiatry, London University. His primary interest in the field is mental health aspects of juvenile and adult criminality. He is Chairman of the Institute for the Study and Treatment of Delinquency and Vice-Chairman of the Howard League for Penal Reform. His publications include: "Female Offenders," *Brit. J. Hosp. Med.* (1971), and "Mental Health Aspects of Shoplifting," *Brit. Med. J.* (1971).

In the last ten years there has been an increasing interest in, and research on the criminality of women. There has been a considerable increase in female crime, but it seems doubtful that this is a reason by itself, rather than being related to the changing status of women in society, spearheaded by the women's liberation movements and consequent legislation aimed at providing women with equal rights. Recently Carol Smart published *Women, Crime, and Criminology: A Feminist Critique* (1977), while in 1968 Frances Heidesohn, a woman sociologist, could write, "one might well be forgiven for wondering whether the deviance of women is a non-problem both to the social scientist and society in general, because so little effort has been devoted to studying it." From the latter point of view one must ask whether the growing interest is going to be very helpful to women offenders, though perhaps Smart would take pride in seeing women dealt with by the courts as severely as men.

In describing the present state of female crime I have been greatly helped by Miss Nancy Goodman, who has made a detailed analysis for the Council of Europe. She is not responsible, however, for the interpretations put upon these statistics, which are mine. Throughout this section I shall refer to the situation in England and Wales rather than Britain; the Scottish legal system is quite different from the English, and comparisons are difficult. England and Wales have the advantage of a unified system of criminal statistics, even though there are many relatively independent police forces and there are certainly some local variations in police practice in prosecuting crime. These statistics are divided into "indictable" offenses (broadly, those which must be tried by the higher crown courts or for which the offender can claim trial by jury) and nonindictable offenses tried only by magistrates. A few offenses are "hybrid." Magistrates, however, deal with the vast majority of indictable offenses, which include, for example, all forms of theft. The police can issue a "caution" for minor indictable offenses if the accused admits the offense; they can therefore count as convictions. Altogether, 31 percent of females are cautioned, half of girls up to 16 and women over 60, but 5 to 10 percent at other ages.

The reader will probably not need to be reminded that the relation of criminal statistics, even when punctiliously and uniformly recorded, to the dark figure of unrecorded and undetected crime is very uncertain. The relationship varies from one crime to another. As far as the popular property crimes are concerned, the newer methods of collecting confidential self-report studies of young people are rather reassuring, that is, that those committing frequent and persistent offenses tend to be caught and that the undetected do not do it so often or for so long. Legislative changes also have affected them. Thus, the Theft Act of 1968, operating from 1969, codified theft and receiving and fraud offenses and increased the number of indictable offenses, including "taking and driving away an automobile." The Criminal Damage Act of 1971 also made some forms of "malicious damage" indictable.

In the years 1963–1977, females of all ages found guilty have increased 2⅓ times, or with cautions threefold; while males, though much more numerous, have increased 1¾ times. In relation to 100,000 population, and taking 1963 as a base line of 100, females guilty cautioned were 282 in 1977 and males 178. The male/female ratio has fallen from 7 : 1 in 1963 to 5 : 1 in 1977. There has, therefore, been a considerable absolute and relative increase in female convictions for indictable offenses, though it has not risen above 18 percent of male crime.

If one concentrates upon females alone, it is very easy to make alarming assumptions about the increase. But for a more balanced appreciation of the "crime wave" among females, one must look at it in relation to the total crime problem, especially in relation to age. Figure 1 shows the persons under 21 found guilty or cautioned for indictable offenses per 100,000 of the relevant age group during the last fifteen years. The peak is at 14 for girls and 15 for boys, but, as we saw, those cautioned amounted to 58 percent of girls aged 14 to 16. The male/female ratio is at its lowest in juveniles at the age of 12 when it is only 3.3 : 1, but it rises to a peak at 18 when 7.5 boys are convicted for every girl. It has always been the case that,

Figure 1. Persons aged under 21 found guilty of, or cautioned for, indictable offenses* per 100,000 population.
*Adjusted for changes in legislation

England and Wales

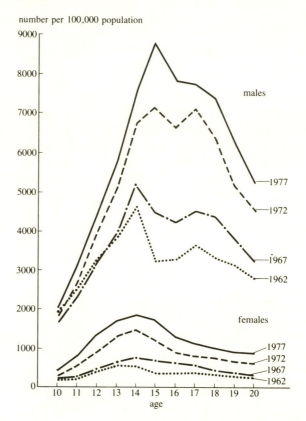

as in most other aspects of life, women "keep going" longer than men. The ratio falls again to 3 : 1 at 40–50, 2 : 1 at 50–60, and even only 1.8 : 1 at 60 or over. This is largely due to shoplifting offenses, which amount to over half of all convictions in the 1960s for men and women. Only 30 percent of men are then cautioned, however, compared with 48 percent of women.

To a large extent, then, the "crime wave by females" turns out to be a remarkable growth of petty theft by schoolgirls, though there has been a substantial increase, at all ages, especially in the younger age groups. A thorough appreciation of the delinquency of juveniles, especially girls, is difficult if not impossible because of the "care" or welfare proceedings which can be brought against them. Girls of 15 or 16, especially the more unmanageable and disordered, with whom I have been familiar for thirty years as psychiatrist to the London Observation Centre, were often not charged for the "crimes" they committed. They tended to be runaways from home, promiscuous, caught in cars their boyfriends had stolen, sharing in the proceeds of burglaries their boyfriends had committed, and perhaps stealing on their own. They were charged with being "beyond control" of their parents or "in need of care and protection" (rather like the American incorrigible minors), and since the Children and Young Persons' Act of 1971, "in need of Care and Control," their offenses being regarded as only one of many elements, together with truancy and absconding, in care proceedings. But their offenses, whatever they may be, are underrecorded. It is these girls who are most likely, when they reach adult jurisdiction age at 17, to be involved in adult criminal behavior. Certainly the figures from 17 onward are much more reliable.

As far as type of crime is concerned, "theft and handling stolen goods" played a much larger part among women than among men. Only a quarter of those found guilty or cautioned for these offenses are females, but they amount to 81 percent of all offenses of women compared with an equivalent proportion of 54 percent of offenses by men. This has remained about the same since 1969. Moreover, in 1977, 70 percent of all the thefts and handling offenses were for shoplifting, and this accounted for 55 percent of all women's indictable offenses, compared with 23 percent and 12 percent, respectively, among men. Rather surprisingly, the proportion of indictable offenses by women which consist of shoplifting has remained remarkably consistent for the last seventeen years, 25 percent of offenses by girls of 17–20, 30 percent of those aged 21–29, 50 percent at 30–40, 60 percent at 40–49, 75 percent at 50–59, and 85–90 percent at 60 or over.

Shoplifting is a fascinating and unique offense. It shows quite clearly all the causes of variation in reporting, detection, and prosecution which probably operate to some extent in all visible crime, but to a grossly exaggerated extent. It is not known to occur unless the woman is caught redhanded; a variable but high proportion of those observed are not arrested; and this occurs in practice only in places where there are store detectives. Many of those arrested are dealt with by threats and warnings by the store manager and, if reported to the police, are merely cautioned. Those finally coming before the courts are a peculiar selection from a particular sex and age group.

Recently it has become an anxiety to shops, and research has been stimulated. If every tenth person entering a store were to be followed until he or she leaves, 1 in 25 customers in English departments stores would be seen to shoplift, and rather more in self-service stores. In the U.S.A. it is 1 in 10 to 15, depending on the type of store. A national security firm estimated that "wastage"—goods unaccounted for—is 10 percent to accident, breakage, and spoilings; 30 percent, theft by delivery services, 40 percent, theft by sales staff; and 40 percent theft by customers. Each is difficult to detect or uneconomic to prosecute in the individual case. In one incident within my knowledge, a truck fulfilled an order for twelve crates of drinking glasses. By accident only eleven were delivered, but when the driver came back with apologies the next day with a twelfth, the reception clerk told him to take it away, since he would get into trouble for not counting the first part of the delivery. It is even reported that managers of large chain stores, whose pay is partly dependent on their takings, steal back from the public by the procedure of "bunching"—conniving with the assistant at the till to charge every customer for an extra item. The managers of one chain expressly forbade this practice.

The predominance of women is probably due to the fact that they predominate in places where there are detectives. The proportion of men, however, is steadily rising. Nowadays men shop more often with their wives, and as the tool shops, motor accessory shops, and the like, get bigger and employ security, these men are arrested more often. Bookshops arrest men only; women hardly ever steal books, apart from occasional students. The age figures on distribution of those arrested compiled by security firms, as opposed to figures compiled by courts, show that shoplifting is much like any other form of theft, with a graph very similar to that in Figure 1, the vast majority being children and young poeple from 12 to 15, though it does not decline among adults as rapidly as crime in general.

The most important feature of shoplifting is probably that it is an occupational theft for women, whose business is to spend money on housekeeping. Similar offenses by other women, secretaries who steal stamps and stationery or telephone their friends, or men in all industries who take home valuable waste metal, allegedly "damaged" goods, cooks in restaurants who take "surplus" food, dockers who take care to drop a few crates on the quayside and are allowed to take home the contents are difficult or impolitic to detect and are not separately recorded when they are. This sort of stealing is morally downgraded as "pilfering." In some respects, this is justified, because for each person it is only on a very small scale. Housewives spend $50 legitimately and steal only $5 worth of luxury food. They are observed week after week, and if they get bolder and steal 30 percent of what they pay for, they are arrested, though the earlier evidence is not admissible in court.

Theft and handling of stolen goods are the commonest property offenses, but a third group—fraud and forgery—fairly often involve women, who are responsible for 22 percent of convictions for these offenses. These offenses increased faster in women in recent times; between 1969 and 1977 they rose by three quarters (13 to 23 per 100,000) compared with a third (62 to 86) in men. In many ways, one would expect this to be much more widespread than it is, as larger numbers of women, married and unmarried, earn their living and have checkbooks and bank balances of their own. But to a surprising extent, England remains a cash rather than checkbook society. Security vans still transport large sums of money to pay factory workers, to the exasperation of the police and the encouragement of the armed robber. Cash payments for odd jobs or part-time jobs to evade income tax is practiced on a very wide scale. Some of the largest department stores do not bother to detect shoplifters because their losses from unpaid debts by women with accounts with them are so much more important, and the cost of litigation is so high that surprisingly large debts are written off rather than recovered. These do not count as fraud or false pretenses. Forging the checks stolen from a checkbook during a burglary is fairly common by both men and their girl friends. Among women who receive fairly long prison sentences—and a year or more counts as a long sentence for women in England—fraud and false pretenses account for about one third in one recent study, and in one includes blackmail and "demanding money with menaces," a much larger proportion. If wage clerks or bookkeepers, receptionists at hotels or offices defraud their company systematically of fairly large sums of money, they are likely to be sent to prison even if first offenders, and appear socially well adjusted in all other respects. The ease with which such women can obtain the same sort of job again is remarkable, helped by stolen, headed notepaper, and forged testimonials. There is, however, a very different group composed of dull and ill-educated women from large, poor families who illegally apply for every sort of sickness, unemployment, or special sort of public benefit, of which there is a vast variety today. It may be very difficult to decide whether this is due to criminal intention or mere ignorance.

Many criminologists, however, have been concerned mainly with the extent to which women are taking to the sorts of crime which used to be almost exclusively male—personal violence, burglary, and robbery, for example.

Between 1969 and 1977 offenses of violence have increased much faster among women, by 200 percent (from 6.4 per 100,000 population to 18.9). Among men it has increased by 76 percent (107 to 188), though the male rate is still ten times that of the female. About a third of these female violent offenders are girls under 17, compared with one sixth of male offenders. Similarly, burglary and robbery by females has risen much faster than by men (39 percent against 7 percent increase), but not as fast as all indictable offenses by women (92 percent). On the other hand, women found guilty of all forms of homicide—murder, manslaughter, attempted murder, threats or conspiracy to murder, and infanticide—have remained remarkably steady at about 60 to 70 cases a year for the last nine years.

There is no doubt that personal violence is very inadequately measured by court appearances and criminal statistics, especially in the young. Dr. West has shown in his monumental study of 400 boys in deprived areas of London from the age of 8 to 20—which included self-report interviews at 18 or 19, as well as full information from school, parents, police, and social workers—that a high proportion admit considerable violence for two or three years from about 14 to 17, with frequent fights alone or in groups, often with reinforced boots, bicycle chains, combs, and so on, as weapons, even involving fights with police, without any convictions for these and indeed any other offenses. Seriously delinquent youths are concentrated among these violent boys, though their arrests are often only for property offenses. This behavior comes to a fairly rapid end at 18 or 19, when they start going steady with girls; and it seems clear that both the police and the magistrates wisely turn a blind eye to this, because for the majority it is essentially temporary and subcultural.

Violent offenses by girls have a rather different character, consonant with their social groupings. It is apt to be accompanied by considerable emotional instability, expressions of anger and hostility mixed with panic, and accompanied by suicidal attempts, floods of tears, apologies, and the like. Clinically, in dealing with delinquent girls of 15 and 16 there appears to be some increase in physical violence, with small knives or large nail files being added in their handbags, which occasionally produce serious wounds. There is an increased rate of violent behavior in women's prisons. Women seem to resist arrest more violently, joining in with their boyfriends, or snatching handbags from old ladies or wealthy foreign visitors in the main shopping centers. Recently a gang of four girls had a tallyho game which consisted of hunting old ladies down the road with wolf noises, but sometimes stealing their handbags. One old lady fell and broke her hip. A recent survey showed that most young shop assistants say they would be too frightened to stop a shoplifter they observed because of potential violence. My favorite case is the middle-aged shoplifter who resisted arrest by standing in front of a large counter full of crockery, hurling cups, plates, and teapots at the staff so accurately that they could not get near her.

One type of violent crime in which women seem to be involved almost as often as men is "terrorism," whether political assassination, bomb throwing, hijacking, hostage taking, or other politically motivated crimes. Some of these offenses are of course nonpolitical property crimes, the result of gang feuds, or things of that kind. But in these instances women do not figure so clearly. Political terrorism is greatly encouraged by the wide publicity it receives on radio and television. Most European countries seem to be affected, though in some groups, such as the Red Brigade in Italy, and the Baader-Meinhof group in Germany, it is difficult for the foreigner to understand the exact political objective, except protest against a society which is thought by them to be completely corrupt. Depending on one's point of view, these movements are composed of terrorists or brave and determined patriots, as in the French resistance to Hitler in the last world war. Women have always been readily involved. Women are very useful as inconspicuous messengers and in maintaining safe houses for those on the run. A special feature, mentioned recently by a middle-aged "retired" terrorist, is that a recruit may join for relatively common romantic or enthusiastic motives, but soon knows so many secrets that attempts to withdraw are greeted by threats of reprisals or even death. They can go forward but not back.

In England political terrorism has been severe in Northern Ireland, but strenuous efforts by the police have largely prevented a spread to England itself. Since 1969, homicides "attributed to terrorist activities" have been recorded separately. The number has varied from 1 or 2 to 10 a year, though there were 43 in 1971. It is not known if men or women were involved. Some of them were assassinations or attempts by members of foreign movements against compatriots living in England.

Drug offenses are another category in which females figure rather frequently. Like all others, these offenses depend upon the definitions of the law, which in this field have been changing fairly rapidly. The Misuse of Drugs Act of 1971 attempted a more sophisticated approach to differentiating the more dangerous drugs from others in the penalties provided, and even provided for a schedule which would allow new drugs to be added rapidly in their appropriate classes of danger without waiting five to ten years for legislation to be passed to control their use. This was partly the result of the introduction of LSD and the various increasingly effective "mind benders" which found their way into Europe, as well as STP and the other alphabetical additions. It was also stimulated by the observed effect of the epidemic of destruction caused by methedrine, an amphetamine which in intravenous injection caused extremely rapid habit formation and dependence, at its height when I surveyed the population in the London Women's Prison in 1967. It is now unobtainable except for its small useful purpose, that is, to raise the blood pressure of anesthetized patients in the operating theater.

Since the act came into force in 1971, the masculine/feminine ratio of convictions has been fairly constant, but possibly increasing gradually for women, from 6.6 men to 1 woman in 1974 to 6.1 men to 1 woman in 1976. There is undoubtedly a difference in sex preference in this field. Male offenders are used to alcohol and a free expression of aggression to overcome their difficulties. Women, however, with their habitual tendency to suffer without so much freedom of action, may be under greater pressure to make life tolerable either by alcohol or the tranquilizers prescribed in large quantities by their doctors. The situation is undoubtedly changing more rapidly than in other aspects of social sexual differences. Women who arrive in prison seem almost universally dependent on some drug or other, either alcohol, tranquilizers, or sedatives in various mixtures.

Penology

The last statistical aspect of the sex differences relates to the punishments imposed by the courts. Though convictions of men have greatly increased and those of women even more rapidly, the sentences imposed by the courts on women have remained remarkably constant in the last fifteen years. The main changes have been technical. Just over half of all women convicted of indictable offenses are fined. This also applies to 50 percent of men; 20 percent are put on probation, an increasing proportion of these being called "supervision" by the social services, as the probation service has withdrawn from the juvenile field; 20 percent receive an absolute or conditional discharge; a steady 3 percent have been sentenced to imprisonment; and 4 percent (since 1968 when the sentence became available) to sentences of imprisonment suspended for a stated period.

Women are committed to prison for various reasons, probably more frequently in England and Wales than in many European countries. This may seem surprising, since only 1 woman is finally sentenced to imprisonment or Borstal for every 33 men. Moreover, the sentences are usually short, the vast majority serving three to six months (effectively, two or four months with remission). Studies of the social psychology of women in prison, such as Giallombardo's *Society of Women* or Ward and Kassebaum's *Women's Prison* therefore do not apply in English prisons or probably in most European countries, because so few women are sentenced in the prime of life

(20 to 30) for five to ten years, during which these adjustments have to be made. These studies are nevertheless of great theoretical interest because they explore the marked sex differences in the response of men and women to confinement in institutions, and they are reported in miniature or incomplete form in English prisons. Essentially this difference lies in the fact that men in prison organize themselves (whether their captors like it or not) on a power basis, the tough and ruthless among them dominating the rest, who are disposed on a pecking order of those of lower and lowest status. Women, on the other hand, tend to reproduce family life in interpersonal relations, with women in the position of mothers, fathers, sisters, and lovers. However, it takes three to five years of imprisonment to develop such patterns, except in a marginal form.

The "daily average population" of women in prison institutions in 1977, which included those convicted of indictable and nonindictable offenses, was 1,358—about 3 percent of the male figure. This is what prison governors have to cope with, a vast range from the trivial to the most serious. Inevitably, the "daily average" emphasizes the longer-sentenced women. One life sentence woman, serving probably seven to ten years, occupies the bed of 42 or 60 average prisoners serving a three-month sentence.

Receptions into prison give a measure of the daily amount of work of the staff and of the activities of the courts. It is this number which arouses the greatest controversy. Over 7,000 women and girls over 17 were admitted in 1977, a third of them before trial, a quarter convicted to await sentence, and a quarter sentenced to imprisonment. Only a quarter of the untried ultimately receive a prison or Borstal sentence, and many of the convicted, but unsentenced, are in the same position later on. Many of these are for relatively trivial offenses by young women under 25, remanded for three weeks for physical (e.g., VD), psychiatric, and probation reports. There may be no problem about the offense, but the magistrates want to take the most constructive course to prevent further offenses. It is easy to forget, however, that it amounts to a sentence of three weeks in prison. Using the criteria for granting bail developed by the Vera Institute in the U.S.A. (being in a job, having a home, not being aggressively dangerous, liable to abscond, etc.) one of my colleagues (S. Dell) calculated that two thirds of the cases could have been bailed. Magistrates sometimes counter these arguments by saying that the fact of a woman having been three weeks in prison enables them to be more lenient when she finally comes to court and that it would take more than three weeks to obtain a report from a psychiatrist in the Health Service. These are perhaps domestic problems, and it is still true that justice is more speedy than in most European countries.

One type of woman in prison causes concern—the 856 cases (not necessarily different women) sentenced to a short period of prison for defaulting upon the payment of fines, usually for public drunkenness, but at times for prostitution. Many of these cases refer to the same woman being sent to prison several times in the year. Various plans to divert this group of inmates have not been successfully applied.

There is a further controversial group—prostitutes. In most respects, the magistrates seem to deal with female offenders more leniently than with males, but prostitutes are a notable exception. Prostitution itself has not been an offense for a great many years, but soliciting in public is. In 1954 the Wolfenden Committee was set up to consider the law in relation to prostitution and homosexuality. It reported in 1957: the recommendation in relation to prostitutes was accepted and enacted almost at once in the Street Offences Act; the recommendations about homosexuality were also accepted, but no less than thirteen years later, after a great deal of public controversy! At the time of the committee's appointment there had been an increase in street soliciting. Kinsey, who visited at that time, said that the soliciting was "more aggressive than in any European country he had visited." The "last straw," as there so often is in such questions, was when an American officer, walking with his wife, who was heavily made up, complained that a prostitute had attacked his wife with the stiletto heel of her shoe, supposing her to be a prostitute "horning in on her beat"! Till then, prostitutes persistently soliciting were fined only a few pounds, often every few days, and so clogged the courts. The new act provided that a woman who persistently solicited in public should be given an official warning by the police twice; on the third or subsequent offenses there was discretion to pass a sentence of up to three months imprisonment. Keeping or living in a brothel still was liable to imprisonment. The act achieved its purpose rather well. Prostitution went underground, into clubs, bars, or night clubs or through contacts arranged through taxi drivers, hotel porters, and travel agents. The process was accelerated by the boom in the tourist industry, and to a surprising extent the needs of international commerce, which made it necessary for the largest and most respectable corporations to provide for the evening and nocturnal entertainment of their guests. Everything was at least out of sight and out of mind, except in VD clinics where the 250 included several very conventional and respectable business executives who "had not wished to seem backward or stuffy at such a gathering."

The act, however, had one unfortunate consequence, that there was an alarming increase in prostitutes sentenced to prison for up to three months (rarely less) for refusing to be warned, even though they were a very small proportion of all prostitutes. Those who employed them always committed no offense; it was an act of sexual discrimination. In practice, the courts have returned to the old practice of repeated fining, without deciding to impose a prison sentence. Recently, consideration has been given to the possibility of prosecuting their "curbcrawling" partners, who annoy ordinary women by drawing up in a car at the curb beside them and inviting them to get in. Devising an effective law to prevent this is extremely difficult, and a bill has now been introduced into Parliament to end the imprisonment of women for soliciting. Prostitutes have started a trades union to complain about unfair tax arrangements. Prostitution undoubtedly plays a large part in the lives of the socially incompetent or psychopathic women who are detained in prison. Ten years ago in confidential interviews with every fourth female entering one of the London prisons in a year, we found that a history of present or past prostitution was present in between 24 and 35 percent, in all the different groups; and was 62 percent among those admitted for default of payment of a fine, but only a minority had been fined for soliciting itself; 40 percent of them were middle-aged, chronic alcoholics, fined for public drunkenness. Such women often have a period of past prostitution, subsequently marry, and are then abandoned because of steadily increasing alcoholism. A great many ordinary property offenses or frauds, from trivial to extremely sophisticated, were committed by women with this past or present history. This should hardly be surprising. Male recidivists are just as often persistently promiscuous and owe their convictions largely to the inability to make stable sexual relations.

Fifteen years ago it was penal policy or planning that the imprisonment of women would gradually dwindle to nothing. When a parole system was introduced in 1968, the numbers fell further, from a daily average of sentenced prisoners of 763 to 627. However, the numbers have steadily increased to 1064 in 1977. There is little sign that sentences are getting longer; 76 percent get six months or less, 85 percent not more than a year, and only 5 percent over four years; and this has been almost the same for ten years. It is just that the total number of women sentenced to immediate imprisonment has gone up quite sharply in the last three or four years; from a steady figure of about 1100 a year they rose in 1975 to 1976 and 1977 to 1472, 1771, and 2071 for all types of offenses.

Mental Abnormality

The optimism of the 1960s was partly due to the heyday of the medical, and particularly psychiatric, model of social deviance. Women offenders were seen to be much more often mentally disordered, with psychiatric symptomatology of all kinds, and they were felt to be largely a problem which the Mental Health and Social Services could handle. The new London Prison for Women was described as a medically oriented establishment. The Mental Health Act of 1959 implied great hopes in the progress of psychiatric treatment and defined a category of "psychopathic disorder" which could necessitate hospital detention for treatment, whether they had broken the law or not, if under 21, at all ages if they had. Ten years of experience showed that successful treatment of such personality disorders would need to be highly specialized and inordinately expensive and that National Health resources were fully stretched to provide for the frankly mentally ill or psychotic offenders, who have never been very numerous. Mental illness has less and less stigma, and as drug treatment and maintenance became more effective, the large mental hospitals were gradually closed and replaced by treatment in psychiatric wards of general hospitals for a few weeks and then in the community; or even entirely in the community, with daily visits by experienced psychiatric nurses. Offender-patients, uncooperative, dishonest, and occasionally violent, became ever less acceptable, and just as unpopular in open hospital environments as they are in the community. The hospital service is under great pressure to meet the needs of the growing population of geriatric women who cannot be looked after at home. About one third or a half of schizophrenic psychotics do not recover completely but can be maintained in the community if they seek advice and take drugs regularly. The more unreliable and uncooperative offender-patient forgets to take his drugs, drinks too much, and keeps up his petty theft, but is free in the community in increasing numbers, with occasional short admissions to hospital from which he or she is soon discharged or allowed to abscond when he becomes stabilized.

Mentally disordered offenders are dealt with in three ways under the Mental Health Act. Magistrates can make a "hospital order" to a mental hospital on the advice of two doctors. The doctor concerned can release the patient at any time. The High Court can impose an order "restricting discharge" for a definite or indefinite period until the home secretary consents, when the judge considers the offender might represent a serious danger to the public if released prematurely. These orders may be made to general Health Service hospitals, if they accept, or to one of the four "special hospitals" who offer complete security for patients of "criminal or violent propensities." Two are for the dangerous subnormals and two for the mentally ill, with "psychopaths" fairly equally distributed between them. Those committed to special hospitals by the courts tend to be those disordered offenders who have committed murder or violent sexual offenses, but technical nonoffenders under psychiatric detention who show these characteristics of dangerous and impulsive violence may be transferred to them, as well as convicted offenders in prison who develop a psychosis. All these hospitals are part of the Mental Health Service, and not prisons, and pride themselves on being treatment institutions, though quite secure. The relevance of these arrangements is that of those given simple hospital orders, about 15 percent are females, and of those with "restriction orders" to ordinary or special hospitals nearly 1 in 5 (19 percent) are female, about six times the proportion of women sentenced to prison compared with men.

In the London Women's Prison (for those aged 17 upward), mental and physical disorders are exceptionally high. They are, of course, a selected sample of the more deviant or sociopathic women. Those remanded for a psychiatric report naturally had a high level of sociopathy. But a large proportion are healthy young women aged 17 to 23 remanded for social inquiries about the family and environmental situation, circumstances of the offense, or need for further inquiries. Yet the striking thing is that, however they have arrived, the levels of disorder are comparatively similar. For example the label "physical ill health a major problem" never applied to less than 15 percent and at most 21 percent; "mental ill health a major problem" to 15 to 39 percent, depending on the group; "inpatient mental hospital treatment in the last 3 years, 14 to 26 percent; "inpatient" over 3 years ago," an additional 4 to 10 percent; "history of suicidal attempt(s)," 21 to 29 percent; "alcoholism," 3 to 41 percent; "venereal disease," 9 to 18 percent; "pregnant now," 7 to 16 percent (over half illegitimately); and "past or present prostitution," 24 to 62 percent. There is no certain means of knowing how abnormal these women in custody were, compared with women offenders in general. There is one study, however, of shoplifting (Gibbens and Prince), which dealt with the subsequent convictions and mental hospital admissions of a total sample of 525 women shoplifters appearing before three contrasting courts in inner, suburban, and outer London in 1959. The great majority were not remanded or sentenced to imprisonment. They were followed for up to ten years, but owing to the suspension of the Mental Health index of admissions to mental hospitals, only admissions in the second five years (1964–69) could be studied. Early and single admissions in the first five years were therefore not available. But even for the second five years the rate was exceptionally high. Since, as expected, it varied with the record of previous or subsequent convictions for crime of any kind, they were divided into: (1) those with no convictions before or after 1959—70 percent, and three groups of approximately 10 percent each;

(2) no previous convictions but some subsequently; (3) previous conviction but none since; (4) with convictions both before and after 1959. A very high proportion, therefore, are once-in-a-lifetime convictions. The mental hospital admissions in the second five years for these four groups was 5.8 percent, 12.2 percent, 12 percent respectively, and 19.6 percent and thus not very different from the selected prison admissions. In five cases the diagnosis could not be traced, but for 28 of the 39 remainder it was for depression with suicidal attempts.

The average admission rate was therefore 8.4 percent. They were of all ages from 17 to over 70, but two fifths were between 40 and 60, an age when mental hospital admissions are exceptionally high in women. However, we calculated that the high expectations in normal women was only 2.5 percent, so that the rate for shoplifters was three times higher. Clinically, about 5 to 10 percent of shoplifting women are quite depressed before the offense, though usually not to the extent of needing hospitalization. Many middle-class, "respectable" women are also depressed by the stigma of a criminal conviction for theft.

Discussion

Mental health has been dealt with at some length because it plays a fairly large part in the debate about why women are so much less often convicted than men (leaving aside whether they commit less crime, though I would guess they do). It is also part of the fascinating question of what the difference is between men and women, apart from the obvious and fortunate physical ones. If one accepts that, apart from a very small number of physically related tasks, women can do and achieve everything that men can, they may still always do it in a different way. In some ways one may hope it is so, if civilization is to survive.

In 1977 Dr. Pollitt tried to summarize from many sources what he regarded as "harder" and best-substantiated differences in "sex difference and the mind." Girls have a five-week lead in maturation over boys at birth, and this increases to one year and three months at puberty. Their growth is more resistant to malnutrition and other environmental insults. Since mortality figures for females are lower in almost all areas compared with those of boys, females have a greater life expectancy. They are, however, more vulnerable to endocrine stresses and some pathological disorders.

A major difference is the effect of menstruation. Only 5 percent of U.S.A. high school and college students are free from premenstrual symptoms, but multiparous Scottish students and nurses are as much as 17 percent free of symptoms, though two thirds were irritable and over half depressed. Premenstrually there is a greater risk of failure in exams, misbehavior in boarding schools or in prison, and increased road accidents. The premenstrual four days have perhaps been overemphasized, but the eight days of the paramenstruum (premenstruation and menstruation) contain a quite significant concentration of troubles, far above the 2 : 7 ratio that one would expect. Dalton (1964) maintained that a decreased resistance to bacterial and viral infection, lower pain tolerance, increased allergic reactions, and frequency of pyrexia result in over half the admissions to surgical and medical wards for any reason occurring during the paramenstruum. D'Orban and Dalton (1979) have recently shown that, controlling for sources of error quite carefully, crimes of violence by women (but not of theft) are significantly concentrated in the paramenstruum.

Above all, women who attempt or commit suicide undoubtedly do it mainly in the paramenstruum, as shown by postmortem and many other studies. Moreover, women are admitted to mental hospitals for depression nearly twice as often as men (1.7 : 1) almost throughout Europe and the U.S.A., and this figure resists all social and situational explanations (e.g., that there are more beds available, or that they have no one to look after them at home). Even if one allows that alcoholism in men is often the result of efforts to get more energy and to keep going when depressed, it reduces the ratio to only 1.5 : 1. Suicide is highest in the childbearing ages of 15 to 45; after about 55 the sexes are more alike. Women attempt suicide a great deal more often. Men succeed in committing suicide in a high proportion. Suicide is not easy, and Pollitt suggests that this difference may be due to the inefficiency, thoughtlessness, and absentmindedness of women in this period. If the excess of the paramenstrual period were ruled out, men and women would be equal in the incidence of depression. It seems that the endocrine variations impose a considerable burden on women. It is calculated that the old-fashioned woman who has ten children and breast-feeds each for the accepted long period could have amenorhea (no menstruation) for 27.5 of her productive years, to the greater advantage of her nervous and endocrine system. At least, the tendency of women is to respond to stress of any kind by depression, while men tend to respond by aggression.

This may seem to have little to do with criminal behavior in women which, especially in relation to theft, depends upon the most superficial and artificial definitions of behavior. But one observation in relation to suicide has more important implications. The rapid changes in the legal, economic, educational, and professional status of women have been going on in all

Western countries, but the effects upon female crime have differed considerably. Recent research on suicide, which is increasing fairly steadily in all north European countries, shows that in England the rate of suicide has gone down. In searching for the reasons for this, the study eliminated many of the popular explanations (the effect of the twenty-four-hour Samaritan phone-in movement, the fact that our new North Sea gas from the seabed is much less lethal when people put their head in the gas oven, etc.), but from a number of indices they concluded that *social change* in England has been much slower and less marked than in other European countries, although those of us who live here do not have that impression. Rapid social change liberates some but imposes additional stress on those who cannot make the transition.

The introduction of the contraceptive pill and availability of abortion have liberated women from the consequences of sexual activity and, combined with economic changes, have given them a new self-image. There are half-amusing stories that men of 26 who decide after a traditional period of experimentation that they are in a position to marry find that many girls under 22 are already married, and the remainder whom they want to marry told them that they are willing to become their lovers but do not intend to marry until they have established their careers at about 30 and decide to have children. These are journalistic parodies of real life, of course, but contain a large grain of truth. But this probably only applies to the 10 to 15 percent of the educated middle class. The contraceptive pill or the contemplation of abortion is spreading to social classes 4 and 5 quite slowly. In the thirty years during which I worked in the remand home for juvenile girls of 15 and 16, I always offered the possibility of abortion to those illegitimately pregnant who were severely maladjusted and incapable of looking after their children. None accepted the idea until the last three or four years, even when pregnant as the result of indecent assault or rape by a stranger. They always said they would not want to keep the child and would hand it over to the local authorities, but would certainly want to bear it. It was, one felt, the only area in which they thought they could succeed, in contrast to the massive failures elsewhere; and of course no attempt was ever made to discourage them. The rapid, if relatively small, increase in female crime in the 13–16 age period is more likely to be due to changes in the Juvenile Court Law, which leaves few powers to the magistrates to do more than commit them to "care" of the local social services for social support. More sophisticated and intelligent girls will say frankly that after 17 they will have to change their ways; until then there is nothing much anyone can do to prevent them from carrying on. Although this may seem to authoritarians to be excessively permissive, it pays off in practice because at 17 and 18 most of them take a much more realistic view of life, free from exasperating parents, and set their sights upon a reasonable husband. Apart from a few very disordered girls, they disappear from the criminal scene. As Lee Robins has shown, they become a problem to other authorities, have repeated illegitimate pregnancies, and so on. When I followed up the adult convictions of 350 girls of 15 and 16 whom I had seen (the more disturbed ones) fifteen years later, 25 percent had had adult convictions (usually once for shoplifting or small theft), 6 percent had been sent to prison and 10 percent had convictions for prostitution. But of a six-month sample of all 485 juvenile girls (10–17) coming before the six London juvenile courts during an overlapping period, 13 percent had minor adult convictions, 2 percent had been in prison, and 2 percent had convictions for prostitution. What the results of the upsurge in delinquency in the juvenile period, recorded in Figure 1, may be, as these girls get older, is a matter of conjecture. If social change is in fact slower in England, it will work through gradually and, in any case, depend on the state of society in their adult life. There are few reliable studies of the current changes.

The great difference in the criminality of the two sexes must surely depend mainly on the fact that the gender roles of males and females in society are most strongly differentiated (and indoctrinated from very early years) in social classes 4 and 5, and it is from here that most ordinary delinquency and adult crime comes. Attempts to show that this is not so, or that the middle class commits as many or as serious offenses, have been unsuccessful, in spite of attempts to show that this is largely a matter of police prejudice. With education this difference tends to disappear, and it becomes increasingly difficult for psychological tests to detect the difference between the sexes in social outlook, expectation, and attitude, except in special vocabulary tests with words describing the fabric materials, colors, and so on, such as crepe de chine, organza, and eau de nil. Gender role changes—the husband actually preferring to do the cooking or expecting to do the washing regularly—is very common in the middle class but still unthinkable, until recently, in social classes 4 and 5.

Environmentalists can point to the fact that gender roles in society are inculcated almost from birth. Children misclassified in their sex allocation because of abnormalities in the external genitalia are upset to be allocated to the opposite sex after the age of 4 and, after 9, usually have neurotic and personality difficulties when transferred to their correct sex. Surgeons have come to appreciate the need for early diagnosis.

A quite recent and careful study of the attitude to, and experience of, delinquency of boys and girls from similar families shows that girls were quite heavily protected. They knew other delinquent peers much less often, and were much more condemnatory about crime and especially criminal female associates.

There is little doubt that girls tend to identify with their mothers more closely, and if the mothers are stable and competent and present a reliable image, they can resist the influence of fathers and brothers with a substantial criminal record in the belief that these are just foolish male attributes which do not apply to themselves. A recent study of a large group of normal schoolgirls showed that those who lost their fathers after the age of about 10 or 11, provided it was by disease or accident, tended to rally around their mother, and the family in fact became even more cohesive. It was entirely different if the loss of the father was by desertion or divorce.

A factor which has been little studied in real detail is the factor of criminality in parents and siblings. West's study of the development of criminal behavior among 400 boys in a deprived area of London, followed from 8 to 20, carefully checked the recorded convictions of fathers, brothers, mothers, and sisters, a task involving recording the full name and date of birth of all of them.

A criminal conviction was recorded in 28.2 percent of the boys themselves, 26.7 percent of their fathers, 13.3 percent of their mothers, 37.4 percent of their brothers (who were usually older), and 7.6 percent of their sisters. The sisters usually were older but not above 24 or 25, and in those days half of all female convictions tended to occur later in life. The study was orientated toward boys and, like several others, has found that a high proportion of all criminality came from a relatively small proportion of all the families. For example, 11 percent of the families were responsible for nearly half of all recorded convictions.

So far as concerns the association of a criminal mother with her sons, 54 percent of the sons had convictions, but this was only partly attributable to the mother, because half of these mothers were married to criminal fathers. Of the boys who had a convicted mother but unconvicted father, 33 percent had a conviction by the age of 20.

The effect of a convicted mother upon her daughter(s) was rather closer: 28.8 percent of their daughters had a conviction, compared with only 5 percent of the daughters who did not have a convicted mother. Among convicted fathers, 17 percent of the daughters had a conviction, compared with 6 percent of daughters with unconvicted fathers. If both parents were convicted, 61 percent of their sons had convictions.

Any real explanation of the recent trends in female crime must depend upon research of this kind, of which there has been very little, rather than upon the wide range of unsupported theories being put forward.

References

Criminal Statistics. H.M.S.O., 1977.

Giallombardo, R. Society of Women. Wiley & Sons, 1966.

Gibbens, T. C. N. "Female Offenders," Brit. J. Hospital Med. (September 1971): 279.

Gibbens, T. C. N., and C. Palmer and J. Prince. Mental Health Aspects of Shoplifting, Brit. Med. J. Vol. 3 (1971): 612–625.

Gibbens, T. C. N., and J. Prince. 1962 I.S.T.D. 34 Survey St., Croyden, London.

Goodman, N., and J. Davies. Girl Offenders Aged 17 to 20 Years. H.M.S.O., 1969.

Goodman, N., and J. Price. Studies of Female Offenders. H.M.S.O., 1971.

Goodman et al. Further Studies of Female Offenders. H.M.S.O., 1975.

Heidensohn, F. Brit. J. Sociol. Vol. 19 (1968): 160.

Home Office Working Party on Vagrancy and Street Offenses H.M.S.O., 1974.

Morris, R. R. Brit. J. Criminol. Vol. 5 (1965): 249.

Mott, J., and M. Taylor. Delinquency among Opiate Users. H.M.S.O., 1975.

Pollitt, J. Sex Differences and the Mind. Proc. Roy. Soc. Med. Vol. 70 (1977): 145.

Smart, C. Women, Crime, and Criminology, A Feminist Critique. London: Routledge, 1977.

Special Hospital Research Unit No. 15 H.M.S.O., 1979.

Ward D., and Kassebaum. Women's Prison. London: Weidenfelt and Nicholsohn, H.M.S.O., 1979.

West, D., and D. P. Farrington. The Delinquent Way of Life. London: Heineman, 1965, 1977.

5. Changing Patterns of Female Criminality in Germany

W. MIDDENDORFF AND D. MIDDENDORFF

Wolf L. Middendorff is Professor at the University of Freiburg and a member of the Max-Planck Institute for Foreign and International Penal Law. He is a Lecturer at the Department of Justice in Stuttgart and a District Court Judge in Freiburg. His primary interest in the field is historical criminology and traffic criminology. His publications include books and articles about juvenile delinquency, sociology of crime, crimes of violence, terrorism, historical criminology, and traffic criminology.

Dorothea E. J. Middendorff is lecturer and research assistant. She is affiliated with the Herder Publishing House in Freiburg. Her primary interest is in the field of historical criminology and female delinquency. She is interested in university studies in history and romanistics. She has worked for different radio stations, newspapers, and reviews and has been the author of radio features, plays, articles, and books.

In the criminological literature it is often said that female criminality has risen enormously and that, especially female violence, is the new phenomenon of our days. We shall attempt to examine these opinions in the light of the current situation in Germany.

The Statistical Picture

The police statistics for the Federal Republic of Germany show that in 1977 the number of all cases which have come to the attention of the police has increased 7.5 percent over the rate of the previous year. The offense rate for all cases was 5,355 for 100,000 inhabitants.[1]

For murder and manslaughter (attempts included) 2,598 cases were recorded, that is, 6.7 percent less than in 1976. The percentage of female suspects in 1977 for all offenses was 18.7 percent. The percentage differed for the different offenses; for murder and manslaughter the female percentage was almost half of the middle rate, 9.7 percent. Women who had committed theft without aggravated circumstances ranked in the first place. Here the female percentage was 31.5. The increase, compared with that of the previous year, was 9.4 percent. Fraudulent conversion ranks second, with a percentage of 21.5. This is a clear indication of women's participation in business life in higher positions. In the third place are offenses of insult, with 20.8 percent of female participation, followed by embezzlement with 20.1 percent, fraud with 19.8 percent, and drug offenses with 18.9 percent. According to the German statistics, women committed mostly offenses against property, violence playing a minor role.

In other European countries crimes of violence seem to be more important. A Hungarian study, for instance, done by Gabriella Rasko, shows that 26 to 35 percent of all offenders committing crimes against life are women. The rate has slightly decreased in the past fifty years. Gabriella Rasko has studied killings, committed by women, which belong to the main type characterized by a prolonged crisis situation between persons ordinarily living under the same roof.[2] We have conducted similar research dealing with the historical and psychological aspects of the *crime passionnel* in Germany and other European countries, including some of the very few cases acknowledged in the U.S.A. as *crime passionnel*.[3]

For both sexes in 1977 dangerous and grievous bodily injury and slight bodily injury with intent increased by 5.9 percent and 13.4 percent, respectively. The female participation is 9 and 10 percent, respectively. There are some indications that violence, as far as bodily injury is concerned, plays a much more important role in the family than in former years. It was estimated that bodily injuries are committed in 60 percent of German families.[4] Researchers in this field believe that in more and more cases men are the victims who never complain about it because it would be against honor and self-estimation of a man to confess that he was beaten by a woman. The dark figure is therefore probably very high.

There is no doubt that violence often is connected with, or the result of, excessive consumption of alcohol. In Germany we have probably almost 2 million alcoholics, of whom one fourth are females. Not only in Germany, but in many countries, the alcohol consumption of women and women's alcoholism have increased disproportionally during the last few years, compared with alcohol consumption of men. The danger of addiction of women has increased more than on the average. Therefore, it is not surprising that offenses committed by women under the influence of alcohol increased significantly during the last years, as indicated by a recent study done in Hamburg. The percentage increase in alcohol criminality of women is higher than that of men. Remarkable also is the considerable increase of female juvenile delinquency. On the whole, alcohol criminality of women in Hamburg indicates the tendency toward equalization of men.[5] Female juvenile delinquency, on the whole, has almost doubled in the last decade in Germany.[6]

The developments regarding bank robbery are of special interest. Otto Pollak in his classic *The Criminality of Women* found in 1950 that, as far as robbery was concerned, the material was scarce. There were only a few cases reported showing women as accomplices of male offenders who used them as watchers or decoys. In Germany the situation has changed only slightly. In one study, concerning bank robberies, done in Freiburg (1964–66), the percentage of women offenders was 3.3, much lower than the percentage of female offenders in general. Women participation was limited to helping male perpetrators. The German Police Statistics for 1977, however, show a female participation in bank robbery of 6.4 percent. Compared with the previous year, the percentage increased by only 0.3 percent. A study done in Austria found a female participation of 10 percent, but the numbers are too small to permit any important conclusions.[7]

One recent German case may be mentioned which shows a psychological relationship among robbery, fraud, and terrorism. At Ulm, Württemberg, a 30-year-old housewife and mother of five children phoned the cashier of a bank telling him that she was a member of the criminal police and, in her capacity as an undercover agent, was then standing with a group of terrorists outside the bank and holding some hostages. In order to save human lives, she asked the cashier to hand over all the money to a woman soon to appear inside the bank. She herself went into the bank and got—without any difficulty—all the money she had asked for and later paid all her debts with this money. She was sentenced to three years in prison.

The female percentage of victims of bank robbery in 1977 was 39.7 percent. One may ask why the percentage was not higher, since robbers may believe that it is easier to rob the so-called weaker sex. In reality, women are not as weak as imagined. We have many examples proving that the reactions of women tellers are completely unpredictable. Their range of behavior is much larger than that of men, and it ranges from quickly delivering all money, to just doing nothing, to total resistance even when it is completely useless. According to American experience, the number of screamers is large. "The automatic yelper, who lets go involuntarily, from surprise, is not much a problem . . . the aboriginal, or ritual screamer is a little more troublesome. Her scream is a notice to all males that a poor defenseless female is in distress, and what are they going to do about it? Worst of all screamers is the hysterical screamer. This one takes a kind of a fit—clenches her eyes shut and lets loose at the top of her voice, and anything done to calm her is only likely to make her worse, if possible."[8] In Germany, in August 1978, at Dortmund, two robbers stormed into a bank and asked for all the money. The female cashier answered coolly: "I cannot decide this question, I have to ask my boss." The robbers were completely surprised and left the bank without money.

Terrorism and Political Murder

Terrorism and political murder are very old forms of criminality in which female participation likewise is not new. I refer, for example, to the life and death of Charlotte Corday who killed Marat during the French Revolution.[9] In France, even in our times, Charlotte Corday is often compared with Joan of Arc, the national saint and hero whose life was recently told in an excellent way by Felix Grayeff.[10]

Among the Russian revolutionaries of the last century were a number of women.[11] Tatjana Leontieff, for example, killed a Frenchman in Switzerland whom she believed to be the Russian minister of the interior.[12] Vera Zasulich, the child of impoverished nobility, taught illiterate workers in the radical St. Petersburg "Sunday schools." Outraged by the arrest and humiliation of her revolutionary comrades, she concealed a pistol in her bag and lined up with petitioners awaiting the governor, Trepov, to shoot him on his arrival. The governor was severely wounded. Vera Zasulich was acquitted by a jury of lay judges; the acquittal was reversed by the tsar; and she finally left Russia.

Vera Figner, daughter of a well-to-do forester, abandoned her long dreamed of medical career to "go to the people." Beautiful, elegant, educated, able to mix with all social circles, she was indomitable in her revolutionary zeal, tunneling by night with her comrades to lay mines along a route the tsar might take. During her trial, both the judges and the public listened with uncommon attention to her revolutionary confession. She received the death penalty, but her sentence was subsequently commuted to life imprisonment. After twenty years, she was released from prison.[13]

Comparing the Russian revolutionary women with the German terrorists of today, we find many similarities and some differences. The Russian women mostly came from well-to-do families. They tried to go to the people—without apparent success. They were idealists who tried to change the course of history, although without success. They succeeded only in alarming state power and strengthening the police. It is an old experience, shown in many criminological studies, that the impact of terrorism and assassination on the political system tends to be low. "On most occasions assassinations result in utter failure as far as the political aims of the conspirators are concerned, especially if these conspirators expect to profit politically from their deed."[14]

As far as we can see, German terrorists show similar features; but there is one striking difference: Russian terrorists, especially the women, behaved courageously in court and displayed much dignity. They did not show any signs of fear and defended their actions eloquently. German terrorist women of today in court usually use four-letter language and insult judges, who sometimes have no choice other than to exclude the defendants from the trial.

Criminological studies of German terrorists are practically nonexistent, first because there are not enough terrorists to enable statistical empirical research, and second because the terrorists constantly resist any psychological and psychiatric examination and completely refuse to answer any questions. Therefore, the only method which can be applied in dealing with this problem is the trained understanding of the historian and the psychologist. We can only paint a portrait and develop some characteristic features.[15]

Let us first give an example of the life and death of a German terrorist woman who seems to be quite typical of the first terrorist generation after World War II.

Gudrun Ensslin, a leading member of the Baader-Meinhof gang, was born in 1940 as a clergyman's daughter in the south of Germany. Her parents, slightly Marxist, very pious, puritans, unstable, aggressive, and antibourgeois, educated her to be against rearmament and for reunification of the two Germanies, and she soon was concerned with social problems, especially the sufferings of the Third World.

She acquired a contempt for the base materialistic greed of bourgeois society. She was rather good in school and a pious child and teenager. In June 1958, under a scheme of the International Christian Youth Exchange, Gudrun went for one year to Warren, Pennsylvania, where she attended the local high school. She fell in love with an American boy but found much fault with American society, developed many prejudices, and found, as many people with strong prejudices do, what she looked for. In 1960, she took her baccalaureate, won a prize for "social engagement in pupil-code-termination," and went to a university to study German literature and pedagogy. In her fourth university semester she met Bernward Vesper, a young leftist and son of a Nazi poet and fell in love with him. Much later he became a drug addict and committed suicide, leaving a book behind which told of his desolate life.[16] They announced their official engagement in 1965 to please the clergymen-parents, as they said. They changed over to Berlin University, which was at that time more than today a sort of leftist, progressive, and rebellious university. Gudrun wrote poems for the paper *Konkret,* the editor of which was Ulrike Meinhof who later became the leader of the famous and dangerous gang. Ulrike Meinhof returned the poems, dismissing them as "hysterical." Gudrun Ensslin and Bernward Vesper both worked hard for the German Social Democratic party, and when this party formed the Grand Coalition with the Christian Democrats in 1966 they left this party disappointed, and they demonstrated against the war in Vietnam, singing "The International." Their son Felix was born in May 1967, and they wrote a placard, attached to the handle of the baby carriage: "When I am big, I'll carry machine gun with me always. Use your head"! Gudrun, the mother, soon fell out of love with her baby's father because she became more and more unstable, restless, and aggressive; she took a leading part in a porno film, attended demonstrations, and got into trouble with the police. After the death of Benno Ohnesorge, a student who had been shot in 1967 by the police during a demonstration against the Shah of Iran, she became hysterical and cried that they all would be killed by those pigs. The famous German poet Grass said of her: "She was idealistic with an inborn loathing of any compromise. She had a yearning for the Absolute." Motherhood, she felt, was like a trap. So she abandoned baby Felix. Her mother later excused her, saying that in any case Gudrun had looked after the son for eleven months! Then she met Andreas Baader, three years younger than she, a spoiled, violent, good-looking, and sexy boy who was known as a playboy for his reputedly enormous success with women. His father had died during the war, and the beautiful little boy had been raised by women only. In 1967 Baader met the white-faced, intense, shrill-voiced Gudrun, and she fell in love—was lost, as some people said who knew her well. It was a sort of marriage between her fanaticism and his unscrupulousness. They hated West German society. In 1968 they set two Frankfurt department stores on fire while laughing and joking, as witnesses told later. The damage amounted to 80,000 marks. They were apprehended by the police and arrested, went on trial, and were sentenced to three years' imprisonment. The court psychiatrist stated: "[Gudrun Ensslin] was capable of hating in a very elementary fashion, she was the backbone of [the] group, she is arrogant, ruthless and coercive. She would sell her own brother. Hers was the kind of fervor which old religious wars . . . had been fired with." Ulrike Meinhof wrote at that time: "The progressive significance of department-store arson does not lie in the destruction of the goods, it lies in the criminality of the action, in lawbreaking." As they all said of it, "the bold breaking of the law is progressive." Already in 1880, Peter Kropotkin, the most gentle of the nineteenth-century anarchists, wrote: "Everything is good for us which falls outside legality." In 1969 Gudrun Ensslin was put on parole. The parole of Baader was revoked later, but Baader fled together with Gudrun to France, Italy, and for a short time to Jordan for guerrilla training, which was no great success, since Baader did not like it and Gudrun was not liked by the Arabs, who found her too domineering. The Germans were regarded as a criminal gang and Baader as a coward.

Earlier, in the spring of 1970, the fugitives had arrived secretly in Berlin. They had to be hidden, sheltered, and fed. When Baader was arrested, Ulrike Meinhof freed him by violence. A man at the library where Baader had been allowed to study was badly wounded. Ulrike Meinhof and Gudrun Ensslin met at a time of Ulrike's weakness and need for acceptance, since she had divorced her well-to-do husband and was afraid of the broken home because she had two little girls for whom she wanted a real home. There were many similarities between the two women. Both had been devout Protestants and ardent pacifists, they had read the great romantics of German literature, played the violin, won scholarships from the Study Foundation of the German People, and studied pedagogy. They both liked publishing, they had a child and children, respectively; and they had been disappointed by a husband and a lover, respectively, and by the Grand Coalition. They both committed themselves to the antiauthoritarian movement, became politically active, protested against the bomb and rearmament; and both possessed the temperamental quality of absoluteness.

Gudrun now participated in several cases of bank robbery, driving the getaway car. Another terrorist woman, Beate Sturm, who dropped out of the gang, said of that time: "The women were truly emancipated. We could do many things better than the men. We felt we were stronger, for instance, and much less anxious than they. We were also far less aggressive and never quarreled." The terrorist gang obtained more and more members, and there were fights with the police all over Germany; there were bank robberies and kidnappings and the attack on the German embassy in Stockholm. And there was the killing of Federal Attorney General Buback, the murder of Dr. Ponto and that of Dr. Schleyer and two American army officers in Heidelberg, and of many German policemen. In return for Dr. Schleyer's life, his kidnappers requested among others the release of Gudrun Ensslin.

Baader was arrested for the third time after a hard fight in 1972, and one week later Gudrun was arrested in a Hamburg boutique, where one of the saleswomen had discovered a gun in her jacket and had called the police. A second gun was later found in her bag.

The trial against the Baader-Meinhof gang, of which perhaps Gudrun was the most important member, took place in Stuttgart-Stammheim where a special security prison had been built for about $4 million. The trial was one of the most difficult in the Federal Republic of Germany, since the defendants and their lawyers used every conceivable type of resistance and legal device. The defendants were accused of an aggregate of 6 cases of murder, 59 cases of attempted murder, of bank robbery in many cases, and of being members of a criminal society. Twice Gudrun Ensslin went on a hunger strike. In April 1977 she was sentenced to three times life plus fifteen years, but, as Ulrike Meinhof had done before, she committed suicide by hanging herself in prison on October 18, 1977, after the Mogadishu hijacking had failed. Baader killed himself by shooting.

Gudrun Ensslin's life and her involvement in terrorist activities was a leap of an old unsatisfactory life into a new, exciting one, in which the sexual relationship with "Baby" Baader certainly played a domineering role, but also her need for belonging to a group.

In Gudrun's case—as in Ulrike's—society was a symbol of her own failings, and her committing of herself to a life outside the law was a venture to overcome, not governments, not systems, but private despair. It may be added that instability, too much sensibility, fanaticism, immaturity, and finally an underlying weakness are often the reasons why a person becomes involved in an antilegal life.

The Search for Causes

It has been mentioned that Gudrun Ensslin was driven to radicalism mostly by her personal difficulties, as was Ulrike Meinhof. Criminological research, especially in relation to political murder and terrorism, generally confirms that not political ideology but personal frustration is the main reason for such acting out.[17] Moreover, hardly any crime can be reduced to one single cause or one motive only. The criminal is driven by many motives, by a mixture of ingredients, which he often does not realize himself exactly.[18]

The first generation of German terrorists after World War II was, on the whole, more ideologically motivated. German terrorists, like terrorists in many other countries, gave innumerable explanations for their violence, and these rationalizations are frequently related to three basic concepts:

1. Society is sick and cannot be cured by half measures of reform.
2. The state is in itself violence and can be countered and overcome only by violence.
3. The truth of the terrorist cause justifies any action that supports it. While some terrorists recognize no moral law, others have their own "higher" morality.

We speak today of the third terrorist generation since 1968, the so-called silent generation. Because these terrorists are driven by a pure activism, their crimes—murder or kidnapping for instance—are in themselves the aim and do not serve as a means to attain a higher ideological or political goal.

The current generation of terrorists may be more dangerous than previous ones, because the terrorists frequently do not live underground but work during the day in a bourgeois way and become terrorists in the evening, and leisure-time criminals. As it was, they were called in newspaper articles the "fine people across the street."

In Germany the female percentage in terrorism is much higher than in criminality in general. Among 22 activists of the first generation 12 were women. These women did not just help the men; they acted in the same way the men did. Among 35 German terrorists who were urgently wanted by the police in 1977, 17 were women.

Additionally, it should be mentioned that women terrorists are often more courageous and cruel than men and that they act more coolly and more deliberately. This same experience was made by the British ambassador to Uruguay, Jackson, who had been kidnapped by Tupamaros.

There are many theories circulating among experts and the public in search of an answer to the question: What is it that makes a human being become a terrorist? Where is the turning point between a demonstrator, for instance, and a terrorist? Is it possible to predict the future career of a sympathizer with terrorism? Will he or she ever go over the invisible borderline?

At this point, we can only offer some tentative explanations and suggestions. In 1978 the German researcher Dr. Grossarth Maticek interviewed 84 left- and right-wing radicals, who were not yet terrorists, about their sexual behavior, and he compared their answers with those in the interviews of nonradical students. The result was that the radicals—perhaps the potential terrorists?—had a disturbed and unsatisfactory sex life.

Professor Parry, and the best-known American experts on international terrorism, refer to H. G. Wells, who defines human history as a race between education and catastrophe. Parry adds: "In fact, the kind of half-baked schooling modern terrorists have, is one of the chief causes that could take the planet to its extinction." Parry continues that more than ever before, the radical activism of the youth is an attempt to discover an "identity" or merely to fight their way out of their own sheer boredom. According to another opinion, terrorism is one kind of a person's "total surrender before the strain of decision-making in conditions of uncertainty and overchoice or an explosion of frustration." Terrorists are "supersimplifiers." Many feel guilty for being born to, and reared in, wealth and privilege, luxury, or at least comfort. Compared with former times, this sense of guilt is tremendously heightened today, both individually and collectively.[19]

Female Aggression

It is not necessary to prove that acts of criminal violence derive from the amount of aggression a person has accumulated. Obviously, the potential for aggression in the personality of women is higher in our days than it was in former times. This statement only refers to the European situation, but it may be that one will find similarities and differences between the American and the European situation.

There is vast agreement in Europe that female aggression is increasing in different fields of life. By way of example:

1. Take the behavior in traffic. Females, especially younger ones, are more and more guilty of speeding, driving recklessly and without any attention to the rights of other drivers. Whether they have learned their driving behavior from male drivers or by themselves, cannot be decided.

2. There is, naturally, now more aggression needed in professional life, since more women than ever before have jobs where they compete with men.

3. There seems to be more aggression nowadays in criminal women than before. For instance, there is more active leading in bank robbery and also more use of firearms than before.

4. In publications and generally in the mass media, women are writing, talking, and behaving in a much more aggressive way.

5. In the new fashion trends, which, however, are mostly designed by men and always have shown general philosophical and political trends of the respective time, there is obviously a sort of aggressive new look with more boots and leather clothing, military-style, and the hair under cheeky caps.

The question arises: Why is there—so strikingly—much more aggression in females nowadays? We want to present, though very cautiously, the following suggestions and questions:

1. Perhaps women have been at all times as aggressive as they are nowadays, but perhaps they have shown their aggression in a different way, within the family group or in similar close relationships, or by changing over to depression and even mental illness. Recent studies tried to explain these signs of aggression by relating them to the suppression and frustration of women in former times. On the other hand, self-control was stronger, perhaps due to the more important role of education and to society's expectations of women.

2. If this is true, and the frustration-aggression theory, as seen by our time, was working in that way, why does aggression not decrease rather than increase today, when women have gained more freedom and liberty than ever before?

In conclusion, we would also like to draw the attention of the criminological community to two subjects which have been grossly neglected by the experts: traffic offenses and crimes of espionage committed by women. There are indications that presently women, as we said before, are driving more recklessly and that women increasingly are driving under the influence of alcohol. As regards espionage, there has been an upsurge, at least in Germany, during the last years, especially by women. There is, however, a complete lack of studies about the personality of spies, both male and female.

Notes

1. The Federal Republic of Germany has a population of 61,395,600.

2. Gabriella Rasko, *Crimes against Life Committed by Women in Hungary,* chap. 8, *infra.*

3. Wolf Middendorff, Der Fall Simone B.: *Historische und kriminal-psychologische Studie zur Totung aus Leidenschaft,* Goltdammer's Archiv fur Strafrecht, 4/1978, pp. 97–118.

4. *Der Spiegel,* 27/1968.

5. W. Naeve and F. Schulz, "Offences Under the Influence of Alcohol by Women," lecture at the 32d International Congress on Alcoholism and Drug Dependence, September 3–9, 1978, Warsaw, Poland.

6. Gunther Kaiser, *Kriminologie,* 3d ed. (Karlsruhe, 1976), p. 87.

7. Franz Csaszar, *Der Uberfall auf Geldinstitute, Eine kriminologische Untersuchung* (Wien, 1975), p. 138.

8. Everett DeBaun, "The Heist—The Theory and Practice of Armed Robbery," in H. Knowles, *Gentlemen, Scholars and Scoundrels,* (New York: Harper, 1959), pp. 365–366.

9. Wolf Middendorff *"Die Frau als politische Morderin, Historische internationale und zukunftige Aspekte" Kriminalistik* (Februar–Marz 1977): 78–81, 120–124.

10. Joan of Arc, *Legends and Truth,* (London, 1978).

11. Cathy Porter, *Fathers and Daughters-Russian Women in the Revolution* (London, 1976).

12. Wolf Middendorff, *Der Fall Tatjuva Leovtieff, Archiv fur Kriminologie,* 5 and 6 (1977): 163–174.

13. Five Sisters. *Women Against the Tsar*. Ed. and trans. by Barbara Alpern Engel and Clifford N. Rosenthal (London, 1975). The memories of five revolutionaries of the 1870's.

14. Murray Clark Havens et. al., *The Politics of Assassination*, (New Jersey: Englewood Cliffs, 1970), pp. 148–149.

15. See Wolf Middendorff, "Die Personlichkeit des Terroristen in historischer und kriminologischer Sicht," in Wolfgang Bohme (Hrsg.), *Terrorismus und Freiheit* (Heidelberg, 1978), pp. 9–41.

16. *Die Reise,* Jossa, 1977.

17. See Wolf Middenforff, *Die Gewaltkriminalitat unserer Zeit* (Stuttgart, 1976), pp. 39 et seq.; and Klaus Mehnert, *Jugend im Zeitbruch* (Reinbek bei Hamburg, 1978), p. 285.

18. Susanne von Paczensky (Hrsg.), *Frauen und Terror* (Reinbek bei Hamburg, 1978), pp. 26 and 28.

19. Albert Parry, *Terrorism from Robespierre to Arafat* (New York, 1976), pp. 527–530.

CHAPTER THREE

SOCIALIST COUNTRIES

1. The Criminality of Women in Poland

D. PLENSKA

Danuta Berger Plenska is Assistant Professor at the University of Warsaw (law faculty). Her primary interests in the field are legal and criminological aspects of recidivism and female criminality. She is interested in women's criminality in Poland and has written three articles on female criminality. Her publications include: *Zagadwienia Recycline in Prawie Karnym* (Warsaw, 1974); and numerous articles on recidivism, property crime, and other penal law problems.

1. Women's criminality as compared with men's is statistically as insignificant in Poland as in many other countries irrespective of the difference in socioeconomic development and political systems. It is insignificant insofar as the proportion, the gravity, and the violence are concerned. The proportion of women among known offenders, as well as the structure of female criminality in Poland, are similar to those in most Western countries. The only difference is that in Western countries these statistics show a rising incidence of female criminality. This is believed to be linked to the social and economic transformation of women's conditions which have been noticeable in Europe and in America, as well as to the new wave of the feminist movement. These changes in the socioeconomic status of women began in the Eastern European socialist countries in the late 1940s. It might, there-

fore, be interesting to see the impact of these changes on female criminality in these countries over the period of the last thirty years. This perspective does not imply that Polish developments, which I shall describe as a good example of the process, are going to be reproduced in Western societies. There are, indeed, many important differences, not only of a political and economic, but also of a cultural, social, and psychological nature. Nevertheless, the observations on the phenomenon of female criminality in light of the relatively emancipated socioeconomic condition of women in Poland in the course of the last thirty years can contribute to the discussion going on in Western countries on the interrelation between the feminist movement, and its impact on the redefinition of women's roles and attitudes, and the changes in quantity as well as quality of the criminality of women.

2. The emancipation of women in Poland and in other Eastern European socialist countries started soon after World War II. It was an economic, socio-occupational emancipation; cultural and psychological changes have not really followed accordingly. The life style and the status of women, however, have evolved gradually in relation to their massive entrance into the labor force. There were particular historical and economic reasons for the social demands on women as a labor force. The description of the Polish situation can serve as an illustration of the process which took place in all other Eastern European countries. The phenomenon of a massive absorption of women into the labor force in Poland can be understood mainly because of:

(a) the need to reconstruct the country, largely destroyed as a result of the war;
(b) the transformation of the country from a primarily agricultural society into an industrial one;
(c) the need for women to assist in supporting their families because of generally low wages;
(d) the large propaganda campaign during the 1950s which emphasized women's vocational activities outside the household.
(e) the creation of a new set of social values, e.g. professional activity has become for women, as for men, the main basis of social status.

Administrative and legislative measures tended to support women's striving for professional work: planned rates of women's annual employment, large access by women to the universities, leaves for bringing up children, and so on.[1] These factors, in combination, have resulted in full employment opportunities for women in Poland, a situation which still persists. They have facilitated women's entrance into vocational labor at a rate higher than anywhere in the world. In 1970 to 72 the percentage of women in the total working population was, for Poland, 46 percent; for Rumania, 45 percent, Czechoslovakia, 44.5 percent; Bulgaria and the German Democratic Republic, 44 percent; Hungary, 41 percent; Denmark, 39.5 percent; Japan, 38 percent; U.S.A., Great Britain, and the Federal Republic of Germany, 37 percent; for Italy, only 27 percent.[2]

The majority of women in Poland work outside the household. In 1970, 62 percent of women living in the cities, of productive age (18–59) worked outside the home, compared with 85 percent of men. Among women between 20 and 59 years of age, 75 to 79 percent worked. In large industrial cities this percentage is even higher and reaches a level of 84 percent of the women of productive age, compared with 96.5 percent for men.

The interesting feature of women's vocational activity in Poland is that women do not stop working after having married and having had children. In 1970, 71 percent of all women employed were married (this ratio is also high in Western countries: in the U.S.A., 60 percent; Canada, 58 percent; France, 55 percent; Belgium and Great Britain, 53 percent). Among women aged 25–40 having one child, 75 to 80 percent worked outside the household; among those having two children, 70 percent; three children, 65 percent; and even among mothers of four children, 58 percent worked. The relative percentage for France is only half that much.[3]

In Poland certain occupations are beginning to be dominated by women (which has implications regarding the subject of this chapter). In 1972 women represented 75 percent of all persons employed in medical and welfare services, and 76 percent in financial and insurance institutions. They represented 72 percent of salespersons; 67 percent of people employed in education, science, and culture; and 56 percent in administrative institutions and in the administration of justice.

3. After this brief description of the socioeconomic status of women in Poland, I shall present the general features of female criminality in Poland over the last three decades and try to sketch the relationship of their emancipated position to their criminality. First, I will describe the evolution of this phenomenon, based on the official statistics of persons convicted by courts.

The female/male ratio in crime was 1 to 4 in the late 1950s, 1 to 5 in the early 1960s, and 1 to 7 in 1968. From the early 1970s it was 1 to 9. If we take the number of people sentenced per year between 1921 and 1930, women represented about 18 percent of the total number of convicted persons; in 1937, 16.7 percent; in 1951, 25.9 percent; in 1954, 24.1 percent; in 1959, 21.3 percent; in 1961, 19.3 percent; in 1963, 17.3 percent; in 1968, 12.9 percent; in 1970, 10.6 percent; in 1975, 11.2 percent; and in 1977, 10.2

percent. We observe, then, an interesting trend: an increase in the ratio of women's criminality in the 1950s as compared with the ratio in the 1930s. Then there is a steady decrease which from the 1960s drops far below the level observed in the prewar period. In short, we notice a decrease of 250 percent in female crime (based on the number of convictions by courts) between 1951 and 1977. The incidence of crime among the women of Poland, after the first decade of socioeconomic emancipation was reduced to its previous insignificant dimension.[4]

Persons sentenced Among Sex; Number, Increase Index, and Coefficient Per 10,000.

	Women		Men		Coefficient Per 10,000	
Year	Number	Increase Index	Number	Increase Index	Women	Men
1951	49,834	100	143,608	100	52	172
1954	45,765	92	143,826	102	48	173
1959	60,861	122	219,900	153	63	249
1963	47,079	94	224,464	156	45	245
1968	28,453	57	192,067	133	24	182
1970	17,644	35	148,405	103	15	138
1975	18,143	36	143,143	99	14	122
1977	14,059	28	123,788	86	11	102

Source: Adapted from Statystyka Sadowa, Warszawa, 1976 and 1978.

The number of women sentenced by the courts has decreased since the early 1960s not only in its absolute number, but also in the more appropriate measure of a rate per 10,000 of the total population. A decrease in the number of men sentenced by the courts appears only in the 1970s, due mainly to changes in legislation and penal policy. It is far less pronounced than the relative decrease in female offenders. The rate for women was, in 1951, 52 per 10,000. It grew to 63 in 1958, then gradually dropped to 45 in 1963, to 24 in 1968, and to 11 in 1977. It is now one fifth of what it was in the 1950s, whereas for men this rate grew from 172 in 1950 to 245 in 1963, then dropped to 183 in 1968, and only in the 1970s has it decreased to 102. It is quite clear from these statistics that the rate for men has gone down much less than the rate for women.

In sum, although the Polish data show some increase in women's participation in crime as registered in court statistics in the 1950s, as compared with the 1920s and 1930s, we must also note the steady and substantial decrease of female convictions in the 1960s and 1970s, a far more significant decrease than that experienced by men.

This observation poses an intriguing question: Why has women's emancipation in Poland, after the first decade of the socioeconomic changes, stopped producing an increase in female crime while it has not done so in Western countries? I can venture some tentative explanations. To begin, I wish to underline the fact that at first the increase in women's criminality was largely of an economic type, involving petty offenses against socialized property by women employees, managers, or salespersons. It was correlated to the massive entrance of women, in the late 1940s and 1950s, into vocational activities, mainly as salespersons, bookkeepers, and clerks. Later decreases may be partly perceived as a result of both legislative changes (mainly by the law of March 21, 1953, depenalizing petty offenses against social property), and changes in criminal policy, namely more lenient prosecution of other minor economic offenses since the mid-1950s. The changes affected the number of convictions against women, since the previous increase was due, primarily, to these particular offenses.

These legal changes, however, explain the question only partially; thus, we are left with certain sociocultural or psychological reasons. It has to be pointed out that, after the first decade of stormy social changes, the church and other social control agencies regained their influence and forced women into the old patterns of feminine roles. Hence, sociocultural and psychological liberation have failed to follow the socioeconomic one.[5]

Even though the majority of women work, household and childrearing have remained totally female chores. Alcoholism in women has been widely discouraged by the social control agencies while being totally accepted in men. Presently, alcoholism is cited by all criminological research in Poland as the main factor for criminality. The fact that this is not a problem for women can be another reason for their decreasing crime rate.

Finally, one can point to the juridical explanation for the low rate of women's criminality: the Polish penal code—like any other penal code—is primarily oriented toward masculine deviance. Acts against the person, the majority of which in Poland are committed under the influence of alcohol, as well as violent crimes against property, and traffic offenses, are rarely committed by women. Even in the economic crime category in 1977 women represented only 11.1 percent of persons convicted for usurpation of social property and 9.1 percent of those convicted for all kinds of larceny against private property. These two categories cover 55 percent of all convictions in Poland in 1977.[6]

There are no "female crimes" in the Polish code, except for infanticide, which is a very rare crime at present (statistics for the 1970s do not register any act of that kind). Abortion has been legal in Poland since 1956. Prostitution, soliciting, and similar "morals" offenses are not penalized, and shoplifting is much less widespread since the trade system is more traditional (there are fewer self-services and opportunities for stealing).

In a country where criminal acts are defined mainly with male deviant behavior in mind, women do not have too much of an outlet for their criminal activity—except for their newly acquired opportunities concerning the management of goods and funds. Data presenting the female ratio in the total number of persons convicted for particular offenses in 1977 are demonstrated in the accompanying table.

Type of Offense	Absolute Numbers			Percentage	
	Total	Male	Female	Male	Female
Total convictions	137,847	123,788	14,059	89.8	10.2
Offenses against public safety and safety in traffic:	8,435	8,241	194	97.7	2.3
Traffic offenses	7,492	7,358	134	98.2	1.8
Offenses against life and health	13,997	13,317	680	95.1	4.9
Homicide	327	294	33	89.9	10.1
Causing death unintentionally	270	258	12	95.6	4.4
Causing serious bodily injury	488	465	23	95.3	4.7
Causing other bodily injury	6,219	5,989	230	96.3	3.7
Taking part in a brawl or a beating	6,436	6,125	311	95.2	4.8
Exposing human life to an immediate danger	63	59	4	93.7	6.3
Offenses against liberty:	2,416	2,280	136	94.4	5.6
Illegal threat and compelling	509	431	78	84.7	15.3
Rape	1,251	1,250	1	99.9	0.1
Offenses against honor and personal inviolability	2,380	2,305	75	96.8	3.2
Defamation and insult	366	332	34	90.7	9.3
Violating a personal inviolability	2,014	1,973	41	98.0	2.0
Offenses against the family, guardianship, and youth:	15,795	15,384	411	97.4	2.6
Mistreating a member of the family	8,084	7,954	130	98.4	1.6
Inducing a minor to drink	35	32	3	91.4	8.6
Evasion of payment for support of child	7,634	7,374	260	96.6	3.4
Offenses against social property:	40,347	35,860	4,487	88.9	11.1
Usurpation of social property	16,328	15,090	1,238	92.4	7.6
Usurpation of entrusted social property	6,099	4,129	1,970	67.7	32.3
Usurpation of social property of considerable value	406	324	82	79.8	20.2

Type of Offense	Absolute Numbers			Percentage	
	Total	Male	Female	Male	Female
Usurpation of social property in agreement with other persons	1,519	1,236	283	81.4	18.6
Stealing by breaking and entering or by audacious manner	8,674	8,515	159	98.2	1.8
Temporary stealing of motor vehicle	601	601		100.0	
Receiving stolen goods	4,005	3,342	663	83.4	16.6
Offenses against private property:	35,229	32,010	3,219	90.0	9.1
Stealing	14,418	12,451	1,967	86.4	13.6
Appropriation	825	718	107	87.0	13.0
Fraud	1,186	1,015	171	85.6	14.4
Audacious stealing by breaking and entering	10,216	9,712	504	95.1	4.9
Robbery	3,458	3,352	106	96.9	3.1
Temporary stealing of a motor vehicle	1,874	1,871	3	99.8	0.2
Receiving stolen goods	2,272	1,958	314	86.2	13.8
Economic offenses:	4,135	1,721	2,414	41.6	58.4
Mismanagement causing serious shortage in entrusted social property	1,009	435	574	43.1	56.9
Minor speculation	3,040	1,216	1,824	40.0	60.0
Fiscal offenses:					
Illegal foreign currency traffic	1,539	1,055	484	68.6	31.4
Custom offenses	209	157	52	75.1	24.9
Offenses against the functioning of state and social institutions:	6,732	5,984	748	88.9	11.1
Assault on a public functionary	3,166	2,972	194	93.9	6.1
Insulting a public functionary or not performing dutifully a public function	263	192	71	73.0	27.0
Corruption	610	520	90	85.2	14.8
Against the administration of justice:	1,877	1,696	181	90.4	9.6
False testimony	569	444	125	78.0	22.0
Against documents:	1,864	1,484	380	79.6	20.4
Document counterfeiting	804	653	151	81.2	18.8
Certifying an untruth by a public functionary	846	652	194	77.1	22.9
Against public order:	935	745	190	79.7	20.3
Illegal firearms possession	231	228	3	98.7	1.3
Illegal border crossing	312	187	25	88.2	11.8
Illegal selling of alcohol	240	99	141	41.3	38.8

This table demonstrates the structure and importance of women's participation in crime in Poland, based on statistics of convictions by courts. Thus, in 1977 women represented 10.2 percent of the total criminality. Their ratio was higher than random in offenses linked to women's new opportunities in the management of various units of the socialized economy, access to social funds, and goods and performance of public functions. We find 58.4 percent women among the total convictions for so-called economic offenses, such as mismanagement, misuse or shortage of entrusted social property, petty speculation, and so on; 32.3 percent for usurpation of entrusted social property; 30.3 percent for fiscal offenses (of which 31.4 percent were convicted for illegal traffic of foreign currency); 20.2 percent for large usurpation of social property, 18.6 percent for such usurpation committed in agreement with others (both crimes being possible within one's activity or function in a unit of the socialized economy); 22.9 percent for certifying an untruth by a public functionary; 20.4 percent for all offenses against documents; 27 percent for abusing or not performing public functions dutifully and 14.8 percent for corruption.

Outside these new socioeconomic roles, women in Poland participate in global crime in a very insignificant proportion. They represent a totally insignificant part of persons convicted of violent crimes. In crime against life and health, women represent 4.9 percent of all convictions; and of these, for murder, 10.1 percent; for unintentional killing, for causing bodily injury, or for taking part in a brawl or a beating, 4.8 and 3.7 percent, respectively. Women's ratio in these crimes has diminished even over the last few years. For instance, in 1971 women represented 6.7 percent of persons convicted for offenses against health and life. In other offenses against persons their participation is also minimal: from 5.6 percent in assault on a public functionary, 2.3 percent in offenses against personal inviolability, and 1.6 percent in convictions for mistreating a member of the family.

We find a higher percentage of women in offenses committed by verbal aggression or expressions: 15.3 percent in convictions for illegal threat, 13.1 percent for insulting a public functionary, 9.3 percent for other insults, 22 percent for false testimony.

Women form a totally insignificant proportion of persons responsible for traffic offenses (1.8 percent), temporarily stealing a motor vehicle (0.2 percent), or illegal possession of firearms (1.3 percent), typically male offenses, consistent with male cultural attractions and attributes. Violence within the family, as well as violent crimes oriented toward the property of others, also remain men's domain. Women represent only 2.6 percent of persons convicted for audacious stealing or breaking and entering, and 3.1 percent for robbery (almost always guilty of aiding the male perpetrator).

Women have no substantial part in the most common offenses in Poland which are nonviolent acts against private and social property. Such offenses amount to one half of all convictions. In 1977 women represented only 7.6 percent of persons convicted for appropriation or larceny of social property (not connected with management or protection of such property) and 13.0 to 14.6 percent for offenses against private property. In this category we again find a greater participation of women in acts which are of a helping, accessory nature, or in receiving stolen goods, where they represent 58.4 percent of all convictions.

The analysis of the statistics of persons convicted by the courts shows that women's participation in crime in Poland is not only nonsignificant but "inconsistent." It is linked to both traditional and emancipated roles of women. In "traditional" crime, women have a marginal place, consistent with socially learned roles and behavior. They are involved in nonviolent activities, in acts concerning verbal aggression, or in helping and accessory functions in male crimes. They are absent from crimes linked with traditionally male roles: drinking, battery, driving, violence, and possession of firearms. In "new" economic crime, however, women's participation is more significant, as a consequence of the new roles and opportunities acquired in their socioeconomic emancipation.

4. The data presented above give us information about the importance of women's presence in total convictions for particular types of offenses, but they do not tell us about the structure of female criminality as a separate phenomenon. The subject has been so overlooked that comprehensive published court statistics do not have an appropriate table. The research I have done in this respect is based on statistical forms for the computation of court statistics. For 1975 I found that female crime is composed of the following: 30 percent, offenses against social property; 24 percent, offenses against individual property; 19 percent, other economic offenses (such as misuse or mismanagement of entrusted social property, or so-called minor speculation); 8 percent, offenses against the functioning of state and social institutions (which are mainly insulting a public functionary, usually a police officer, and petty abuse or not dutifully performing a public function); 6 percent, against life and health; 2 percent, against family and youth; 1 percent, against liberty; 1 percent, against honor and personal inviolability; 9 percent, other offenses.

Female criminality is thus composed of 73 percent property and economic offenses, which offense categories represent 48.6 percent of the total criminality in Poland. Hence, women's criminality in Poland is nonviolent and nondangerous. Three quarters of it is composed of economic and property offenses, and to a large extent this is related to the professional and vocational roles of women in Poland.[7]

From these data we can begin to ascertain the interrelationships between the process of socioeconomic emancipation of women and changes in female criminality. I would risk the hypothesis that transformation in women's social and economic status is more reflected in the "new" structure of their criminality than it is in its absolute quantity or seriousness. These transformations originate from at least three different factors. One is related to changes in behavior and attitudes of women themselves, one to men's perception of women and their activities, and another to the definitions that legislators and administration of justice agencies give to women's behavior.

The factors related to changes in the position of women can produce, on the one hand, an increase in women's crime. New social roles as employees, managers, bookkeepers, and public functionaries increase the opportunities for economic crimes. Women become involved more and more in embezzlement, larceny, fraud, financial, and white-collar crimes. The statistics show that in these types of criminal activity women's participation, in Poland, reaches a much higher level than their random proportion in criminality. Transformation in women's self-perception may also produce, on the other hand, a change in the form of their behavior; for example, more traditionally "male," violent acts.[8] However, this has not yet occurred in Poland, perhaps because of the fact that in Poland women's socioeconomic emancipation has not led to any deeper cultural and psychological reorientations.[9]

On the other hand, socioeconomic emancipation diminishes women's feelings of dependence, frustration, helplessness, and victimization. Since these emotions are the typical basis for women's violent crimes, such as homicide, infanticide, and assault, these crimes should gradually decrease. Such a decrease can already be noted in Poland. In 1937 women represented 10 percent of people convicted for crimes against life and health: in 1971, 6.7 percent; in 1977, only 4.9 percent.

The changes in reported female criminality result also from an evolution in the perception of women's gender roles, their deviance and criminality. The legalization of abortion and more liberal attitudes toward unmarried mothers remove the previously existing feminine crimes of illegal abortion and infanticide from the statistics. A less pronounced "double standard" of morality diminishes women's social marginality and deviance, especially prostitution and alcoholism, the two main factors in women's past criminality.

Parallel to changes resulting in the reduction of women's acts which are defined as crimes, one can notice modifications in law and criminal policy concerning typically male criminal behavior. Some acts have been made criminal because of paternalistic, protective attitudes toward women. The best examples in Poland may be the law penalizing evasion of financial support for one's child, a law which applied almost exclusively to men and constituted, in the 1970s, 5.0 to 5.5 percent of the total criminality, or the offense of mistreating a member of the family (almost exclusively wife battery, which accounts for 6 percent of male crime).

On the other hand, some unlawful acts committed in large proportion by women are considered nondangerous and have gradually been decriminalized and removed from the penal code. This is the case in all petty offenses against private or social property, minor economic offenses, petty fraudulent manipulations, deceiving the purchaser or the supplier, or minor speculation.

This section has presented information on the volume of female criminality in Poland, its dynamics over the years, and its structure as compared with male criminality. I have attempted to propose some social, cultural, psychological, as well as juridical factors resulting in low, insignificant and decreasing female criminality in Poland, in spite of the fact that, for the past thirty years, there has been a socioeconomic emancipation of women.

Notes

1. Z. Dach. *Praca zawodowa kobiet w Polsce* (Warszawa: Ksiaka i Wiedza, 1976), pp. 91–101.

2. *Year Book of Labour Statistics* (Geneva: ILO, 1973).

3. Z. Dach, (1976), p. 98, K. Wrochno. *Problemy pracy kobiet* (Warszawa, 1971), p. 39.

4. Fifteen percent of total arrests in the U.S.A. in 1972, 19 percent of the arrests for "crime index" crimes; in Canada, 16 percent of persons convicted; in Great Britain 14.5 percent. See F. Adler, "The Interaction between Women's Emancipation and Female Criminality: A Cross Cultural Perspective" *Int. J. of Criminology and Penology* (1977) 5: 104.

5. Freda Adler also suggests this explanation of the above analyzed question. See F. Adler, (1977), p. 107.

6. See Statystyka Sadowa Warszawa, (1977).

7. Rita J. Simon also believes that social and economic emancipation of women in the U.S.A. leads to their larger involvement only in property offenses. She shows that the much-discussed increase in the ratio of women's arrests is due almost wholly to the fact that women commit more property offenses. The percentage of women arrested for crimes of violence presents neither an upward nor a downward trend. For instance, among all arrests for these crimes women formed the following percentages: in 1953, 11.9 percent; in 1956, 13.5 percent; in 1963, 10.3 percent; in 1972, 11 percent. The striking rise is observable mainly in larceny. It is also important in forgery, fraud, and embezzlement. See R. J. Simon, *Women and Crime* (Lexington, Mass.: D. C. Heath (1975), pp. 36–47. The same trend is visible in Canada where

women's criminality consists of 34 percent of offenses against property. The increase in female criminality is also due to these offenses, since it has been as high as 35 percent in the period from 1960. The number of women convicted for crimes against person has grown only by 30 percent and for violent crimes against property by 50 percent. See M. A. Bertrand, *La Femme et le Crime* (Montreal: L'Aurore, 1979), pp. 70, 75, 107.

8. Such is the suggestion of Freda Adler whose book, *Sisters in Crime* (1975), presents this thesis. Recently this conviction was presented by Rita James Simon and Navin Sharma: "Greater visibility and participation in criminal activities on the part of women may be one of the unintended by-products of the women's movement. Not only has the movement provided a rhetoric that has emphasized similarities between sexes, and an image of the female that legitimizes her desire to compete with men in business, political, and educational worlds, but it has also been effective in getting women to move from the kitchen or the typing pool to the executive suite or the lecture hall. Once women have started working at changing their image and life style, it should not be surprising that some would seek shortcuts to monetary success and independence through deviant careers." See R. J. Simon and N. Sharma, "Does the American Experience Generalize?" in F. Adler and R. Simon, The Criminology of Deviant Women (Boston: Houghton Mifflin, 1979), pp. 391–396. Laura Crites disagrees with the opinion of the effects of the women's liberation movement on the rise of female crime or the nature of it. See L. Crites, "The Female Offenders: Myth vs. Reality," in *The Female Offender* (1976), pp. 36–39.

9. The same supposition is expressed by F. Adler, (1977), p. 107.

2. Crimes Against Life Committed by Women in Hungary

G. RASKO

Gabriella Rasko is Clinical Psychologist, Chief Collaborator, and Researcher at the National Institute of Criminology and Criminalistics. Her primary interests in the field are criminology, contemporary trends in criminology, female criminality, clinical criminology, and victimology. Her publications include: *Sociology and Criminology* (1973); *Theories of Bourgeois Criminologists on Women's Delinquency* (1975); *Psychological Examinations of Female Convicts* (1976); *Sex and Criminality: A Historical Outline of Certain Forms of Women's Criminality* (1977); *The Bourgeois Victimology of Today Reflected by Two International Symposiums* (1979); *Monograph: The Criminality of Women* (Budapest, 1978); and longer studies in the yearly anthology of N.I. of C. and C.

In most countries the proportion of women in crimes committed against persons is not large. However, within this category the proportion of crimes against human life is not small, moreover in many countries it is greater than the proportion of women in total criminality. Such a situation can be found in many prominent capitalist countries, as well as in Hungary and Czechoslovakia. As a matter of course the proportions are higher in the countries where statistics combine infanticide and homicide, but even where this is not so, the rate of women committing crimes against human life is higher than their proportion in total criminality.

In Hungary 26 to 35 percent of all offenders committing crimes against human life are women. Their rate has slightly decreased in the past fifty years, as before World War I the proportion of women was 37 percent.

At the same time, bourgeois criminologists have often pointed out the fact that in our age, as compared with the 1930s, female criminality against life has greatly increased—at least as concerns leading industrialized countries. Thus, in the U.S.A. and the Federal Republic of Germany the increase is more than 100 percent.[1]

The American criminologist MacDonald refers to the fact that the proportion of male and female killers varies first of all according to the cultural background. "The female share of the total amount of crime is greatest in those countries where women are most emancipated. It reached a vanishing point in those countries of the East and Middle-East, where their social experience is rigorously circumscribed."[2] The dominant role of the culture over race is shown, for example, by the fact that, according to the survey by Wolfgang, the frequency of homicides among black women in the U.S.A. is higher than that of white men, but the index for black women in Africa is lower than that of white women in Philadelphia.[3]

Even if one disregards the quantitative analysis of the proportions of female participation in crimes against human life, it is worthwhile to deal with these issues in order to make an international comparison, not only because of the general importance of this type of crime and its outstanding danger to society, but because there are characteristic morphological and psychological differences between male and female offenders within this category. Besides that, I am of the opinion that comparison of various national surveys on homicides is interesting because it may reveal the role of the different cultures. Moreover, there is more than one common base for comparison than in the case of other more pointedly society-specific types of crime.

The basis of the present report is a complex criminological research conducted by the Hungarian National Institute of Criminology and Criminalistics for a number of years, surveying the material of 125 female offenders of the past decades convicted of intentional homicide or attempt. Infanticide, which according to the Hungarian law qualifies as homicide, was separately examined. The research based on the records of the investigation and the trial was supplemented by psychological and sociological examinations conducted in prison, comparing the results of the examinations of the offenders with those of a control group consisting of persons having committed crimes against property.

A. I attempted to classify the research material on the basis of situational and psychic inner and outer circumstances regarded as decisive factors, and drew up the *constellation types,* discussed below.

1. The literature on female criminality agrees that the majority of killings committed by women belong to an easily definable main type which can be characterized by a prolonged crisis situation with respect to persons both physically and psychologically close to each other or living in a common household. The victims here are from among relatives, first and foremost the husband, common-law husband, or lover; second, the child; third, parents and other related persons. The crime always originates from a personal relationship with the victim and is usually triggered by deep despair which increases until the offender's range of possible action narrows down and practically no other alternative remains for her apart from killing. Criminologists discussing this category, which has such a great importance in female crime against life, often underline the role of provocation, which is particularly significant in the case of victims of the first type. Thus, von Hentig expressly mentions that "in the case of these family killings the situation is often doubtlessly similar to self-defence."[4] Seelig calls these female offenders "crisis criminals," and MacDonald writes: "Provoked beyond all measure, the long-suffering wife of the alcoholic tormentor may take her revenge in an impulsive act of violence."[5] Horoszowski calls attention to the fact that from the analysis of the motives of female offenders in this group and, from the circumstances, it is evident that the offender acts in a situation in which the provocation of the victim is, as a rule, much stronger than in the case of male offenders committing similar crimes of conflict. In the case of such female offenders their reaction, as Horoszowski states, develops in the course of long frustration and humiliation often related to the alcoholism of the victim.[6]

This type of provocation, however, is only one, but doubtlessly the most important variable; it can be called an emotional domestic conflict situation. Such situations were found in 47 of the investigated cases. About half of them—which was a quarter of the total number—were situations in which the husband, common-law husband, or lover could be considered to be a provocative victim of the killing.

Surveys described in the foreign literature report similar proportions concerning the percentage of female killers committing their crimes in conflict situations. These results are significant, as they show a great similarity in different countries and different times: Roesner (1938), 46 percent; Wolfgang (1958), 65 percent—although more distant relatives and acquaintances are also included in this number. But the close personal relationship is a common factor: Bluhm (1958), 52 percent; Krause (1966), 67 percent; the victims classified as by Wolfgang, the study of the Baltimore Criminal Justice Commission (1964), 45 percent; Cole and Fisher (1968), 67 percent where the circle of related persons was interpreted in a wider sense; and the two studies by Ward (1969), 50 percent.[7]

In spite of the somewhat different aspects of the surveys, it can be stated that in the typology of killings committed by women the principal type here described has a predominant role, since it constitutes about half of the total number of killings committed by women in the different populations.[8]

The psychological mechanism of such acts committed in an emotional domestic conflict situation can be characterized—on the basis of the results of the study of the National Institute of Criminology and Criminalistics—by the accumulation of suppressed aggression as a result of prolonged experiences of frustration, then its explosive manifestation, usually triggered by an everyday provocation suffered without any counteraggression earlier, or by other events which cannot be considered extraordinary at all. In the case of premeditated acts, the slowly but irresistibly accumulating hostility or thirst for revenge or escape lead to a deepening emotional desolation until it becomes general, that is, it extends to other interpersonal relationships. The method of the action itself—especially in the case of prolonged frustration— is often cruel and goes beyond the extent necessary to extinguish life.

It does not follow from these facts that in the constellation defined as the main type, the offenders are all "martyrs" and their acts should always be considered as "attempts of escape." Only in half of the examined cases was the female perpetrator exposed to prolonged provocation—usually because of alcoholism and brutality—but in at least a quarter of these cases the behavior of the perpetrator also contributed to the permanent conflict. Thus, on the basis of the survey it can be established that although the killings committed in an emotional domestic conflict situation are predominant in half of the cases, and are characteristic of the female criminality of homicide, it cannot be stated that the unbearable situation created by the victim is equally characteristic.

2. The nondomestic conflicts are different in their character from the above-mentioned main type, but they are also characterized by a thirst for revenge and the feeling of hostility to the extreme. Such situations emerged

in the case of abandoned paramours, quarrels between distant relatives, and in day-by-day conflicts among neighbors. These cases, however, are singular, in that they do not have such common features as the previous or the subsequent constellations. Besides, neither their number nor their proportion are significant.

3. The so-called extended suicide is also a characteristic form of homicide committed by women, although it is small in number; it also is committed in an emotional conflict situation. But it is different from the main type inasmuch as the victim is not the same person who induces the conflict. Its essence is that the doer does not see any way out of the situation and prepares for suicide, but, not wanting to abandon the person who needs her care, most often her child, kills that person. The killing having been completed, the doer cannot or, in some cases, does not want to commit suicide.

4. In the fourth group I include those situations and motives where the doer is burdened with heavy obligations toward the victims, and the killing means an escape therefrom. This effort to escape from burdensome obligations, however, is not only a concept of motivations; it also is characteristic of a special situation, mostly typical of women. In the majority of cases, the perpetrator, who has a difficult life anyway, has to take care of a helpless or crippled person, toward whom she also feels hostility. Thirteen percent of the examined cases had to be classified as falling into this constellation. Such cases were naturally more frequent in the past, but they also occur at present. The criminogenous situation arising from the coincidence of the burdensome obligations and the primitive personality incapable of fulfilling them can be considered a constellation typical of women even today, partly because it is still women who have the immediate duties of taking care of such persons, and partly because in such cases women have fewer practical and psychological possibilities of changing the situation.

All four types are characterized by the fact that the sphere of motivations is determined by the emotional conflict which, with few exceptions, pertains to persons close to the perpetrator. Nevertheless, it is desirable to separate them from each other, since the differing circumstances, the relationship with the victim, and especially the role of the victim in the events basically define the crime in all its complexity. From the point of view of criminology it is not indifferent whether the deed takes place as the last link in the chain of prolonged domestic provocations, as in the case of a typical murder of a husband, or is an extended suicide, or an escape from burdensome obligations, even though all of these cases are emotional conflict homicides. But they doubtlessly have such common characteristics which sharply distinguish them from the following group.

5. The homicides committed for profit differ not only in their motives but also as to the situation, the features of the execution of the crime, the behavior after the deed, and especially the psychology of the perpetrator. Her type of personality and her relationship with the victim are basically different. Fifteen percent of the examined offenders belong to this group. But this proportion cannot be considered to be a fair representation, since only 4 percent of all homicides were committed for profit in Hungary in recent years, and their number is on the decrease. In the past, the rate of crimes of this type used to be much higher, and the decrease was brought about necessarily by socioeconomic changes. The material for this investigation had to be collected from several decades past, and this accounts for the relative frequency of this type in the sample. It is a fact that most of the cases belonging to this group come from material prior to 1960. Among present cases of homicide committed by women, those committed for profit are extremely rare. The situation on a world scale is different. In the developed capitalist countries within the growing category of homicides committed for profit, the infrequent but still more and more numerous crimes committed by armed women, alone or with accomplices, are particularly conspicuous.

6. The remaining small number of cases which cannot be classified into any of the previous categories constitute a mixed group, into which acts of insane persons and other cases of special motivation belong.

Finally, it can be stated that the group distribution of the 125 offenders in the investigated sample proves the well-known experience that crimes against human life committed by women in emotional conflict situations, mostly in connection with related persons in the wider sense, constitute the majority of the cases. Beside these, the acts committed for profit and the group of crimes with mixed motives are not significant, the less so the more recent the sample is.[9] In sum, the proportions of the different constellation types are shown in the accompanying table.

Origin of Killings

	%
1. Conflict and domestic	47
2. Conflict but nondomestic	9
3. Extended suicide	8
4. Escape from burdensome obligations	13
5. For profit	15
6. Mixed group	8

The first three are basically one category: varieties of conflict killings, where the victims belong to the same group of interrelated persons. They constitute 77 percent of the cases. Here I must emphasize again that the majority of the first group, considered to be the main type, that is, one quarter of the whole sample, forms that basically homogeneous unit, that I consider the most characteristic of homicides committed by women: the explosive manifestation of suppressed aggression accumulated in the course of prolonged provocation.

B. Treating the sample as a whole, let me point out some characteristics of the subjective side of the act that can form the basis of an international comparison; for example, the *participation in the act*.

In the literature of criminology the female offender was generally characterized by remaining in the background, by the predominance of the role of the instigator, and the accessory by passivity in general. This was also regarded as applicable to crimes against human life, except for infanticide. Recent data prove the opposite to be the case. The majority of women found guilty of homicide are convicted as single offenders. This is reflected by the different representative surveys. According to two surveys of Ward and Jackson (1969), U.S.A., in 77 percent of the total number of cases the convicted women were single offenders. Totman reports similar proportions. Suval and Brisson (1974) also emphasize that women commit their killings mostly alone, the proportion of single female murderers being higher than that of male murderers.[10] The proportions found in my sample are shown in the accompanying table. It is to be noted that in only 5 of all these cases did the court convict the offender as instigator of the crime.

	Number	%
The murderess was a single offender	88	70.4
She was one of two	19	15.2
She was one of three	14	11.2
She was one of four	4	3.2
Total	125	100.0

The facts concerning the social and educational background of the offenders, examined from many aspects, are less suitable for international comparison. It must be noted, however, that the majority of the middle-aged or older offenders, both in the past and in our days, grew up in very primitive and harsh circumstances. Nearly two thirds of the female offenders were raised in primitive rural surroundings, in an environment poor in intellectual stimuli, where the influence of the macrosociety could not reach them, and they were exposed to the insulating and depressing atmosphere of the immediate surroundings. Most of them worked from their early youth both in the household and agriculture, got married early, bore children, and by the time they reached their more mature years, they became weary and apathetic women. In most cases this was aggravated by a bad marriage, in which these women spent years, often in circumstances where they, rather than the alcoholic husband, had to keep up the family.

Such severe conditions have a multiple criminogenic effect. The primitive, isolated environment, poor in stimuli, narrows down the individual's ability of choice and decision to a great extent in conflict situations, as he or she does not know any alternatives which might lead out of the conflict. In addition to this, he or she is affected by the traditional, almost suggestive peasant system of values, that is, being bound to the locality and sticking to the existing circumstances, which is especially true in the case of women. Divorce, moving to another place, finding a job, and the like, as alternative solutions to the situation do not occur to these old-fashioned peasant women, for both actual and psychological reasons. Turning to violence is closer to their personality, as the slighter forms of this pattern of behavior are well known to them because of the smaller or greater brutalities of the father and other male members of the family in their childhood and those of their own spouses later on.

Most of the female offenders in our sample were middle-aged women of a very low educational level, without any trade or personal income. Two thirds of them came from the poor peasantry of the past and the lowest layers of the working class. Many of them came from the most backward areas; their possibilities for leaving behind the life style of the past were worse than the average. The professional and intellectual conditions can hardly be compared with the Western surveys of the same topic, partly because of the basic differences in the sociocultural structure, and partly because our survey involves a very long range of time. Nevertheless, it is interesting that in respect to one of the significant factors, the predominance of the lack of a trade, the results in most countries are very similar. According to Cole and Fisher's survey published in 1968 (U.S.A.), containing data of 112 convicted female killers, 81 percent of them were characterized as unskilled, whereas in the Hungarian sample this proportion was 75 percent.[11]

The average age of female killers, especially in infanticide, all over the world is higher than that of female offenders in general. There is a certain age difference compared with males committing homicide. MacDonald emphasizes that "women are more likely to be offenders at later ages than men." Totman noted the same. In addition to general data, she also refers to those of Wolfgang, according to whom most of the female convicts were about 30 years of age. According to surveys by Suval and Brisson, two thirds of female killers are older than 30, while this proportion was 27.6 percent in the case of offenders convicted of crimes against property. In their sample, female offenders convicted of homicide were also older than males who committed the same crime.[12] The accompanying table represents the age distribution of the present survey:

	Number	%
Juvenile, 14–17 years	1	0.8
Young adult, 18–25 years	26	20.8
Adult, 26–40 years	50	40.0
Middle-aged, 41–60 years	41	32.8
Old, 61–75 years	7	5.6
Total	125	100.0

Beside the large number in the age group of about 30, the proportion of middle-aged women is relatively high. This is not surprising if we consider that most of the acts are the result of emotional conflicts which emerged after many years of frustration with ever worsening interpersonal relationships.

As regards the personality structure of the perpetrators, the criminological examinations based on the records were supplemented by different projection and performance tests, exploratory clinical interviews, and sociological surveys conducted in prison. The results were reported in a separate study. Here only some of the main aspects can be mentioned.

Nearly three quarters of the examined female offenders were considered by the court to be sane; 20 percent were found of limited sanity; and about 5 percent were found to be insane. Sanity and insanity being rather more legal than psychological concepts, these data do not reveal too much about the personality structure of the offenders. Our complex studies proved that the psychological factors are in a close and decisive correlation with the role the offenders played in their immediate environment, usually inherited from the past. This role was a passive one, despite the hard work they performed in their families. They were deprived of possibilities of self-fulfillment and of adequate information about the wider social environment. As a result of the frequent psychic deprivations, a certain type of emotional desolation and alienation emerged, which was accompanied by an attitude of egotism and ruthlessness, more intensive than usual, in the majority of cases.

The above-mentioned mechanism of aggression can generally be found in the case of women committing crimes against life in the sense that while men are more inclined to react immediately to the frustration, especially the ones affecting their own persons and their aggression is open and ready, women are more inclined to slower reactions. Women's aggression develops over a long period of time, and is latent for long. These women are usually capable of living in an actually or seemingly humiliating situation for a long time. However, the repressed aggressive tendencies accumulate over time, and the inhibitions built up of role conventions, fears, and everyday repressions break through: the criminal act takes place.

The typical female killer of the surveyed sample was a primitive personality raised and living in backward circumstances whose intellectual level was substantially lower not only than the average but lower than that of the control group of female offenders committing crimes against property. At the same time, their emotional structure was poorly differentiated, and their impulsivity was much higher than the average. Their lack of education, their dependence, and their sticking to the rigid life style made them almost incapable of action and determined the narrow parameters of the offense.

The psychological examination conducted in the prison underlined the conclusion that most of the women convicted of crimes against human life showed personality disturbances which originated from before the imprisonment. Such were extreme introversion, disturbed ability to make contacts, general inhibition, general imbalance and tension of the nervous system, general lack of interest and deficiencies of adaptation. It is particularly interesting from the criminological point of view that they could control their emotions to a lesser extent than the members of the control group. They were at the mercy of their passions, and at the same time they rigidly stuck to the most acceptable patterns of behavior.

On the basis of the tests[13] it could be established that both the neurotic and the psychotic features were more significant in the case of offenders convicted of crimes against life than in the case of those convicted of crimes against property.

C. The characteristics of the objective side of the act, which were also surveyed in detail—for example, the time and place of the act, the means and methods employed, the behavior after the deed, the cover-up of the deed, together with the judicial qualification of the act and the sentence imposed—are to a great extent culture specific, and so less adequate for international comparison. Nevertheless, I want to treat the questions of the means and method of committing the act briefly, inasmuch as, co-jointly with other factors, they point to the change which can be regarded as typifying female criminality in our days.

When committing their crimes, more than two thirds of the female offenders in the sample employed direct physical force, that is, methods involving bloodshed, strangulation or drowning, beating or kicking to death. Less than one third of the offenders employed more indirect and passive methods, such as poisoning, neglect, or shooting. It must be noted that cases of poisoning, the frequency of which in the past was pointed out by Otto Pollak in his work about female criminality as one of the arguments to his theory about the perfidious and disguised nature of women's crime,[14] grow rarer and rarer as we near the present. Killings with firearms occur in Hungary only exceptionally.

The means and methods are greatly defined by availability and by the nature of the offenders' everyday functions and skills. The homicide tools at the disposal of the women constituting our sample are: kitchen knives, axes, hammers, the electric cord of the iron. Peasant and working women are used to applying these tools, and they have the physical power to use them.

Women in an emotionally strongly influenced conflict situation usually employed methods involving bloodshed, especially in crimes against provocatively interacting victims. Such acts constitute nearly half of the cases in the sample. Within this group it is noticeable that the perpetrators overact, their actions involve more effort than necessary to take the victim's life— for example, where the victim was killed with ten to fifteen blows, or by many stabs or many blows, each of which could have caused the victim's death. These overacts were not, however, the manifestations of some extreme cruelty, but partly expressed the fear of the offender as to what would happen if the victim, superior to her in physical strength, did not die, took revenge, and everything began again. Besides, in my opinion it is indicative of the long repressed aggression induced by prolonged frustration that, if once it breaks through the barrier of inhibiting mechanisms, it takes destructive, raging forms appearing in unrealistic repetitions.

The methods of the act manifested by physical force, and often sheer brutality, the predominance of the single offenders, the experience that the majority are stubbornly consistent in their actions, and the fact that in the case of accomplices the woman often has an initiating and planning role prove that the typical female killer of the past decades in Hungary cannot in the least be characterized as staying in the background and preferring perfidious, passive methods, as was so commonly believed by public opinion and the literature about women committing crimes against life.

It seems, however, not only that the Hungarian surveys, including the present investigation, but that similar Western studies prove that open violence comes to the fore in the case of women today, though to a lesser extent than in the case of male offenders.[15]

Because of space limitations I could only outline some of the most important conclusions of our much wider, comprehensive study which considered many aspects, and used material accumulated over several years of empirical research. I limited myself to the facts which are relevant to an international comparison. Considering the growing significance of female criminality on an international level in the past few years, it would be interesting and desirable to conduct a harmonized cross-cultural research program with similar methods and sampling, in the fields most suitable for comparison.

Notes

1. Gustav Heinemann, for example, in his introduction to the book of H. Damrow, *Frauen vor Gericht,* (Frankfurt a.M., 1969), emphasizes that "the proportion of women committing killings is much higher nowadays than it used to be in the thirties. At that time it was 12.5 percent, now it is 25 percent." Armand Mergen, in his book, *Kriminologie* (Berlin-Frankfurt, a.M., 1967), p. 275, writes that "the killing criminality of women seems to be on the growth in our age, their proportion between 1926 and 1930 was 12 percent, now it is 25 percent.

2. John MacDonald, *The Murderer and His Victim* (Springfield, 1961), pp. 31–22.

3. Jane Totman, "The Murderess," *Police* (1971), 6: 16.

4. Hans von Hentig, *Zur Psychologie de Einzeldelikte,* II. (Tubingen: Der Mord, 1956), p. 275.

5. Ernst, Seelig, *Lehrbuch der Kriminologie* (Darmstadt, 1964), p. 132; MacDonald, *op. cit.,* p. 71.

6. Pawel Horoszowski, "Homicide of Passion and Its Motives," in *Victimology: A New Focus* (Lexington, Mass., 1975), vol. 4, p. 12.

7. Klaus Sessar "The Familiar Character of Criminal Homicide," in Victimology: A New Focus (Lexington, Mass., 1975), vol. 43, p. 29; Marvin Wolfgang, *Patterns in Criminal Homicide,* (Philadelphia, 1958).

8. Although I do not possess any results of research referring only to women from the socialist countries, in the Soviet Union, V. A. Serebriakova in her study entitled "Female Criminality as a Subject of Criminological Research," *Voprosy Borby prestupnosti* (1975), 22: 27–30; and Pesic Vukasin, in his study entitled *"Murderers in Yugoslavia,"* based on the survey of 1000 homicide cases, published in 1973, emphasized that, in the case of female offenders, killing situations based on domestic conflict are much more frequent than in the case of men.

9. In the case of men the situation is different. Gunther Bruchkner, reporting his research in

Zur Kriminologie des Mordes (Hamburg, 1961), p. 18, states that in his sample only 20 of the 80 men convicted for homicide were conflict killers, while 42 committed their crimes for profit.

10. Hoffman-Bustamante, "The Nature of Female Criminality," I, *Issues in Criminology* (1973), vol. 8, no. 2; Totman, *op. cit.,;* E. Suval and R. Brisson, "Female Criminal Homicide Offenders," *International Journal of Criminology* (1974), 2: 31.

11. K. E. Cole, G. Fisher and S. S. Cole, "Women Who Kill," *Archives of General Psychiatry* (1968), Vol. 19 (July): 1–8.

12. MacDonald, *op. cit.,* p. 31; Totman, *op. cit.,* p. 17; Suval and Brisson, *op. cit.,* p. 26. Solonge Troisier, in the article "La ciminalite feminine," *Revue internationale de criminologie et de police technique,* X–XII (1975): 377, makes a similar statement concerning French female convicts.

13. Catiel 16 PF, Eysenck P. Q., Szondi test/two profil/"Luscher test, Ravan IQ test."

14. Otto Pollak, *The Criminality of Women* (Philadelphia, 1950), pp. 16 ff.

15. Wolfgang, *op. cit.;* Bustamante, *op. cit.*

CHAPTER FOUR

AFRICA

1. A Preliminary Study of Female Criminality in Nigeria

O. OLORUNTIMEHIN

Olufunmilayo Oloruntimehin is Senior Lecturer and Member of the International Sociological Association (Research Committee on Deviance and Social Control and Sociology of Law). She is interested in the criminology of contemporary Africa. She is also interested in the areas of juvenile delinquency, crime, social reaction to deviance, and interrelationships between law and society, especially in Nigeria. She has served as a consultant to the United Nations Crime Prevention and Criminal Justice Branch and as the rapporteur of the United Nations Interregional meeting of experts on Crime Trends and Crime Prevention Strategies, Ottawa, 1978.

Introduction

At the present time there is no significant work on female criminality in Africa. In this era, when the interest of the world is directed to women's affairs, including criminality, it is believed that a study of female criminality in Nigeria is desirable. The aim of this study is, therefore, to examine as much as possible the role of women in the area of crime in Nigeria. Authors such as Adler,[1] who have recently written on female criminality, have claimed not only that the rate of crime among women has risen in recent years but that the degree of violence of female criminality had moved rather closely to that of male criminality. One would like to see to what extent such claims can be upheld within the context of Nigerian society.

It would also be desirable to deal with questions such as the following: What relationship has the socioeconomic development of a society to the level of female criminality? To what extent does the cultural and social situation of women contribute not only to the level but also to the nature of crimes perpetrated by women? What peculiarities can be observed in the pattern of female criminality in Nigeria?

Until very recently the lack of interest in the area of female criminality by scholars and even policymakers was remarkable in many societies. While there is no intention to elevate female criminality to a level of a new social problem by raising a high degree of "moral panic," it is necessary to direct people's attention to it as an important aspect of the field of criminology. This is highly desirable in Nigeria where very little is known about female criminality and basic information such as criminal statistics is very difficult to obtain.

The Nigerian mass media have recently developed a keen interest in the area of criminality. Thus, a considerable amount of useful information on female criminality can be obtained from the mass media to supplement whatever information can be derived from official sources.[2] For example, the official criminal statistics do not indicate with any degree of clarity the nature of criminal behavior usually engaged in by women. The mass media, however, tend to provide information which could aid a fruitful discussion of the nature of female criminality. It is believed that even the criminal statistics can provide a reasonable basis for the understanding of female criminality in this society, provided they are obtainable, carefully studied, and interpreted. The problem with official criminal statistics in Nigeria is that they are very difficult to obtain. For example, the most recent published official statistics that have relevance to female criminality are those for the year 1974. One is aware that a series of significant changes must have taken place in the area of female criminality between 1974 and the present time. Some forms of behavior, such as hoarding and profiteering, and certain forms of illegal dealings in foreign exchange which were commonly engaged in by women, have become criminalized in Nigeria since 1974.[3] However, it is believed that the limitations the lack of up-to-date statistical data can create in the understanding of female criminality can be somewhat rectified by mass media information. It seems that the information from the mass media about criminality could actually lead to a better understanding of the nature of female criminality—for example, the types of offense and the socioeconomic background and occupations of the offenders—in other words, figures about crimes involving females which are usually presented in the official criminal statistics. Thus, it is believed that with the supplementation of the official criminal statistics with the information obtained from the mass media, a reasonable understanding of female criminality in Nigeria can be attained.

One proposition that is generally accepted in the study of crime and criminals is that the total number of female criminals is less than the total number of male criminals. This proposition seems to hold, whatever the ideology of the particular society, whether it is capitalist, socialist, communist, or fascist.[4] The fact that there is a difference in known male and female criminality is undisputed. The available data in Nigeria support the proposition of a significant difference between the level of male and female criminality (see Appendix 1). These data deal with the rate of committals to prisons in all the states of the Federation of Nigeria between 1968 to 1974 by sex. Between 1968 and 1969 a total of 104,028 males, or 97 percent, and 3,468 females, or 3 percent, were committed to prison. In 1969–70, 156,979 males, or 96.4 percent and 5,933 females, or 3.6 percent, were committed to prison. In 1971–72, 265,522 males, or 96.1 percent, and 10,391 females, or 3.9 percent, were sent to prison. In 1972–73, 96,222 males, or 96.9 percent, and 3301 females, or 3.1 percent, were sentenced to imprisonment. Between 1973 and 1974, 111,523 males, or 96.8 percent, and 3,697 females, or 3.2 percent, were committed to prison. It is remarkable that between 1968 and 1974 the percentage of males sentenced to imprisonment did not fall below 96 percent while that of females did not rise above 3.9 percent.

It should be noted, however, that if the data on arrests of criminals were available, the difference between the total number of male and female offenders arrested within the period under discussion would not likely be as significant as the difference between male and female offender convictions. This is because a considerable number of female offenders tend to be involved in misdemeanors and relatively less serious crimes which were likely to have entailed minor penalties, such as fines and suspended sentences. For example, a considerable number of females found guilty of assault without any grievous harm and those involved in prostitution were likely to be fined or have their sentences suspended rather than being committed to prison.[5] In spite of this fact, the proposition that the total number of males involved in criminal behavior is greater than that of female criminals remains undisputed.

The difference in the level of male and female criminality could be explained in Nigeria from the point of view of differing cultural pressures on the female as compared with the male. In this society the female is culturally defined as a sober, submissive, tender, and passive figure. Such ideas have had a significant effect on the advancement of female education in this society. Many parents, especially fathers, believed that education for the female was a wasted effort, since the female would end up as a cook in the home. The women have generally had fewer opportunities to interact with both noncriminal and criminal attitudes and activities than men. This is because the sphere in which the male could be expected to move in current society is so much wider than that of the female. It seems that women have not been found to be generally involved in violent gun-wielding methods of achieving criminal desires, primarily because the opportunities of learning such attitudes and activities are very limited and also because the image of the female as culturally defined does not conform to the practice of such activities. For example, since the Anti-Robbery and Firearms Decree was promulgated in 1970, hundreds of males involved in armed robbery had been tried and found guilty by various anti-robbery tribunals and executed by the firing squad. Only one woman had been found guilty and condemned to death by the tribunal.[6] The situation seemed to have been unusual enough to arouse comments from some members of society in the mass media generally. The basis of these comments was that it was difficult to believe that a woman accused of armed robbery actually had the motivation to commit that crime.[7]

Many female offenders tend to be involved in criminal behavior which required much less violence than armed robbery, such as assault, shoplifting, receiving stolen goods, smuggling, and so forth. Many of the cases of murder involving women were not carried out by means of instruments such as a gun or a dagger but rather by the use of the kitchen knives, by heavy wooden or iron materials, or even by poisoning.[8] While one is aware of the possible effects of certain forms of social change, such as urbanization, industrialization, education, and modernization, on the attitudes and roles of women in this society, it is believed that such factors had only had minimal influence as far as the involvement of females in violent forms of criminal behavior is concerned. The impact of such factors in relation to female criminality seems to be more significant in the area of crimes such as drug peddling, smuggling, corruption, and illegal foreign exchange transactions.

Some sex-specific crimes such as abortion, child abandonment, and infanticide, which are committed mainly or only by females, could be regarded as resulting directly from the situation of the female as child producer and rearer. Although the dark figure in relation to these forms of criminal behavior is very high, there is adequate evidence from the mass media to show that the degree of female criminality involving these crimes is rather high.[9] One could even suggest that this category of criminal behavior is likely to contribute a very high percentage to the total rate of female criminality in this society, provided the dark figure is controlled. The perpetration of these crimes is heightened by the need for single girls or women to avoid the economic responsibilities for illegitimate children in addition to preventing the disruption of much-valued education among a considerable number of such females. This situation has been further escalated by the lack of any significant policy of adoption and also by the lack of any form of welfare service for unmarried mothers and their children in this society. It should be noted that the above forms of criminal behavior, which, as has been suggested, constitute a highly significant part of female criminality in this society, rarely involve violence. They do not require much strength or force or skill, expertise, or training in violence. Any form of socialization into a delinquent subculture or a sophisticated criminal organization is entirely unnecessary in such cases.

In the case of child stealing, which can be distinguished from kidnapping especially where the act involves a baby, most of the female offenders who engage in this form of behavior are usually motivated by the desire to possess a baby which they could not produce by the normal biological process. This criminal act also has some cultural undertone in that the norms of society tend to discriminate against the childless female and relegate her to an inferior status, regardless of her socioeconomic status. The condition of some childless women, especially those who are involved in polygynous relationships, can be so unbearable as to arouse the motivation to acquire a child by unnatural and illegal means. Some women engage in kidnapping children directly or receiving and selling into slavery kidnapped children. This could involve some planning and dealing with a syndicate. However, child stealing and kidnapping do not usually entail violence or any form of expertise in the use of force. What is often required is a sufficient amount of wits to be able to manipulate the mother of a baby or to entice a child.[10]

The few women who have been found to be connected with armed robbers were used only as means to achieve the desires of the males. For example, such women were used as bait to entice victims who were later robbed of their cars and other property by armed robbers. The women also receive and dispose of some of the stolen goods. Women have rarely been found to be directly involved in any gun-wielding attack on victims of armed robbery.

The data for young persons committed to prison in the Federation of Nigeria between 1968 and 1974 (see Appendix II) show a significant difference between the level of involvement in criminal behavior by juvenile males compared with that of juvenile females. For example, looking at the section on juveniles under 16 years, between 1968 and 1969 a total of 283 male juveniles, or 100 percent, and zero percent of female juveniles were committed to prison. In 1969–70, 226 male juveniles, or 91.1 percent, and 20 female juveniles, or 8.9 percent, were sentenced to prison. Between 1970 and 1971, 479 male juveniles, or 90.3 percent, and 52 female juveniles, or 9.7 percent, received prison sentences. In 1971–72, 508 male juveniles, or 89.2 percent, and 68 female juveniles, or 11.8 percent, were committed to prison. In 1972–73, 378 male juveniles, or 94.5 percent, and 21 female juveniles, or 5.5 percent, received prison sentences. In 1973–74, 586 male juveniles, or 96.1 percent, and 22 female juveniles, or 3.9 percent, were committed to prison.

Data in the section on juveniles between 16 and 20 years show that between 1968 and 1969 a total of 4,256 male juveniles, or 97 percent, and 133 female juveniles, or 3 percent, were committed to prison. In 1969–70, 4562 male juveniles, or 94.6 percent, and 264 female juveniles, or 5.4 percent, were sentenced to prison. Between 1970 and 1971, 10,552 male juveniles, or 94.8 percent, and 581 female juveniles, or 5.2 percent, received prison sentences. In 1971–72, 9422 male juveniles, or 95.3 percent, and 468 female juveniles, or 4.7 percent, were committed to prison. In 1972–73, 12,976 male juveniles, or 95.1 percent, and 674 female juveniles, or 4.9 percent, received prison sentences. In 1973–74, 14,191 male juveniles, or 95 percent, and 762 female juveniles, or 5 percent, were committed to prison.

Although there are no available data to indicate the types of crimes committed by both male and female juveniles and the degree of seriousness of such crimes, one could suggest that the forms of criminal behavior engaged in by the former are likely to be more serious than those by the latter. The crimes committed by the males are also likely to involve the use of violence more often than is the case with the females. The types of offense likely to be committed by females below 16 years are shoplifting, other forms of theft such as stealing from employers by maidservants, and child abandonment.[11] Those females who were between 16 and 20 years old could have been involved in the peddling and use of drugs in addition to the forms of criminal behavior already mentioned in connection with juveniles under 16 years. Males of both groups under 16 years and 16 to 20 years, on the other hand, were likely to have been involved in crimes such as burglary, arson, and armed robbery, in addition to all the forms of criminal behavior referred to previously, with the exception of child abandonment.[12]

Appendices III and IV contain data on the terms of imprisonment issued by magistrates and high courts in two states of the Federation of Nigeria, namely East Central and Western states, between 1971 and 1973, according to sex. The main purpose of using these data is to examine the degree of seriousness of female criminality. The two states selected were chosen on the basis of the availability of recent data, since for some of the other states similar data for the years 1971, 1972, and 1973 were not available. Even if such data could not be obtained for every state, it would not be necessary to include them all in this study.

The intention, as far as the data on the terms of imprisonment is concerned, is not only to compare the situation of the male, both adult and juvenile, with that of the female of both groups, but also to concentrate on the section which deals specifically with females. It is believed that while the explanation to be made could be done effectively by concentrating on the section for the female alone, a more fruitful result can be achieved by such comparisons.

Appendix III shows that for 1971, 152, or 63 percent, of the adult female offenders sentenced to prison by the magistrate courts of the East Central State received short-term imprisonment of between one and six months. No female juvenile was given any term of imprisonment. Only 1,567, or 30 percent, of the adult males and 10, or 37 percent, of male juveniles committed to prison by the same courts received short-term imprisonment. In 1972, 306, or 75 percent, of adult females sent to prison by the magistrate courts received short-term imprisonment. No female juvenile was sentenced to prison by the courts. Two thousand and forty-eight, or 52 percent, of adult males received short-term imprisonment. No male juvenile was sentenced to prison. For the same year, 5, or 71 percent, of the adult females, and 42, or 25 percent, of the adult males sent to prison by the high courts received short-term imprisonment. In 1973, 39, or 42 percent, of adult females and 1935, or 49 percent, of the adult males committed to prison by the magistrate courts got short-term imprisonment. For the same year, 7, or 58 percent, of adult females and 15, or 7.4 percent, of adult males sentenced to prison by the high courts received short-term imprisonment.

Appendix IV shows that for 1971, 12, or 63 percent, of adult females and 530, or 60 percent, of adult males committed to prison by the magistrate courts of the Western State received short-term imprisonment. In 1972, 17, or 77 percent, of adult females and 658, or 58 percent, of adult males sent to prison by the magistrate courts got short-term imprisonment. In 1973, 15, or 83 percent, of adult females and 214, or 32 percent, of adult males committed to prison by the magistrate courts received short-term imprisonment. For the analysis of the data on length of sentence from both the East Central and Western states, it is clear that the majority of female offenders sent to prison between 1971 and 1973 received short-term imprisonment ·while a majority of the males received longer terms of imprisonment. An attempt to interpret this in the light of the application of the criminal code of Nigeria would show that the majority of women tend to be involved in forms of criminal behavior referred to as misdemeanors and simple offenses, while few women are involved in felonies and more serious offenses. On the other hand, a majority of men tend to engage in offenses described as a felony and related serious offenses.[13]

Appendix II shows the rate of recidivism recorded from all the prisons in the Federation of Nigeria between 1969 and 1974 according to sex. Between 1969 and 1974, the data on inmates who had had one previous conviction were as follows: 1969–79, 2,165 males and 16 females; 1970–71, 3,227 males and 51 females; 1971–72, 5,819 males and 100 females; 1972–73, 7,240 males and 104 females; 1973–74, 7,993 males and 67 females. During the same period, the following was the position of inmates with two previous convictions: 1969–70, 1,778 males and 1 female; 1970–71, 2,646 males and 15 females; 1971–72, 3,906 males and 23 females; 1972–73 5,125 males and 17 females; and in 1973–74, 5,299 males and 26 females. Between 1969 and 1974 the following were the data on inmates who had had three or more previous convictions: 1969–70, 1,429 males and 4 females; 1970–71, 2,658 males and 9 females; 1971–72, 2,669 males and 9 females; 1972–73, 3,886 males and 14 females; and in 1973–74, 4,012 males and 4 females.

The above data on recidivism show that a very high percentage of female offenders are first offenders. Most of these offenders tend to be scared away from engaging in further criminal behavior by their first conviction. It could even be suggested that for a considerable number of the female offenders the event of being processed through the criminal justice system itself was adequate to prevent them from engaging in further criminal activities. Few women are likely to be motivated toward adopting a criminal career.

Appendix I shows a steady increase in the number of females committed to prison between 1968 and 1972 as follows: In 1968–69, 3,468 females were committed to prison, while in 1969–70 the number rose to 5,933 (an increase of 71 percent). In 1970–71 it rose to 8,295, with an increase of 56 percent. In 1971–72 it rose to 10,391, with an increase of only 25 percent.

However, in 1972–73 the number declined sharply to 3,301, with a fall of 68 percent. In 1973–74 the number rose a little to 3,697, with an increase of 12 percent (which is still a fall of 64 percent compared with the figure for 1971–72). Thus, the above analysis shows that there has been no phenomenal rise in the level of female criminality. In fact, the sharp decline after the period 1971–72 seemed to be more significant than the increase. From the data available and already analyzed there seems to be no basis to support Adler's thesis of the phenomenal rise in female criminality as far as this society is concerned. In addition, the claim that females are now involved in all categories of criminal behavior and have tended to achieve a more equal footing with the males in the criminal hierarchy has not been upheld by our data.[14] This situation might have been the result of the fact that the campaign for the emancipation of women was never taken seriously in this society by either women or men. Thus, it seems that whatever the influence this social movement might have had on women's social and antisocial behavior in societies such as the United States of America, this cannot be detected in Nigerian society.

Rather than focus on women's emancipation for the explanation of the females' involvement in criminal behavior, it seems that one can achieve more fruitful results by examining the relationship between socioeconomic development of the society and female criminality. There had been a significant increase in the number of literate women in this society since the independence of 1960. The increase in the level of literacy among females has been accompanied by a substantial attempt to secure job opportunities which were previously monopolized by males.[15] Women are now involved in university and high school teaching and administration. They are also found in the various ministries of the civil service at both state and federal levels. Women also form a substantial part of hospital services and administration in the various states of the Federation of Nigeria. They are also employed by private companies such as banks and commercial firms. Since most occupations tend to provide opportunities for engaging in deviant behavior, one could suggest that as women become a larger part of the work force, more of them are likely to be involved in criminal behavior. For example, a number of women have been processed through the criminal justice system for forgery, corruption, embezzlement, and the like.[16] There is, however, no basis for claiming that the level of involvement of women in such forms of behavior has risen to that of the men.

It should be noted that, with regard to the quality of the position of women, the situation has not changed significantly. While there are more women working than before, this category seems to constitute a very small percentage of the women. Among those who are working, many are more often nurses than doctors, and secretaries rather than heads of establishments. Since there tends to be a correlation between leadership roles in work positions and the opportunity to engage in criminal behavior, such as embezzlement and corruption, it is unlikely that women can compete favorably with men in the perpetration of these crimes. Thus, while the rate of female criminality has been affected by the fact that more women had taken jobs in various spheres of society, this situation cannot be said to be the result of any conscious efforts on the part of women to attain equality with the men. It is likely that this condition had arisen as a result of the influence of some socioeconomic aspects of a rapidly developing society.

No discussion of female criminality in Nigeria can avoid some reference to the role of women in what can be regarded as the crimes which have assumed much significance in recent times in this society, namely hoarding and profiteering; smuggling, especially of prohibited goods, and illegal transactions in foreign exchange. These forms of behavior became very noticeable within the last few years due to the degree of damage believed to have been done to society and its members. For example, hoarding and profiteering were legislated against because of their significant contribution to inflation through the creation of artificial scarcity. This situation led to much suffering among the masses, whose purchasing power was drastically reduced as a result of very high prices of essential consumer goods such as milk, and sugar. Smuggling became recriminalized, first because much foreign exchange was being lost by this country through the importation of certain goods, such as textiles, tobacco, spirits, and so on, and second, because a lot of revenue was lost by the government through evasion of customs duties, in an attempt to conceal the prohibited goods from government officials and sometimes to avoid the payment of the very heavy duties which had been established to discourage the importation of some goods.

Some forms of foreign exchange transactions were legislated against as a result of the high rate at which the foreign exchange reserves of this country were being drained through illegal dealing in foreign exchange. This action was taken by the federal government in order to protect the level of the country's foreign exchange reserves, as well as to maintain a favorable balance of trade with foreign markets. However, this situation required an official control of the amount of foreign exchange which could be exported by individuals, corporations, and the like. Such control led to a drastic limitation of the means of purchasing foreign goods, especially prohibited ones. A considerable number of businessmen and businesswomen affected by the government's policy tend to engage in illegal methods of securing adequate foreign exchange to keep their business going.

There are no official criminal statistics to indicate the rate at which both males and females become involved in the types of criminal behavior discussed above, possibly as a result of delay in the publication of criminal statistics. The mass media, however, contain useful information about these "new" crimes and the rate at which people commit such crimes. Hoarding and profiteering are more often engaged in by women who are generally involved in the business of retailing essential consumer goods. This tends to correlate with the traditional role of women as traders in this society.[17] Many of the cases of hoarding and profiteering dealt with by the courts through the price control boards involved women.[18]

A few Nigerian women had been involved in smuggling marijuana across national borders for sale. One such woman was arrested in London.[19] As far as the smuggling of prohibited goods, such as textiles, spirits, and jewelry, into the country was concerned, many of those involved were women. For example, a considerable number of people processed through the courts for smuggling through the Board of Customs and Excise were women.[20] Some of the men who were arrested for this offense were paid agents of some wealthy female traders in big cities such as Lagos.[21]

Some women, especially traders who require much more foreign exchange to purchase imported goods, some of which had been prohibited, engage in some form of illegal foreign exchange transactions. Some of them purchase the required foreign currencies from black markets located in the various big cities such as Lagos and Kano. The foreign currencies are then smuggled out of the country to various foreign countries for the purchase of certain goods which are usually smuggled into the country and sold to consumers at exhorbitant prices. A number of women have been processed through the courts for being involved in this form of foreign exchange transaction.[22]

Conclusion

An attempt has been made in this preliminary study to examine the limitations of a study of female criminality in this society, especially with regard to the nonavailability of comprehensive official criminal statistics. In spite of this problem, a picture of the situation of female criminality has been presented. Using the rate of commitment of offenders to prison, it has been shown that the rate of female criminality seems to be much lower than that of male criminality. The data on recidivism have also been analyzed and demonstrate that most female criminals tend to be first offenders and that only a very small percentage of female offenders adopt criminal careers.

Based on the data on the length of imprisonment and the information obtained from the mass media, it has been suggested that women tend to be involved in relatively less serious forms of criminal behavior. Women are rarely involved in violent, gun-wielding crimes. Many of the crimes committed by women seem to be closely correlated with their cultural and social positions in society. In addition, it has also been suggested that any noteworthy increase in the degree of involvement of females in criminal activities is likely to be the result of the influence of socioeconomic factors on the role of women in a rapidly developing society, rather than of any conscious effort to achieve equality with males, or the success of the campaign for the emancipation of women. Finally, the contribution of women to the "new" forms of criminal behavior such as hoarding, profiteering, and illegal foreign exchange transactions have been examined.

It is believed that while no final conclusion can be derived on the basis of this study, by virtue of the limitations already discussed, some significant questions have been raised about female criminality in Nigeria. Such questions should lead to more comprehensive studies on the subject.

Further studies on female criminality could focus on the following. There could be case studies of female offenders in selected prisons all over the Federation of Nigeria to examine some of their socioeconomic characteristics, such as level of education, occupation, family background, and relationship, the types of crime committed, and their attitude toward crime and punishment and to the law in general. In addition, female recidivists could be studied to discover the nature of female recidivism; and victim surveys could be carried out in various parts of the country, specifically dealing with female criminality, to examine the magnitude of hidden criminality among females, to find out the types and nature of the offenses generally committed by women and how they are being dealt with. Is there any significant difference in the types of offense committed by working women compared with nonworking women? Do the offenses committed by these two groups of women differ from those committed by women who are relatively isolated from the public, that is, women kept in purdah? To what extent are the offenses committed by women handled informally rather than by the criminal justice system? What forms of informal methods are usually used? With regard to which particular offenses are these informal methods likely to be applied? Furthermore, studies could be carried out on female criminality among societies with similar cultures and/or similar levels of socioeconomic development. Thus, although the findings of this study may be regarded as preliminary and inconclusive, their implications for future research, both on the national and the international level, seem to be considerable.

Notes

1. Freda Adler, *Sisters in Crime* (New York: McGraw Hill, 1975), and "The Interaction between Women's Emancipation and Female Criminality: A Cross Cultural Perspective," *International Journal of Criminology and Penology* (1977), 5:101–112.

2. The information given in the official criminal statistics does not provide an insight into the nature of female criminality, nor the socioeconomic backgrounds of the offenders.

3. See *Price Control Board Decree* 1977, no. 1, which repealed the Price Control Decree 1970, as amended by Price Control Amendment Decrees 1971 and 1974. *Exchange Control (Anti-Sabotage) Decree* no. 57, 1977; see also "Death Now for Smugglers," *Daily Times,* Saturday, May 14, 1977, no. 21551.

4. Jocelynne A. Scutt "Toward the Liberation of Female Lawbreakers," *International Journal of Criminology and Penology,* vol. 6, no. 1 (February 1978): 5. See also Carol Smart, *Women, Crime and Criminology* (London: Routledge and Kegan Paul, 1977).

5. See "Two Women Bound Over for 6 Months Guilty of Assault Charge," *Daily Times,* Thursday, July 2, 1970. See also "Bad Day for Free Women," *Lagos Weekend,* December 10–12, 1976.

6. "Woman to Face Firing Squad," *Daily Times,* Friday, May 4, 1979, no. 22167.

7. "Spare the Life of Anat," *Nigerian Tribune,* Saturday, June 9, 1979, no. 8354. It seemed that the pleadings from the public to spare the woman's life had influenced the decision of the administrator for Lagos who has the final say on the sentence of anybody accused of armed robbery in that state, since the death sentence on Anat was commuted to fourteen years imprisonment. See "Ukiwe Shows Clemency-Saved," *Daily Times,* Friday, June 15, 1979, no. 22209.

8. Unpublished study on homicide in Western Nigeria by the Institute of Behavioral Sciences, University of Ibadan, 1969.

9. See "Abortion Rate Becoming Alarming," *Sunday Times,* February 12, 1978. See also "Cases of Abandoned Babies Worry Bendel Police," *New Nigerian,* Monday, June 18, 1979, no. 4141.

10. See "Pregnant Mother Disappeared with Day-Old Baby," *Lagos Weekend,* Friday, April 2, 1976. The woman was "pregnant" with pieces of rags which she stuffed under her blouse, a device to outwit those who might suspect her of possessing a newborn baby. See also "Woman on Child Theft Charge," *Daily Times,* Saturday, June 27, 1970. Unlike the above case, this is a case of kidnapping of a 10-year-old girl, possibly for sale into slavery.

11. O. Oluruntimehin, "A Study of Juvenile Delinquency in a Nigerian City," British Journal of Criminology, (April 1973): 157–169. See also O. Oloruntimehin, "A Note on Juvenile Delinquency Statistics in a Nigerian City," *Ghana Journal of Sociology,* vol. 8, no. 1 (July 1974): 61–79.

12. See "Shoplifting, the Menace, Lagos Shop Loses £N100,000," *Sunday Punch,* June 20, 1976, Vol. 171.

13. See Criminal Code Chap. 42, Vol. II, Laws of Federation of Nigeria and Lagos, 1958. Although the judge's discretion and the possibility that these judicial officers could be more lenient with women in sentencing criminals should be considered, the significance of the difference between the length of sentences of women compared with men is highly remarkable.

14. Adler, *op. cit.,* pp. 101–112.

15. R. D. Mickelwait and C. F. Sweet, *Women in Rural Development. Westview Special Studies in Social Political & Economic Development* (1976). See also "Women Employment—

Nigeria Labour Ministry (1976). *Report on Survey on Working Women with Family Responsibilities* (Lagos, 1971).

16. See "V.I.P.'s Mum Gets £N250 Monthly Kickback," *Daily Times,* Friday, September 26, 1978, no. 21042. Also "Rector to Refund £N30,000—Probe Uncovers Package Deal," *Daily Times,* Thursday, February 12, 1976.

17. Bolane Awe, "The Economic Role of Women in a Traditional African Society," in *La Civilisation de Femine dans la tradition Africaine* (Colloque d'Abidjan 3–8 Juillet, 1972).

18. See "Profiteering, 3 Jailed 30 Months," *Daily Sketch,* Wednesday, February 23, 1977, no. 4071

19. See "Woman, Brother Arrested for Indian Hemp," *Daily Times,* Tuesday, July 14, 1970.

20. See "4 Women Held for Smuggling," *The Punch,* Monday, March 26, 1979, vol. 3, no. 742. See also "Business Woman Charged with Smuggling," *Sunday Times,* April 29, 1979, no. 1538.

21. See "The Shock Find," *Daily Times,* Saturday, March 3, 1979, no. 22114.

22. See "Nigerian Held Over £N3m Cheques in London," *Daily Times,* Wednesday, March 28, 1979, no. 22135. See also "Lagos Socialite Jailed," *Punch,* Tuesday, March 20, 1979, vol. 3, no. 737.

Appendix 1. Committals to Prison.

States	1968–69 Male	1968–69 Female	1969–70 Male	1969–70 Female	1970–71 Male	1970–71 Female	1971–72 Male	1971–72 Female	1972–73 Male	1972–73 Female	1973–74 Male	1973–74 Female
East Central	—	—	599	6	9,846	243	19,448	628	12,605	440	12,571	486
South Eastern	—	—	2,662	190	6,385	403	11,006	712	9,120	421	7,362	302
Mid-Western	26,988	1,232	32,095	1,773	36,626	2,094	42,082	2,384	7,533	409	8,292	425
Western State	22,940	991	31,238	1,276	38,800	1,555	46,837	1,878	12,012	376	14,901	382
Lagos State	31,230	740	42,477	973	53,660	1,206	61,974	1,416	15,886	231	17,044	314
Rivers State	—	—	—	—	832	32	3,429	165	4,013	217	4,374	202
North Central	10,269	265	16,337	511	20,966	713	26,481	931	8,602	245	0,000	445
North Western	—	—	3,878	217	6,357	380	10,140	489	8,278	272	7,303	286
Benue Plateau	12,601	240	19,351	488	13,521	737	32,028	980	10,279	389	14,367	484
Kano State	—	—	2,850	132	6,785	320	1,203	53	1,218	28	2,108	39
Kwara State	—	—	2,455	223	4,346	361	6,287	485	2,680	123	2,903	142
North Eastern	—	—	3,037	144	5,259	251	4,607	270	3,996	150	7,036	185
Total	104,028	3,468	156,979	5,933	215,183	8,295	265,522	10,391	96,222	3,301	111,523	3,697
Grand Total	107,496		162,912		223,478		275,913		99,523		115,220	

Source: Adapted from Federal Ministry of Internal Affairs, Nigerian Prisons Service, Lagos.

Note: Above information is based on figures of persons committed to prison at the end of each of the previous financial year. To this, is added each month's new committals up to and including figures for the last month of the financial year.

Appendix II. Recidivism—All Prisons.

Type of Conviction	1969–70		1970–71		1971–72	
	Male	Female	Male	Female	Male	Female
One previous conviction	2,165	16	3,227	51	5,819	100
Two previous convictions	1,778	1	2,646	15	3,906	23
Three or more previous convictions	1,429	4	2,658	9	2,669	9
Total	5,372	21	8,531	79	12,394	132

Type of Conviction	1972–73		1973–74	
	Male	Female	Male	Female
One previous conviction	7,240	104	7,993	67
Two previous convictions	5,125	17	5,299	26
Three or more previous convictions	3,886	14	4,012	4
Total	16,251	135	17,304	97

Young Persons Admitted to Prison.

	Age Group					
	Under 16 Years			16–20 Years		
Period	Males	Females	Total	Males	Females	Total
1968–69	283	—	283	4,256	133	4,389
1969–70	226	20	246	4,562	264	4,826
1970–71	479	52	531	10,552	581	11,133
1971–72	508	68	576	9,422	468	9,890
1972–73	378	21	399	12,976	674	13,650
1973–74	586	22	608	14,191	762	14,953

Source: Adapted from Federal Ministry of Internal Affairs, Nigerian Prisons Service, Lagos.

Appendix III. Persons in Prison by Sex and Length of Sentence: East Central State.

Sex and Length of Sentence	1971 Magistrate Courts Adults	Juveniles	1971 High Courts Adults	Juveniles	1972 Magistrate Courts Adults	Juveniles	1972 High Courts Adults	Juveniles	1973 Magistrate Courts Adults	Juveniles	1973 High Courts Adults	Juveniles
Male:												
Under 1 month–3 months	728	8	—	—	1,232	—	28	—	1,066	—	2	—
Over 3 months–6 months	839	2	2	—	816	—	14	—	869	—	13	—
Over 6 months–9 months	657	2	4	—	481	—	3	—	914	—	12	—
Over 9 months–12 months	778	2	6	2	530	—	11	—	458	—	15	—
Over 1 year–3 years	984	12	25	—	681	—	59	—	375	—	97	—
Over 3 years–5 years	201	—	37	—	123	—	36	—	206	—	28	—
Over 5 years	72	—	39	—	63	—	13	—	—	—	36	—
Life	—	—	—	—	—	—	1	—	—	—	—	—
Subtotal	4,259	26	113	2	3,926	—	165	—	3,888	—	203	—
Female:												
Under 1 month–3 months	85	—	—	—	195	—	3	—	25	—	4	—
Over 3 months–6 months	67	—	—	—	111	—	2	—	14	—	3	—
Over 6 months–9 months	44	—	—	—	30	—	1	—	11	—	2	—
Over 9 months–12 months	22	—	—	—	36	—	—	—	21	—	1	—
Over 1 year–3 years	22	—	—	—	15	—	1	—	6	—	2	—
Over 3 years–5 years	—	—	—	—	10	—	—	—	12	—	—	—
Over 5 years	—	—	—	—	7	—	—	—	2	—	—	—
Live	—	—	—	—	—	—	—	—	—	—	—	—
Subtotal	240	—	1	—	404	—	7	—	91	—	12	—
Grand Total	4,499	26	114	2	4,330	—	172	—	3,979	—	215	—

Source: Adapted from High Court of Justice, ENUGU.

Appendix IV. Persons in Prison by Sex and Length of Sentence: Western State.

Sex and Length of Sentence	1971				1972				1973			
	Magistrate Courts		High Courts		Magistrate Courts		High Courts		Magistrate Courts		High Courts	
	Adults	Juveniles	Adults	Juveniles	Adults	Juveniles	Adults	Juveniles	Adults	Juveniles	Adults	Juveniles
Male:												
Under 1 month–3 months	429	49	—	—	446	—	3	—	150	9	3	—
Over 3 months–6 months	101	1	4	—	212	1	4	—	64	7	2	—
Over 6 months–9 months	49	—	1	—	104	—	1	—	83	1	—	—
Over 9 months–12 months	90	—	8	—	86	—	—	—	85	—	11	—
Over 1 year–3 years	82	—	4	—	187	—	11	—	150	—	13	—
Over 3 years–5 years	65	—	3	—	43	—	7	—	63	—	65	—
Over 5 years	61	—	7	—	45	—	12	—	58	—	83	—
Life	—	—	3	—	—	—	—	—	—	—	—	3
Subtotal	877	50	30	—	1,123	1	38	—	653	17	117	3
Female:												
Under 1 month–3 months	3	—	—	—	14	—	—	—	13	—	—	—
Over 3 months–6 months	9	—	—	—	3	—	—	—	2	—	—	—
Over 6 months–9 months	3	—	—	—	2	—	—	—	—	—	—	—
Over 9 months–12 months	1	—	—	—	—	—	—	—	—	—	—	—
Over 1 year–3 years	2	—	—	—	2	—	—	—	2	—	1	—
Over 3 years–5 years	1	—	—	—	1	—	1	—	1	—	2	—
Over 5 years	—	—	—	—	—	—	—	—	—	—	1	—
Life	—	—	—	—	—	—	—	—	—	—	—	—
Subtotal	19	—	—	—	22	—	1	—	18	—	4	—
Grand Total	896	50	30	—	1,145	1	39	—	671	17	121	3

Source: Adapted from High Court of Justice, Ibadan.

2. Female Criminality in Egypt

A. W. EL ASHMAWI

Abd El Wahhab Kamal Eldine El Ashmawi is Secretary General of the Arab Organization for Social Defence, Cairo. His primary interest in the field is criminological research. He has served as Director of the Social, Youth and Health Departments at the League of Arab States, and as a member of the Egyptian Prisoners' High Council and the Egyptian Social Defence High Council. His publications include: "The Role of Legislation in the Protection of the Family," *Tanmiat El Mogtama Community Development;* "Development and Crime and Social Defense Policy," *Tanmiat El Mogtama Community Development; Crime and Society,* Arabic Edition; "Trends of Crime in the Arab Region," American Society of Criminology Publication.

Although female criminality still is an unpopular concept with Egyptian researchers and readers, it is in fact true that a considerable number of crimes are committed by women. When doing research or statistical study, the researcher frequently overlooks the factor of the sex of the criminal: male or female. The history of crime in modern Egypt, however, relates outstanding incidents about the crimes of women. We have as an example the famous case of Rayya and Sekina, two Egyptian women, from Alexandria, who had become professional murderers with primarily female victims. They were finally arrested, after a long period of criminal activity, tried, sentenced to death, and hanged. In spite of the fact that this case was of great concern to the public, that it was widely covered by the mass media, and that it was translated into broadcasting serials and motion pictures, scientific research in Egypt has been somehow negligent in not carrying out detailed and specialized studies in the field of crimes of women. The majority of official and nonofficial statistics on the different kinds of crime have overlooked whether the criminal is a man or woman.

As far as we know, the study we are presenting here is considered the first of its kind in Egypt, and generally in all the Arab world. We may consider this study a comprehensive one, considering that the life conditions of women in the different Arab countries are somewhat similar. In Egypt alone we find the modern city woman, the village woman, and the bedouin woman. They represent not only the three types of women in the Arab countries but a unity of religion, traditions, and life styles. This study is based on fieldwork carried out during the last three months of 1978 and the first three months of 1979. Samples under study were taken from a group of women prisoners of Kanater Prison, near Cairo, considered the central prison for women in Egypt. Before giving details of the results of this study, we would like to point out some facts which may help in the understanding and clarification of these results.

First: Categories of Women in Egyptian Society

The structure of Egyptian society is characteristically composed of three sharply divided female types. Next to the modern Egyptian women who live in the capital and in the large cities (not unlike European city women) are the Egyptian women who live in comparatively smaller cities, where the social conditions are more like those of a village than a larger city. Along with them live the village women who fall into two groups:

1. Those who are married to well-off husbands and who enjoy a good living without having to go out to work or to do business.
2. Those who, because of the husband's or guardian's limited financial resources, have to share the burdensome work and heavy physical tasks.

And finally, there are the bedouin women. There are still many tribes who live in Egypt under exclusively nomadic conditions which restrict the women to a limited and primitive way of life.

The diversity of the types of women in Egypt has led to the commission of varying forms and dimensions of criminality. By way of example, whereas prostitution is more or less rare among female university and college graduates of the capital, such crimes are found among working women of the middle class whose limited income does not correspond to their expectations of city life. At the same time, prostitution is nonexistent among village and bedouin women. The results of this study demonstrate how much educational and economic standards have affected the trend and frequency of female criminality.

Second: Traditional Characteristics of the Egyptian Woman: Fear of Getting Involved in Crime and Inability to Face Its Consequences

The fear of criminal involvement is due to the physical nature of women in general and to the social conditions under which Egyptian women have had to live. This fear has discouraged many women from getting involved in offenses like white-collar crimes, which would require a break with the traditional passivity of the majority of Egyptian women. However, in spite of this, there are cases in Egypt where women were found to be leading male gangs; and a psychological, social, and biological study of such cases reveals that women heading such operations and gangs usually possess male rather than female traits. We cite as an example narcotic-smuggling gangs and the compulsory tribute claimers who were prevalent some time ago in Egypt.

Third: The Place of Woman in Egyptian Society

The traditional outlook, and the one that is still reflected in many levels of Egyptian society, makes the woman dependent upon a man for the family income (or, as the Egyptian saying goes, "the earner of daily bread"). In spite of her breakthrough into the work force, the Egyptian woman, in many cases, still assumes a dependent and subordinate role, a role which influences the types of crimes she commits. This situation is obvious in certain cases of prostitution where we find that the husband has directed the activities of his wife. In robbery and pickpocketing the women is often the helper rather than the perpetrator. Likewise, in the narcotics business, the woman's subordination in complying with her man's instructions and orders is another vivid example of her dependence upon him. Moreover, she may continue the business after her husband's arrest or imprisonment.

The Study: A Statistical Analysis of Female Crime

In the instant study, a group of researchers administered a questionnaire to the inmates of the Women's Prison of Kanater. The instruments covered both the types of crimes and the processing of the offender through the criminal justice system. Random samples, representative of the types of crimes committed, were taken from the prison population. The figure in the prison daily register revealed that out of 850 prisoners, 600 women were sentenced for prostitution and the remainder for robbery, homicide, narcotics crimes, and others. Those sentenced for prostitution, therefore, represented two thirds of the total number of prisoners. Consequently, the results of this study relate primarily to those sentenced for prostitution. A sample of 70 women was selected which included 55 sentenced for prostitution and 15 for robbery and homicide. The following procedure was used for implementing the data collection: social scientists told the prisoners that they had come to hear their complaints in order to find better solutions for their problems in prison. This approach proved very successful in that it helped to attract the prisoners' interest. They spoke freely and gave useful information for the study, especially after being assured that they could refuse to speak with the social worker if they chose to do so. Strangely enough, all those who were selected insisted on participating in the study.

Below are the results of our study according to the following categories:

   (a) age of the prisoner when committing the crime and at the time of the court sentence;
   (b) social and educational status of the prisoners;
   (c) educational status of the prisoner's parents;
   (d) parental relationships;
   (e) income and financial status;
   (f) personal factors such as unmatched marriages, social surrounding, and friendships.

Age When Arrested and Sentenced

1. Concerning prostitution, the study shows that the age of the majority of the women at the time of arrest was between 20 and 25 years, an age of mental maturity when they should be able to resist temptation and to assume full responsibility for their own conduct. This group represents 50 percent of the total number in the sample. The age of the second group of deviants falls between 18 and 20 years. This group represents about 22 percent of the total number. The deviation of this group was found to be joint between the deviant herself and her guardian. The study shows that the majority of deviation at this age is due to early and unmatched marriage, or to ill treatment of the unmarried by their parents. The third group of deviants are over 30 years of age and represent 11 percent; next is the group between 16 and 18 years of age, who represent 10 percent; and finally those between ages 25 and 30.

2. Concerning homicide and robbery, it was found that the majority of

the deviants were over 30 years old when arrested, that they usually committed their crimes jointly with their husbands, and that the motive for these crimes generally stems from deviancy in their own families.

Age When Deviation Occurs

1. Concerning prostitution, it was found that the majority (45 percent) of deviations occur between the ages of 16 and 18. Women in this group had been engaged in such criminal actions for about three or four years before they were arrested. Similarly, a considerable percentage of those below 16 years of age had started their deviant behavior at an early age. In the majority of cases, the reason for this behavior appears to be due to the absence of the guardian from the house for long periods of time, divorce of the mother, separation of the husband, marriage to a deviant person, or financial need of the family. The majority of women in this group are illiterate, as are the guardians.

2. For other crimes, we have found that in the majority of cases the criminal activity started after the age of 30 and that the reason for the shift toward crime is the deviation of the guardian or financial need. Female perverts, in the majority of cases, were found to be illiterate.

The Social Condition

1. As regards prostitution, a preponderance (45 percent) of the deviants are married. One of the basic problems is with unmatched marriages in which there is a large age difference between husbands and wives (it should be noted that the difference in age was not accompanied by impotence). In some cases, deviance of the wife is due to the long hours of absence of the husband from the house, as well as to the element of temptation or instigation by friends or surroundings.

As for divorced and widowed women, the motive is generally financial need and occurs after the husband leaves and the members of the family are unable to earn a living. Next to these comes the unmarried group. It was found that the deviance of this group is due to the faulty direction on the part of the father or mother, as well as to other bad influences. There were cases, for instance, in which information from the mass media directly influenced the deviant behavior.

2. Concerning criminal attack on property and soul, it was found that 60 percent of the offenders were married and were motivated by their guardians or husbands to take part in the crime.

Educational Standing

1. It was found that 60 percent of those committing prostitution were illiterate and that only 10 percent knew elementary reading and writing; about 14 percent had primary school certificates; 9 percent had a preparatory school certificate; about 5 percent had a secondary school certificate; and a little less than 2 percent had a university or a high degree. In the latter case it was observed that deviance, in general, was due to the separation of the parents, poor parental supervision, or unsupervised freedom.

2. Concerning criminal attack on property and soul, it was found that 73 percent of the cases were illiterate; 13 percent had primary school certificates; 7 percent had preparatory school certificates; and about 7 percent had university or high degrees.

Educational Status of the Family

1. Illiteracy: fathers represent 41 percent, mothers 72 percent, and husbands 72 percent. In spite of these figures, we should not always associate illiteracy with deviance as a general rule. In many cases the illiterate family is governed by good ethical and social norms and traditions.

2. Those who hardly knew how to read and write: fathers represent 30.77 percent, mothers 14 percent, and husbands 26.50 percent.

3. Those who have a primary school certificate: fathers represent 2.5 percent, mothers 3.50 percent, and husbands about 6 percent.

4. Those who have the preparatory school certificate: fathers represent 5 percent, mothers 3 percent, and husbands about 6 percent.

5. Those who have the secondary school certificate: fathers represent 5 percent, mothers 5 percent, and husbands 6 percent.

6. Those who have a university or high degree: fathers represent 15 percent, mothers 2 percent, and husbands 12 percent. It was also observed that female pervertedness is due, in most cases, to the long absence of the father from his house.

Relation Between Father and Mother

The results of the study are shown in the accompanying tables.

The income data provide one of the most important conclusions produced by this study. In the majority of cases we found that the deviance was motivated by financial need as a result of the family's limited income. This in turn affected the women's desire to "show off."

Parental Relationship.

	Father & Mother Live Together		Death of Father		Divorced Father & Mother		Death of Mother		Death of Father & Mother	
Prostitution	36.36%	20	41.82%	23	5.45%	3	16.36%	9	—	—
Other crimes	—	—	53.33%	8	6.67%	1	26.67%	4	13.33%	2

Absence of the Guardian.*

Absence of the Guardian	Usually Present		Absent from 8:00 A.M. to 2:00 P.M.		Works All Day and Is Sometimes Absent	
Prostitution	12.5%	4	25%	8	62.5%	20

*By guardian is meant father, mother, or husband, or whoever is responsible for the woman.

Number of Marriages of the Father.

	One		More Than One	
Father	71.79%	28	28.21%	11

Income.

Average Income	Less Than £E.30.00		£E.30.00 to £E.50.00		£E.50.00 to £E.80.00		£E.80.00 to £E.100.00		Above £E.100.00	
Prostitution	41.82%	23	23.64%	13	10.91%	6	10.91%	6	12.73%	7
Other crimes	40%	6	20%	3	13.33%	2	6.67%	1	20%	3

It was found that the income of 41.82 percent was less than £E.30.00. Calculation of the income was determined by the family's income for the unmarried woman; in the case of the non-working married woman, by the husband's income; and in cases of the working woman, by both husband's and wife's income.

Low income was found to be the strongest cause of deviation, for the perverted woman usually wants to meet her essential needs: good food, clothing, living equally among neighbors, imitating friends.

One might say that this percentage is not high enough to support the strength attached to this factor. We should point out, however, that in many cases of high income there were stingy fathers, mothers, or husbands.

Therefore, the 12.73 percent in the category "over £E.100.00" does not represent the actual financial situation of the offenders.

Furthermore, deviance among those with high income usually exists in cases where the husband works abroad but does not in fact send sufficient money to his wife.

Instigation of Friends

Effect of Friends.

	Instigation of Friends		Friends Not Having an Influence	
Prostitution	74.54%	41	25.45%	14
Other crimes	46.67%	7	53.31%	8

In the case of prostitution, instigation of friends is considered the main cause of deviation (74.54 percent of the deviants). Related to instigation are the working conditions of the husband or guardian, absence for long hours during the day, little supervision, and poor education. This motive is obviously stronger in prostitution cases than in ordinary crimes, where the percentage is only 46.67 percent. There is a tendency to imitate friends in prostitution crimes, and in many cases instigators become active participants in the crime.

Unmatched Marriages

Matched and Unmatched Marriages.

	Matched Marriages		Unmatched Marriages	
Prostitution	53.76%	23	45.24%	19
Other crimes	27.27%	3	72.73%	8

Unmatched marriage was, to a large extent, an influencing factor in deviation. The percentage of "other crimes" exceeds that of prostitution. This is in itself evidence of how great an influence habit and tradition have on deviation.

Two major problems arise as a result of unmatched marriages:

1. In some cases an attempt is made to escape reality after abandoning the husband. In these cases the wife becomes an easy prey for temptation and seduction.

2. In other cases there is participation in criminal behavior with the partner. This is clearly shown in "Other Crimes" and "Narcotics Crimes."

Religious Devoutness/Consciousness

Relation of Religious Devoutness and Crimes.

	Religiously Devout		Not Devout	
Prostitution	14.55%	8	85.45%	47
Other crimes	46.67%	7	53.33%	8

It is hardly necessary to point out the influence of religious devoutness on deviation. The accompanying table points out clearly that the highest percentage, that is, 85.45 percent of the deviants, are not religiously devout.

The absence of religious devoutness leads to more serious deviations. Being religiously conscious–no matter how little—may strengthen a person and protect him or her from pervertedness. It strengthens the person's morals and suppresses his or her animal instincts. It may strengthen his or her will against moments of weakness in daily life.

In this connection it is undoubtedly true, that, if the percentage of non-devout were even lower, the deviation rates would be correspondingly reduced, for both prostitution and other offenses. In the latter case, the percentage is somewhat lower due to the different criminal means which affect the inner feelings of the deviants.

Influence of Mass Media on the Deviant

The Effect of the Mass Media.

	Have An Influence		Do Not Have An Influence	
Ethics, morals, & discipline	38.18%	21	61.82%	34
Other crimes	33.33%	5	66.67%	10

With respect to the mass media, we would like to state that the concept mass media includes all media—broadcasting, TV, movies, magazines, newspapers, and books. The number of cases influenced by the mass media is attributable to the fact that the desire for imitation and popularity weaken one's resistance and may lead to crime.

Other Motives

Other Motivations for Criminal Activity.

Impotence of Husband	Acquisition of Wealh	Imitation of Friends	Alcoholism & Drug Addiction	Sexual Desire & Pleasure
9.9%	92.73%	40%	7.27%	1.82%

Professional Sex Pleasure	Deviation of Guardian	Undesired for Marriage	Deviant Determination
3.4%	9.95%	7.27%	20%

Besides those categorized above, other motives have been recorded and a statistical study was made for each of the 70 cases under study. The results are as follows:

Impotence of the Husband as a Motive for Deviance. Impotence of the husband was not found to be a strong motive (9.9 percent); yet it may be considered an influencing factor in deviations. By way of example, the impotent husband may become a drug addict, and this in turn may lead to the ill-treatment of the wife.

Acquisition of Wealth. Acquisition of wealth is the strongest motive behind deviation, representing 92.73 percent of the total number under study. As previously shown, this is associated with the low educational standard of the majority of the prisoners. We found also that acquisition of wealth was in some cases related to other motives, such as marriage unpopularity, drug addiction, or deviational instincts.

Imitation of Friend. This represents 40 percent of the cases. Imitation of others plays an important role in deviation, considering that imitation of others is a major characteristic of women, in general, no matter what the cost may be.

Drug Addication. Drug addiction was not found to be a strong motive for deviance. The small number (7.27 percent) appeared to be related to the presence of an addict's husband or guardian.

Sexual Satisfaction. This motive was not a strong one.

Determination. This stage of deviation is considered the most dangerous, because the deviant is highly contented and convinced that her behavior is correct and that society is wrong. She is not ashamed to satisfy her living needs through deviant acts. In the majority of these cases returning to prison is often repeated.

Number of Repetitive Deviance.

Number of Times Entering Prison	One Time	Twice	Three Times and More
	68.57% 48	21.43% 15	10% 7

The accompanying table shows the actual influence of prison on these females. We found that 21.43 percent have been imprisoned twice, and 10 percent have been imprisoned three times or more. Adding the two figures gives a percentage of 31.43 percent for those imprisoned more than once. This percentage shows that the role of prison as a reformatory measure and the efforts of the social workers to cure the prisoners and to solve their problems were not satisfactory. This may be due to the weakness of the sentence as well as to the problems faced by the prisoner upon release. Moreover, lack of a steady income may be a chief factor, because in many cases these women are denounced by their families after going to prison, and many wives are divorced and find themselves without refuge. In addition, many suffer a feeling of total loss—a fact which paralyzes their thoughts and senses and makes it impossible for them to return to a normal life.

Geographical Distribution.

	Cairo	Guiza	Alexandria	Canal Cities	Lower Egypt	Upper Egypt
Ethical/moral & disciplinary crimes	38.18%	5.45%	12.73%	10.91%	23.64%	9.09%
Other crimes	53.33%	6.67%	—	6.67%	6.67%	6.67%

It should be noted that the deviants in the accompanying table have been carrying out their activities in Cairo and that the distribution represents the starting point. We also point out that deviance in cities is greater than in villages. In connection with the Canal cities, it is noted that emigration of the inhabitants as a result of war with Israel and being unsettled has had a negative effect on deviance.

The Call of Conscience.

	Intention to Repent	Intention Not to Repent
Prostitution	23.64% 13	76.36% 42
Other crimes	60% 6	40% 6

The figures in the accompanying table greatly affected the researchers' feelings toward the prisoners, for 76.36 percent of the prostitutes declared that they did not intend to repent after their release from prison. Similarly, 40 percent of those who committed other crimes would not repent after their release. Moreover, some of those who declared that they intend to repent after their release may join the non-repenters, though they may not declare it openly. The high percentage of those who insist upon not repenting may be due to the feeling of pessimism they have about their inability to face life and live normally again, that is, that deviance has become a habit and part of their individuality: How will life be after they come out of prison? How will they shape their new daily life? How will they assure their true intention of repentance and succeed in changing the society's outlook of them if they choose to repent? How will they be able to face the family and live among them again? All these were puzzling questions running through their minds. They are trying to defend their perverted behavior rather than face it. Defending their pervertedness reaches such a great extent that the majority of them decide and insist that after their release from prison they will not only resume prostitution but will also encourage others to do so and facilitate their deviance.

CHAPTER FIVE

LATIN AMERICA

1. Argentine Statistics on Female Criminality

J. N. KENT

Jorge Nicolas Kent is Professor of Criminal Law, and has served as Juridical Advisor, Director, and Cabinet Advisor. He is affiliated with the Faculty of Law and Social Sciences at the National University of Buenos Aires, and the Catholic University of La Plata. He is Subsecretary of Justice in penitentiary and postpenitentiary matters, a member of the International Society of Criminology, of the Brazilian Society of Criminology and Correctional Science, and of the National College of Criminological Research of Mexico. He is a national correspondent of the Argentine Republic with the United Nations in matters referring to the prevention of crime and treatment of offenders.

Introduction

Any effort directed at outlining the characteristics of female criminality in Argentina must begin by noting the difficulties involved, particularly those inherent in the compilation of extant data and their comparability.

It should also be noted that Argentina is a vast country in which geographic, climatic, economic, social, and ethnic-cultural conditions vary according to each region, so that criminality has its own identity within each region, a matter which is not always reflected in the statistics.

This work is not an exhaustive study of the etiology of female criminality, but rather a statistical analysis of the data from the country. Explanatory factors are presented along with hypotheses regarding the determinants of female criminality.

Brief Reflections with General Reach

There is no doubt that the figures on female criminality are lower than those for the opposite sex. Undoubtedly this is true for other countries of the region as well, although obviously differentiated by peculiarities of location and by other factors of political and socioeconomic development. This means that variations are to be found from country to country and from period to period. Changing social situations, which lessen the disparity between men and women, may also lessen their disparity in criminal behavior.

Current events on a global scale indicate a continuously increasing access by women to all spheres of life which, for all too long, were exclusively male. This applies to the sharing of responsibility in the public as well as in the private sphere. Women have begun to become active in a gamut of illicit activities. These are often marked by femininity, but responsive to changed circumstances. It has therefore been said that women are neither more nor less criminal than men. They are different.

In an effort to ascertain the causes of female criminality, it is necessary to observe that, to a certain extent, the lower proportion of female convicts in relation to males in prison can be attributed to the definitions of antijuridical conduct, whereby women escape classification as principals and appear only as accessories.

The dark figure of female criminality is, according to the opinion of some authors, higher than that for men. Instigation, complicity, and concealment—criminal acts easily hidden—constitute episodes that are frequently reflected neither in police nor in judicial statistics and intensify the confirmed dissimilarity between the curves of criminality of both sexes. Abortion, infanticide, and shoplifting are female offenses for which it is difficult to obtain accurate data. Any serious investigation of the difference between male and female criminality should take into account the lesser criminality of women in comparison with that of men. While it should recognize the indisputable biological, psychic, and physical differences of both sexes, it should not neglect the concrete framework of social relations within which members of both sexes behave.

Some of the factors which determine the form and dimension of female criminality are marriage, unequal education, feminine socialization, biological makeup, changing opportunities of contemporary life, and the influence of the social environment. A scientific approach should also take into account the menstrual cycle, pregnancy, childbirth and menopause, conditions which affect the psychology of women.

This is particularly relevant as regards crimes like abortion and infanticide during or immediately after childbirth. Certain authors, in the course of their research, recorded that a large percentage of women committed shoplifting during their menstrual period. Likewise, kleptomania has been associated with menopause. Jimenez de Asua states his position in these terms:

> Male pre-eminence can create in a woman a strong sense of inferiority, with all the consequences of "virile protest." This is particularly relevant during the period of menstruation, pregnancy, nursing, and especially during the menopause. During such times she is particularly prone to commit offences like fraud and shoplifting.

During such periods neurological changes occur which manifest themselves in behavioral changes. The woman becomes anxious and impulsive, and is more likely to commit offenses violative of honor and morality. The statistics bear this out. Alfredo Niceforo, in alluding to such transformations, stated:

> civilization, taking the woman from the house where civilizations had her contained, brings her to a shaken life, full of pain and incitement, of temptations and disillusions, the call to take part in the daily fight for life, of opportunities for criminality that before, within the four walls of the house, she did not have. Liberated from familial slavery, she resembles the butterfly that abandons the shade where they live in order to travel toward the light of a great lamp whose call leaves many of them embraced.

Summary of Statistical Findings

1. The entrance of women into business and professional life is a determinant of female criminality.
2. Sentenced women are, to a large extent, accessories rather than principals.
3. The greatest proportion of female offenders has only a primary school education, followed by those considered illiterate.
4. This lack of education is dependent on parental neglect, great distances between home and school, and dropout rates attributable to

the need to supplement the family income, or lack of interest on the part of the student.

5. The age range 21 or older has the greatest incidence of offenses, followed by the age range 18–20, and then by those 16–17.

6. Domestic servants and saleswomen account for the greatest proportion of offenders, while professional women are rarely found in prison.

7. Most criminal conduct occurs in large cities, followed by smaller towns.

8. In terms of motivation, the profit motive ranks first, followed by altercations and by negligence (thus, abortion and practice of medicine without a license are profit motivated).

9. Simple larceny is the most frequent offense, followed by fraud.

10. Within the sphere of fraud crimes, women offenders are generally associated with men, who transmit their skills to women.

11. There is a virtual absence of female offenders in the categories of offenses against public security, public order, security of the nation, government and the constitutional order, and public faith.

12. As regards offenses against public administration, women often make great sacrifices out of love for their male partners and out of a desire to be helpful and wanted.

Conclusion

The statistics permit us to conclude that men are more involved in criminality than women. These figures have been fairly constant. Women are less likely to wind up before a court or in prison. The fact that women are biologically different from men has influenced their social status and destiny. To paraphrase the words of Anselm von Feuerbach:

The differences between the sexes are omnipresent and infinite. It cannot be said that they begin here and end there.

However, Argentina, like many other countries of this continent, is experiencing a great transformation. The period of change will inevitably bring about repercussions in the realm of criminality. The processes of industrialization, urbanization, migration, and social communication cause deviations from expected compliance with legal norms. Increasingly women are becoming more independent, are less dependent on the home environment, and are entering the mainstream.

Epilogue

This phenomenon undoubtedly implies that social factors will influence them in much the same way that they have influenced men. This will inevitably lessen the disparity between male and female crime rates.

The International Days of Criminology, convened at Mendosa, Argentina, in June 1969, made the following recommendations:

(a) The family structure, by means of educational measures, must be adjusted so as to create an awareness about the responsibility of fathers with respect to their children, the need for family planning, and the significance of family stability;

(b) Rural-to-urban migration, especially as to woman, must be checked by creating incentives for staying in rural areas, such as by the creation of educational centers for women. Such centers should train women for gainful employment, as well as in fine arts. They should also provide for sex education. In the cities, sheltered environments should be established for women in need of assistance which would provide material, spiritual, medical, and social assistance and help with respect to employment.

(c) Agencies must be established to provide vocational training for women in need thereof.

(d) Prostitutes and their children should obtain every assistance in the medical, clinical, sociological, psychological, and educational realm, to insure their re-entry into family life and into productive society.

Up until now female criminality has rarely been empirically researched. I trust that this incipient statistical study has enabled me to offer some relevant conclusions. I would like to conclude with the words of Juan Manuel Mayorca:

The human personality will always be a variable combination among the elements which the human being contributes from his birth in conjunction with all the values, pressures and deformities which social life contributes.

Annex 1
Females Sentenced, 1973–77

Sentences 1973–77/Females.

Classification	1973 #	1973 %	1974 #	1974 %	1975 #	1975 %	1976 #	1976 %	1977 #	1977 %
Jurisdiction:										
National	371	25.05	305	22.92	323	26.24	362	24.63	432	21.08
Provincial	979	66.10	986	74.08	846	68.72	1,027	69.86	1,424	69.50
Federal	131	8.85	40	3.00	62	5.04	80	5.44	191	9.32
Military	—	—	—	—	—	—	1	0.07	2	0.10
Petition:										
Trial granted	749	50.57	831	62.43	700	56.87	887	60.34	1,316	64.23
Appealed and confirmed	635	42.88	423	31.78	448	36.39	492	33.47	614	29.97
Appealed and modified	71	4.79	54	4.06	59	4.79	65	4.42	88	4.29
Appealed and reversed	26	1.76	23	1.73	24	1.95	26	1.77	31	1.51
Sentence imposed:										
Conditional sentence	901	60.84	1,024	76.93	889	72.22	1,064	72.38	1,459	71.21
Sentence to be served	390	26.33	198	14.88	228	18.52	289	19.66	451	22.01
Preventive detention	24	1.62	23	1.73	19	1.54	27	1.84	21	1.02
Prison suspended with permanent incapacitation	9	0.61	8	0.60	10	0.81	9	0.61	15	0.73
Prison suspended with fine or to be paid or incapacitation to be served	150	10.13	60	4.51	40	3.25	12	0.81	34	1.66
Prison or fine suspended with incapacitation to be served	5	0.33	12	0.90	37	3.01	58	3.95	56	2.73
Prison or incapacitation suspended with fine to be paid	2	0.14	6	0.45	8	0.65	11	0.75	13	0.63

Sentences 1973–77/Females.

Classification	1973 #	1973 %	1974 #	1974 %	1975 #	1975 %	1976 #	1976 %	1977 #	1977 %
Penal sanctions:										
Death	—	—	—	—	—	—	—	—	—	—
Detention or Life	11	0.74	10	0.75	6	0.49	10	0.68	11	0.54
—more than 5 years	38	2.57	31	2.33	34	2.76	39	2.65	55	2.68
—2–5 years	124	8.37	77	5.79	90	7.31	108	7.35	110	5.37
—up to 2 years	1,127	76.10	1,104	82.95	971	78.88	1,157	78.71	1,644	80.23
—fine and incapacitation	37	2.50	43	3.23	73	5.93	88	5.99	132	6.44
—fine	238	16.07	126	9.47	97	7.88	113	7.69	142	6.93
—incapacitation	112	7.56	67	5.03	81	6.58	59	4.01	97	4.73
Security measures:										
Detention—article 52 C.P.	—	—	3	0.23	1	0.08	—	—	1	0.05
Detention—article 52 C.P. (suspended)	1	0.07	1	0.08	3	0.24	2	0.14	5	0.24
Exile	17	1.15	21	1.58	18	1.46	33	2.24	14	2.15
Tutelary measures:										
Regime of guarded liberty	—	—	—	—	—	0.08	7	0.48	3	0.15
Internment	—	—	—	—	2	0.16	—	—	1	0.05
Corrective (Art. 34, 19, C.P.)	—	—	—	—	—	—	21	1.42	—	—
General dispositions										
Tentative	79	5.33	85	6.39	71	5.77	92	6.26	118	5.76
Criminal co-participation	214	14.44	194	14.58	168	13.65	226	15.37	314	15.32
Confluence (real)	27	1.82	24	1.80	51	4.14	47	3.20	63	3.07
Confluence (ideal)	161	10.87	130	9.77	179	14.54	214	14.56	301	14.69
Confluence (real and ideal)	1	0.07	—	—	5	0.41	9	0.61	18	0.88
Accumulation of causes	9	0.61	5	0.38	27	2.19	13	0.88	23	1.12
Conditional revocation of cond. liberty	—	—	—	—	2	0.16	2	0.14	3	0.15
Conditional revocation of liberty	—	—	—	—	—	—	—	—	1	0.05

Education:

	No.	%	No.	%	No.	%	No.	%	No.	%
Illiterate	94	6.35	101	7.59	87	7.07	93	6.33	96	4.69
Barely educated	117	7.90	94	7.06	97	7.88	87	5.92	175	8.54
Grade school	1,100	74.27	975	73.25	891	72.38	1,035	70.40	1,458	71.16
Secondary school (education)	67	4.52	56	4.21	67	5.44	80	5.44	132	6.44
University	26	1.76	22	1.65	20	1.62	38	2.58	41	2.00
No data included	77	5.20	83	6.24	69	5.61	137	9.32	147	7.17

Civil status:

	No.	%	No.	%	No.	%	No.	%	No.	%
Single	654	44.16	594	44.63	591	48.01	661	44.97	955	46.61
Married	717	48.41	610	45.83	536	43.54	662	45.03	906	44.22
Widowed	71	4.79	78	5.86	57	4.63	77	5.24	84	4.10
Separated	4	0.27	8	0.60	6	0.49	16	1.09	20	0.98
Divorced	2	0.14	4	0.30	5	0.41	5	0.34	13	0.63
Concubinage	22	1.49	36	2.70	33	2.68	46	3.15	54	2.63
No data included	11	0.74	1	0.08	3	0.24	3	0.20	17	0.83

Age:

	No.	%	No.	%	No.	%	No.	%	No.	%
16 and 17	12	0.81	21	1.58	8	0.65	29	1.97	75	3.66
18–20	200	13.50	177	13.30	192	15.60	224	15.24	338	16.50
"Persons of age"	1,269	85.89	1,133	85.12	1,031	83.75	1,217	85.79	1,636	79.84

Names and other nicknames:

	No.	%	No.	%	No.	%	No.	%	No.	%
With nickname(s)	227	15.33	181	13.60	186	15.11	195	13.26	272	13.27
With other names	38	2.57	38	2.93	31	2.52	37	2.52	50	2.45
With other names and nicknames	10	0.67	7	0.53	8	0.65	8	0.54	7	0.34
Without other names and nicknames	1,202	81.16	1,096	82.34	1,000	81.23	1,223	83.20	1,714	83.65
With given name(s)	4	0.27	8	0.60	6	0.49	7	0.48	8	0.29

Nationality:

	No.	%	No.	%	No.	%	No.	%	No.	%
German	3	0.20	—	—	—	—	1	0.07	—	—
Austrian	1	0.07	2	0.15	—	—	—	—	1	0.05
Belgian	—	—	—	—	1	0.08	—	—	1	0.05

Sentences 1973–77/Females.

Classification	1973 #	1973 %	1974 #	1974 %	1975 #	1975 %	1976 #	1976 %	1977 #	1977 %
Nationality:										
Bolivian	8	0.54	15	1.12	17	1.38	14	0.95	10	0.49
Brazilian	6	0.40	3	0.23	4	0.32	6	0.41	5	0.24
Cuban	1	0.07	—	—	—	—	—	—	—	—
Czech	—	—	1	0.08	1	0.08	—	—	—	—
Chilean	23	1.55	20	1.50	37	3.01	42	2.86	62	3.03
Danish	—	—	5	0.38	—	—	—	—	—	—
Spanish	16	1.08	9	0.67	9	0.73	9	0.61	13	0.63
American	1	0.07	—	—	1	0.08	—	—	—	—
French	2	0.14	2	0.15	—	—	—	—	—	—
Greek	2	0.14	—	—	—	—	2	0.14	1	0.05
Hungarian	—	—	—	—	1	0.08	—	—	1	0.05
English	—	—	—	—	—	—	—	—	1	0.05
Italian	12	0.81	9	0.67	11	0.89	17	1.15	13	0.63
Japanese	—	—	—	—	—	—	1	0.07	—	—
Lebanese	1	0.07	—	—	—	—	—	—	1	0.05
Mexican	—	—	—	—	—	—	—	—	1	0.05
Norwegian	—	—	6	0.45	—	—	—	—	—	—
Paraguayan	23	1.55	17	1.27	25	2.03	37	2.52	38	1.85
Peruvian	3	0.20	—	—	—	—	1	0.07	1	0.05
Polish	2	0.14	3	0.23	1	0.08	1	0.07	6	0.29
Portuguese	—	—	7	0.08	1	0.08	—	—	—	—
Rumanian	—	—	2	0.15	1	0.08	—	—	—	—
Russian	—	—	—	—	1	0.08	—	—	—	—
Syrian	1	0.07	2	0.15	1	0.08	—	—	—	—
Swedish	—	—	1	0.08	—	—	—	—	—	—
Turkish	—	—	—	—	—	—	—	—	1	0.05
Uruguayan	10	0.67	3	0.23	9	0.73	14	0.95	7	0.34

	N	%	N	%	N	%	N	%	N	%
Yugoslavian	—	—	—	—	—	—	3	0.20	—	—
Argentinian	362	91.96	1,230	92.41	1,107	88.95	1,320	89.79	1,884	91.95
Other	3	0.20	—	—	2	0.16	2	0.14	2	0.10
"Stateless"	1	0.07	—	—	—	—	—	—	—	—
Swiss	—	—	—	—	1	0.08	—	—	—	—
Naturalization:										
Nationalized foreigner	4	2.37	4	3.96	6	4.84	10	6.67	9	5.45
Without naturalization	165	97.63	97	96.04	118	95.16	140	93.33	156	94.55
Residence:										
Less than 2 years	61	36.09	8	7.92	7	5.64	2	1.33	5	3.03
2 years or more	6	3.55	65	64.36	69	55.65	70	46.67	65	39.39
No data included	102	60.36	28	27.72	48	38.71	78	52.00	95	57.58
Professions:										
Lawyers	—	—	—	—	2	0.16	6	0.41	2	0.10
Agriculture	2	0.14	5	0.38	4	0.32	1	0.07	6	0.29
Aviculture	—	—	1	0.08	—	—	1	0.07	—	—
Butchers	—	—	—	—	—	—	3	0.20	—	—
Merchants	90	6.08	61	4.58	55	4.47	74	5.03	88	4.29
Commissioners	—	—	1	0.08	—	—	—	—	—	—
Construction workers	1	1.07	—	—	—	—	—	—	—	—
Accountants	1	1.07	—	—	1	0.08	3	0.20	—	—
Business brokers	—	—	1	0.08	—	—	—	—	—	—
Chauffeurs	—	—	—	—	1	0.08	2	0.14	3	0.15
Dentists	—	—	1	0.08	—	—	1	0.07	2	0.10
Designers	—	—	—	—	3	0.24	—	—	1	0.05
Teachers	23	1.55	31	2.33	29	2.36	30	2.04	32	1.56
Employees	154	10.40	110	8.26	144	11.70	162	11.02	283	13.81
Writers	—	—	1	0.08	1	0.08	1	0.07	2	0.10
Students	28	1.89	24	1.80	31	2.52	23	1.56	56	2.73
Pharmacists	—	—	—	—	—	—	—	—	1	0.05

Sentences 1973–77/Females.

Classification	1973 #	1973 %	1974 #	1974 %	1975 #	1975 %	1976 #	1976 %	1977 #	1977 %
Professions:										
Photography	1	0.07	—	—	—	—	—	—	—	—
Gastologists	4	0.27	4	0.30	1	0.08	1	0.07	10	0.49
Industry	1	0.07	—	—	1	0.08	—	—	1	0.05
Newspaper vendors	15	1.01	17	1.27	22	1.79	31	2.11	32	1.56
Exempt (from labor)	4	0.27	5	0.38	4	0.32	6	0.41	6	0.29
Doctors (female)	2	0.14	1	0.08	1	0.08	1	0.07	2	0.10
Dressmakers	31	2.09	33	2.47	27	2.19	28	1.90	37	1.81
Midwives	10	0.67	7	0.53	5	0.41	14	0.95	9	0.44
Hairdressers	16	1.08	8	0.60	11	0.89	11	0.75	17	0.83
Journalists	—	0.07	—	—	—	—	1	0.07	1	0.05
Police	—	—	—	—	1	0.08	1	0.07	3	0.15
Homemakers	775	52.32	704	52.89	573	46.56	695	46.28	948	46.26
Seamstresses	—	—	—	—	—	—	—	—	1	0.05
Tailors	—	—	—	—	—	—	—	—	1	0.05
Domestic service	238	16.07	251	18.85	218	17.71	251	17.07	351	17.13
Textiles	3	0.20	2	0.15	2	0.16	3	0.20	2	0.10
Peddlers	1	0.07	1	0.08	—	—	1	0.07	2	0.10
Newspaper vendors	—	—	—	—	—	—	2	0.14	—	—
Commercial travelers	—	—	—	—	1	0.08	—	—	—	—
Other professions	52	3.51	42	3.15	61	4.96	85	5.78	89	4.34
Without profession(s)	28	1.89	20	1.50	32	2.60	32	2.18	61	2.97
The place of act:										
City	1,124	75.89	950	71.37	885	71.89	1,065	72.44	1,628	79.45
Town	338	22.82	350	26.30	316	25.67	371	25.24	383	18.69
Port	2	0.14	8	0.60	5	0.41	7	0.48	10	0.49
County	16	1.08	22	1.65	25	2.03	26	1.77	28	1.37
Island	—	—	—	—	—	—	1	1.07	—	—
No data included	1	0.07	1	0.08	—	—	—	—	—	—

Determining reasons (motives):

	No.	%	No.	%	No.	%	No.	%	No.	%
Carelessness	51	3.44	68	5.11	96	7.80	87	5.92	97	4.73
Need	3	0.20	17	1.27	8	0.65	9	0.61	6	0.29
Profit	814	54.96	694	52.15	615	49.96	709	48.24	1,007	49.15
Opportunity	—	—	23	1.73	8	0.65	12	0.81	14	0.68
Vengeance	—	—	14	1.05	1	1.08	4	0.27	15	0.73
Fight	194	13.10	202	15.18	199	16.17	273	18.57	290	14.16
Quarrel	9	0.61	12	0.90	3	0.24	12	0.81	5	0.24
No data included	410	27.69	301	22.61	301	24.45	364	24.77	615	30.02

Condition at the time of the act:

	No.	%	No.	%	No.	%	No.	%	No.	%
Normal	1,454	98.18	1,289	96.85	1,196	97.16	1,422	96.74	2,019	98.54
Emotional	16	1.08	24	1.80	19	1.54	28	1.90	19	0.92
Alcoholic	4	0.27	—	—	4	0.32	4	0.27	—	—
Drunk	4	0.27	3	0.23	5	0.41	10	0.68	2	0.10
Stupor	—	—	—	—	2	0.16	5	0.34	4	0.20
No data included	3	0.20	15	1.12	5	0.41	1	0.07	5	0.24

Crimes:

	No.	%	No.	%	No.	%	No.	%	No.	%
Against the person (culpable)	48	3.24	63	4.73	94	7.64	85	5.78	86	4.20
Against the person (intentional)	368	24.86	391	29.38	327	26.56	437	29.73	481	23.47
Against honor	4	0.27	9	0.67	5	0.41	5	0.34	8	0.39
Against honesty	27	1.82	15	1.12	18	1.46	17	1.15	18	0.88
Against the civil status of persons	7	0.47	6	0.45	7	0.57	13	0.88	17	0.83
Against personal liberty	20	1.35	12	0.90	21	1.71	23	1.56	40	1.95
Against property	584	39.44	583	43.82	511	41.51	609	41.44	961	46.90
Against common security	19	1.28	18	1.35	17	1.38	29	1.97	26	1.27
Against public order	4	0.27	—	—	—	—	1	0.07	4	0.20
Against the security of the nation	—	—	—	—	—	—	—	—	—	—
Against the government and the constitutional order	—	—	—	—	—	—	—	—	—	—
Against public administration	99	6.68	64	4.81	60	4.87	72	4.90	113	5.51
Against public faith	99	6.68	69	5.18	67	5.44	51	3.47	76	3.71
Special laws	202	13.64	101	7.59	104	8.45	128	8.71	219	10.69

Sentences 1973–77/Females.

Classification	1973 #	1973 %	1974 #	1974 %	1975 #	1975 %	1976 #	1976 %	1977 #	1977 %
Crimes against the person: (culpable)										
Homicide	10	20.83	13	20.63	26	27.66	10	11.76	24	27.91
Injury	38	79.17	50	79.37	68	72.34	75	88.24	62	72.09
Crimes against the person: (intentional)										
Homicide	28	7.61	43	10.99	34	10.40	27	6.18	36	7.48
Homicide (qualified)	21	5.71	20	5.11	12	3.67	17	3.89	16	3.33
Premeditated homicide	4	1.09	—	—	—	—	1	0.23	—	—
Infanticide	11	2.99	8	2.05	6	1.83	6	1.37	9	1.87
Suicide (inducing or aiding in)	1	0.27	—	—	—	—	—	—	—	—
Abortion (committing or aiding in)	63	17.12	67	17.13	53	16.20	70	16.01	77	16.01
Abortion (qualified)	4	1.09	1	0.26	1	0.31	8	1.83	7	1.46
Minor injuries	161	43.75	164	41.94	150	45.87	206	47.13	237	49.27
Minor injuries (qualified)	8	2.17	12	3.07	18	5.50	12	2.75	17	3.53
Serious injuries	18	4.89	24	6.14	21	6.42	38	8.70	25	5.20
Serious injuries (qualified)	7	1.90	1	0.26	5	1.53	8	1.83	4	0.83
Homicide and injuries (produced in a quarrel)	9	2.44	11	2.81	3	0.92	12	2.75	5	1.04
Homicide and injuries produced in a quarrel (qualified)	—	—	1	0.26	—	—	—	—	—	—
Duel	—	—	—	—	—	—	—	—	—	—
Misuse of weapons	21	5.71	23	5.88	21	6.42	24	5.49	27	5.61
Misuse of weapons (qualified)	3	0.81	3	0.77	1	0.31	2	0.46	3	0.62
Aggression	5	1.36	7	1.79	1	0.31	3	0.69	11	2.28
Aggression (qualified)	—	—	—	—	—	—	—	—	2	0.42
Abandonment of persons	4	1.09	3	0.77	—	—	—	—	2	0.42
Abandonment (qualified)	—	—	3	0.77	1	0.31	3	0.69	2	0.42
Withholding assistance	—	—	—	—	—	—	—	—	1	0.21

Crime	No.	%	No.	%	No.	%	No.	%	No.	%
Crimes against honor:										
False accusation	1	25.00	2	22.22	1	20.00	—	—	1	12.50
Abuse	3	75.00	7	77.78	4	80.00	5	100.00	7	87.50
Crimes against honesty:										
Adultery	—	—	—	—	—	—	—	—	—	—
Violation	1	3.70	2	13.33	—	—	—	—	—	—
Violation (qualified)	—	—	—	—	—	—	1	5.88	—	—
Rape	—	—	—	—	—	—	—	—	—	—
Rape (qualified)	—	—	—	—	—	—	—	—	—	—
Corruption	16	59.26	9	60.00	15	83.33	13	76.47	13	72.22
Corruption (qualified)	5	18.52	2	13.33	3	16.67	3	17.65	3	16.66
Dishonest abuse	5	18.52	—	—	—	—	—	—	1	5.56
Dishonest abuse (qualified)	—	—	—	—	—	—	—	—	—	—
Exploitation of prostitution	—	—	—	—	—	—	—	—	—	—
Obscene public exhibitions	—	—	—	—	—	—	—	—	—	—
Obscene exhibitions	—	—	1	6.67	—	—	—	—	1	5.36
Abduction	—	—	1	6.67	—	—	—	—	—	—
Abduction (qualified)	—	—	—	—	—	—	—	—	—	—
Crimes against liberty:										
Felonies against indiv. liberty	9	45.00	1	8.33	4	19.05	4	17.39	7	17.50
Felonies against indiv. liberty (qualified)	4	20.00	1	8.33	5	23.81	2	8.70	3	7.50
Threats	—	—	—	—	2	9.52	4	17.39	17	42.50
Threats (qualified)	—	—	—	—	1	4.76	—	—	1	2.50
Trespass of domicile	7	35.00	7	58.33	9	42.86	13	56.52	9	22.50
Trespass of domicile (qualified)	—	—	—	—	—	—	—	—	—	—
Disclosing of secrets	—	—	3	25.00	—	—	—	—	1	2.50
Disclosing of secrets (qualified)	—	—	—	—	—	—	—	—	2	5.00
Crimes against freedom of work and association	—	—	—	—	—	—	—	—	—	—
Crimes against freedom of assembly	—	—	—	—	—	—	—	—	—	—
Crimes against freedom of press	—	—	—	—	—	—	—	—	—	—

Sentences 1973–77/Females.

Classification	1973 #	1973 %	1974 #	1974 %	1975 #	1975 %	1976 #	1976 %	1977 #	1977 %
Crimes against property:										
Larceny	330	56.51	367	62.95	290	56.75	372	61.09	553	57.55
Larceny (qualified)	26	4.45	10	1.72	11	2.15	9	1.48	39	4.06
Cattle theft	5	0.86	3	0.51	4	0.78	3	0.49	5	0.52
Simple robbery	32	5.48	33	5.66	28	5.48	39	6.40	40	4.16
Robbery (qualified)	47	8.05	24	4.12	29	5.68	43	7.06	61	6.35
Extortion	3	0.51	10	1.72	9	1.76	6	0.99	4	0.42
Extortion (qualified)	—	—	—	—	—	—	1	0.16	—	—
Kidnapping with ransom	—	—	2	0.34	1	0.19	3	0.49	3	0.31
Kidnapping with ransom (qualified)	—	—	—	—	—	—	—	—	—	—
Swindling and other deceptions	110	18.83	109	18.70	101	19.77	100	16.42	153	15.92
Swindling and other deceptions (qualified)	3	0.51	5	0.86	—	—	12	1.97	21	2.19
Usury	—	—	1	0.17	—	—	—	—	—	—
Fraudulent bankruptcy	—	—	1	0.17	—	—	—	—	1	0.10
Encroachment	5	0.86	3	0.51	15	2.94	9	1.48	30	3.12
Damage to property	23	3.94	15	2.57	10	1.96	12	1.97	50	5.20
Damage to property (qualified)	—	—	—	—	2	0.39	—	—	1	0.10
Crimes against common security:										
Moral corruption	—	—	—	—	—	—	3	10.345	—	—
Moral corruption by carelessness	—	—	—	—	1	5.88	—	—	2	7.69
Fabrication or possession of the means of explosive materials and arms	2	10.53	—	—	—	—	3	10.345	1	3.85
Crimes against security of the means of transportation and commerce	—	—	1	5.56	—	—	—	—	—	—
Crimes against the security of the means of transportation from carelessness	—	—	—	—	—	—	—	—	—	—

	No.	%	No.	%	No.	%	No.	%	No.	%
Crimes against the security of the means of communication	2	10.53	—	—	1	5.88	1	3.450	—	—
Crimes against the security of the means of communication from carelessness	—	—	—	—	—	—	—	—	—	—
Piracy	—	—	—	—	—	—	—	—	—	—
Crimes against the public health	—	—	—	—	—	—	—	—	—	—
Propagation of contagious disease(s)	1	5.26	—	—	2	11.76	—	—	—	—
Propagation of contagious disease(s)—from carelessness or negligence	—	—	1	5.56	—	—	—	—	1	3.85
Unfaithful supply of medicines	3	15.79	7	38.88	2	11.76	3	10.345	1	3.85
Illegal trafficking, producing, and for possession of drugs	4	21.05	—	—	4	23.53	3	10.345	—	—
Illegal practice of medicine	7	36.84	9	50.00	7	41.19	16	55.170	21	80.76
Crimes against public order:										
Instigation of the crime	—	—	—	—	—	—	—	—	—	—
Illicit associations	2	50.00	—	—	—	—	—	—	2	50.00
Illicit associations (qualified)	1	25.00	—	—	—	—	—	—	—	—
Public intimidation	1	25.00	—	—	—	—	1	100.00	—	—
Incitation of violence	—	—	—	—	—	—	—	—	—	—
Defense of the crime	—	—	—	—	—	—	—	—	1	25.00
Imposition of ideas by force or by fear	—	—	—	—	—	—	—	—	1	25.00
Crimes against the security of the nation:										
Treason	—	—	—	—	—	—	—	—	—	—
Crimes that compromise the peace and dignity of the nation	—	—	—	—	—	—	—	—	—	—
Crimes against the government and the constitution order:										
Insurrection	—	—	—	—	—	—	—	—	—	—
Sedition	—	—	—	—	—	—	—	—	—	—

Sentences 1973–77/Females.

Classification	1973 #	1973 %	1974 #	1974 %	1975 #	1975 %	1976 #	1976 %	1977 #	1977 %
Crimes against administration:										
Force and resistance against authority	17	17.17	11	17.19	10	16.67	12	16.67	9	7.96
Force and resistance against authority (qualified)	8	8.08	1	1.56	1	1.67	1	1.39	6	5.31
Inducing a public official to fraudulence	1	1.01	—	—	—	—	—	—	—	—
Contempt	3	3.03	7	10.94	5	8.33	3	4.17	7	6.19
False arraignment	—	—	3	4.69	1	1.67	—	—	—	—
Encroachment of authority, titles, or honors	—	—	—	—	—	—	—	—	—	—
Abuse of authority and violation of duties of officials	1	1.01	1	1.56	—	—	1	1.39	1	0.89
Violation of seals and documents	—	—	—	—	—	—	1	1.39	—	—
Violation of seals and documents (qualified)	—	—	1	1.56	—	—	1	1.39	3	2.65
Bribery	—	—	—	—	2	3.33	3	4.17	3	2.65
Bribery (qualified)	—	—	—	—	—	—	—	—	1	0.89
Misappropriation of public funds	2	2.02	4	6.25	2	3.33	1	1.39	10	8.85
Misappropriation of public funds (qualified)	2	2.02	1	1.56	5	8.33	3	4.17	8	7.08
Misappropriation of public funds from carelessness or negligence	3	3.03	4	6.25	—	—	—	—	—	—
Transactions prohibited by public officials	—	—	—	—	—	—	2	2.77	2	1.77
Illegal exactions	2	2.02	—	—	1	1.67	—	—	3	2.65
Illegal enrichments by public officials and employees	—	—	—	—	—	—	—	—	—	—
Prevarication	—	—	—	—	—	—	—	—	—	—
Denial or delay in the administration of justice	—	—	—	—	—	—	—	—	—	—
False testimony	22	22.22	4	6.25	9	15.00	7	9.72	15	13.27
False testimony (qualified)	—	—	—	—	—	—	1	1.39	1	0.89
Harboring a criminal	36	36.36	25	39.07	23	38.33	35	48.61	45	39.82
Harboring a criminal (qualified)	—	—	1	1.56	—	—	—	—	1	0.89
Escape	2	2.02	1	1.56	—	—	2	2.77	1	0.89
Escape (qualified)	—	—	—	—	1	1.67	—	—	—	—

Crimes against the public faith:

	1	2	3	4	5	6	7	8	9	10
Counterfeiting of coins and banknotes and forgery of bonds and credit documents	—	—	—	—	—	—	1	1.96	—	—
Counterfeiting of coins and banknotes and forgery of bonds and credit documents (qualified)	—	—	—	—	—	—	1	1.96	—	—
Forgery of seals, stamps, and marks	—	—	—	—	—	—	—	—	—	—
Forgery of documents in general	20	20.20	22	31.88	23	34.33	18	35.29	32	42.11
Forgery of documents in general (qualified)	—	—	—	—	2	2.98	2	3.92	2	2.63
Adulteration of public documents	—	—	—	—	—	—	—	—	7	9.21
Commercial and industrial fraud	—	—	—	—	—	—	—	—	—	—
Payments of bills of exchange without funds	79	79.80	47	68.12	42	62.69	29	56.87	35	46.05

Crimes against special laws:

	1	2	3	4	5	6	7	8	9	10
Law no. 11.281 (contraband)	3	1.48	2	1.98	7	6.73	10	7.81	2	0.91
Law no. 11.386 (enrollment)	1	0.50	—	—	3	2.88	3	2.34	2	0.91
Law no. 11.723 (information)	—	—	—	—	1	0.96	—	—	—	—
Law no. 12.160 (law of exchange)	1	0.50	—	—	—	—	—	—	—	—
Law no. 12.331 (prophylaxis)	1	0.50	7	6.93	1	0.96	3	2.34	1	0.46
Law no. 12.962 (registry)	—	—	2	1.98	1	0.96	—	—	—	—
Law no. 13.010 (feminie enrollment)	42	20.79	—	—	2	1.92	—	—	—	—
Law no. 13.482 (clandestine immigration)	—	—	—	—	1	0.96	—	—	—	—
Law no. 13.944 (familial assistance)	—	—	—	—	—	—	—	—	2	0.91
Law no. 14.236 (social provision)	—	—	—	—	1	0.96	1	0.78	—	—
Law no. 17.492 (social assistance)	1	0.50	—	—	—	—	—	—	—	—
Law no. 17.671	16	7.92	—	—	9	8.66	11	8.60	94	42.93
Law no. 19.359	—	—	—	—	8	7.69	8	6.25	5	2.28
Law no. 20.771 (drugs)	—	—	—	—	—	—	3	2.34	14	6.39
Law no. 20.840 (subversive activities)	—	—	—	—	2	1.92	5	3.91	9	4.11
Law no. 21.268 (possession and use of arms and explosives)	—	—	—	—	—	—	1	0.78	—	—
Law no. 408 (gambling La Pampa)	6	2.97	—	—	2	1.92	3	2.34	2	0.91
Law no. 806 (gambling Rio Negro)	—	—	—	—	—	—	1	0.78	—	—

Sentences 1973–77/Females.

Classification	1973 #	1973 %	1974 #	1974 %	1975 #	1975 %	1976 #	1976 %	1977 #	1977 %
Crimes against special laws:										
Law no. 4.097 (gambling Formosa)	—	—	—	—	—	—	2	1.56	—	—
Law no. 4.847 (gambling Buenos Aires)	63	30.18	85	84.16	33	31.74	32	25.01	37	16.90
Law no. 5.800	—	—	—	—	—	—	1	0.78	2	0.91
Law no. 5882 (Code of Faltas Cordoba)	—	—	—	—	—	—	—	—	8	3.65
Law no. 6582/58 (registry of automotor)	—	—	5	4.95	11	10.58	2	1.56	—	—
Law on Gambling Azar	68	33.66	—	—	21	21.16	41	32.04	40	18.27
Law no. 15.348/46 (registry)	—	—	—	—	—	—	1	0.78	45	38.14
Recidivism:										
Generic	66	54.54	49	55.65	47	61.04	50	52.09	51	43.22
Specific	12	9.92	14	15.91	12	15.58	14	14.58	22	18.64
Criminal specification	43	35.54	25	28.41	18	23.38	32	33.33	45	38.14
Generic recidivism and amount of criminal process:										
More than 1 tried and 1 convicted	36	54.56	23	46.95	21	44.68	28	56.00	27	52.95
More than 1 tried and 1 convicted	12	18.18	12	24.40	16	34.04	14	28.00	12	23.53
More than 2 tried and 2 convicted	6	9.09	4	8.16	3	6.38	1	2.00	5	9.80
More than 2 tried and 2 convicted	6	9.09	4	8.16	4	8.51	5	10.00	3	5.88
More than 3 tried and 3 convicted	3	4.54	—	—	1	2.13	—	—	1	1.06
More than 3 tried and 3 convicted	2	3.03	1	2.04	1	2.13	1	2.00	5	3.92
More than 4 tried and 4 convicted	—	—	—	—	—	—	—	—	—	—
More than 4 tried and 4 convicted	—	—	3	6.12	1	2.13	—	—	—	—
More than 5 tried and 5 convicted	—	—	—	—	—	—	—	—	—	—
More than 5 tried and 5 convicted	—	—	1	2.04	—	—	1	2.00	1	1.96
More than 6 tried and 6 convicted	—	—	—	—	—	—	—	—	—	—
More than 6 tried and 6 convicted	1	1.51	1	2.04	—	—	—	—	—	—
More than 7 tried and 7 convicted	—	—	—	—	—	—	—	—	—	—
More th.. 7 tried and 7 convicted										

Specific recidivism and amount of criminal process:

More than 1 tried and 1 convicted	6	50.00	5	35.71	9	75.00	4	28.58	11	50.00
More than 1 tried and 1 convicted	2	16.67	3	21.43	1	8.33	7	50.00	8	36.36
More than 2 tried and 2 convicted	2	16.67	—	—	—	—	1	7.14	2	9.09
More than 2 tried and 2 convicted	1	8.33	2	14.29	—	—	1	7.14	—	—
More than 3 tried and 3 convicted	—	—	—	—	—	—	—	—	—	—
More than 3 tried and 3 convicted	1	8.33	3	21.43	2	16.67	—	—	—	—
More than 4 tried and 4 convicted	—	—	—	—	—	—	—	—	—	—
More than 4 tried and 4 convicted	—	—	—	—	—	—	—	—	—	—
More than 5 tried and 5 convicted	—	—	1	7.14	—	—	—	—	—	—
More than 5 tried and 5 convicted	—	—	—	—	—	—	—	—	—	—
More than 6 tried and 6 convicted	—	—	—	—	—	—	—	—	—	—
More than 6 tried and 6 convicted	—	—	—	—	—	—	1	7.14	—	—
More than 7 tried and 7 convicted	—	—	—	—	—	—	—	—	—	—
More than 7 tried and 7 convicted	—	—	—	—	—	—	—	—	—	—

Criminal specification and amount of criminal process:

More than 1 tried and 1 convicted	35	81.40	17	68.00	13	72.21	23	71.88	28	62.23
More than 1 tried and 1 convicted	4	9.30	1	4.00	2	11.11	6	18.76	11	24.45
More than 2 tried and 2 convicted	1	2.32	3	12.00	1	5.56	1	3.12	1	2.22
More than 2 tried and 2 convicted	2	—	—	—	1	5.56	—	—	2	4.44
More than 3 tried and 3 convicted	—	—	1	4.00	—	—	1	3.12	1	2.22
More than 3 tried and 3 convicted	1	—	2	8.00	—	—	—	—	—	—
More than 4 tried and 4 convicted	—	—	—	—	—	—	—	—	—	—
More than 4 tried and 4 convicted	—	—	—	—	—	—	—	—	—	—
More than 5 tried and 5 convicted	—	—	—	—	1	1.56	1	3.12	—	—
More than 5 tried and 5 convicted	—	—	—	—	—	—	—	—	—	—
More than 6 tried and 6 convicted	—	—	1	4.00	—	—	—	—	—	—
More than 6 tried and 6 convicted	—	—	—	—	—	—	—	—	—	—
More than 7 tried and 7 convicted	1	4.00	—	—	—	—	—	—	—	—
More than 7 tried and 7 convicted	—	—	—	—	—	—	—	—	—	—
More than 10 tried and 10 convicted	—	—	—	—	—	—	—	—	2	4.44

Sentences 1973–77/Females.

Classification	1973 #	1973 %	1974 #	1974 %	1975 #	1975 %	1976 #	1976 %	1977 #	1977 %
Defendant's Prior Record:										
Judicial record:										
With antecedents	93	6.84	231	18.58	86	7.45	112	8.15	126	6.53
Without antecedents	1,267	93.16	1,012	81.42	1,068	92.55	1,262	91.85	1,805	93.47
Police record:										
With Antecedents	275	18.57	313	23.52	312	25.35	325	22.11	360	17.57
Without antecedents	1,206	81.43	1,018	76.48	919	74.65	1,145	77.89	1,689	82.43
Family care:										
With family	757	51.12	684	51.39	597	48.50	755	51.36	988	48.22
Without family	624	42.13	543	40.80	546	44.35	580	39.46	927	45.24
Neglected	100	6.75	104	7.81	88	7.15	135	9.18	134	6.54
Antecedents from childhood:										
Good	116	7.83	128	9.62	143	11.62	118	8.03	157	7.66
Bad	12	0.81	10	0.75	8	0.65	9	0.61	15	0.73
Neglected	1,353	91.36	1,193	89.63	1,080	87.73	1,343	91.36	1,877	91.61
Length of the process:										
Up to 6 months	425	28.70	373	28.03	332	26.97	381	25.91	546	26.65
6–12 months	272	18.37	241	18.11	224	18.20	202	13.74	310	15.33
More than 12–18 months	181	12.22	143	10.74	152	12.35	190	12.93	275	13.40
More than 18–24 months	248	16.75	281	21.11	221	17.95	308	20.95	422	26.65
More than 24–30 months	92	6.21	65	4.88	62	5.04	78	5.31	120	5.85
More than 30–36 months	107	7.22	80	6.01	106	8.61	117	7.96	154	7.52
More than 36 months	156	10.53	148	11.12	134	10.88	194	13.20	222	10.83

Annex 2
Comparative Statistics of Criminal Acts with Intervention, 1973–77

National Totals, 1973–77

| Classification of Crimes | Year | Number of Offenses | | 21 Years and Older | | | Number of Offenders | | | Without Identification of Sex and/or Age | General Total of Accused |
| | | Number of Accused | | | | | Under 21 Years | | | | |
		Known	Unknown	Men	Women	Subtotal	Men	Women	Subtotal		
Against the person (culpable)	1973	18,715	3,883	16,856	1,474	18,330	1,639	457	2,096	1,115	21,541
	1974	25,695	5,368	23,257	1,938	25,195	2,181	359	2,540	1,653	27,368
	1975	23,408	4,182	21,403	1,684	23,087	2,111	286	2,397	1,335	26,819
	1976	17,532	3,568	16,733	1,348	18,081	1,267	217	1,484	1,066	20,633
	1977	15,636	3,399	15,334	1,449	16,783	1,544	346	1,890	1,222	19,875
Against the person (intentional)	1973	32,075	7,911	23,464	4,308	27,772	3,452	1,046	4,498	11,033	44,203
	1974	42,330	8,929	31,797	5,480	37,277	4,944	1,134	6,078	12,725	56,080
	1975	39,201	6,879	30,313	5,140	35,953	4,140	816	4,956	11,073	51,982
	1976	33,533	5,765	26,894	4,803	31,697	3,029	742	3,771	8,379	43,847
	1977	28,597	5,059	23,379	4,291	27,670	2,412	612	3,024	7,471	38,165
Homicide (intentional)	1973	1,893	530	2,083	119	2,202	209	23	232	967	3,401
	1974	2,566	784	2,729	224	2,953	282	47	329	1,117	4,399
	1975	2,323	827	2,452	185	2,637	252	23	275	1,481	4,393
	1976	1,988	904	2,183	157	2,340	164	24	188	1,346	3,874
	1977	2,061	552	3,317	133	3,450	121	15	136	956	4,542

National Totals, 1973–77

Classification of Crimes	Year	Number of Accused		Number of Offenses 21 Years and Older			Number of Offenders Under 21 Years			Without Identification of Sex and/or Age	General Total of Accused
		Known	Unknown	Men	Women	Subtotal	Men	Women	Subtotal		
Against honor	1973	116	27	119	6	125	9	—	9	11	145
	1974	99	31	88	14	102	9	—	9	3	114
	1975	193	38	176	4	180	20	1	21	2	203
	1976	165	42	150	7	157	5	—	5	9	171
	1977	109	59	122	6	126	13	—	13	8	147
Against honesty	1973	4,287	807	3,191	276	3,467	875	89	964	1,730	6,161
	1974	4,800	936	3,474	198	3,672	1,152	135	1,287	1,663	6,622
	1975	4,582	639	3,455	186	3,641	1,064	109	1,173	1,318	6,132
	1976	4,339	757	3,612	243	3,855	892	111	1,003	1,318	6,176
	1977	4,477	875	3,709	271	3,980	850	253	1,103	1,489	6,572
Against civil status	1973	52	13	37	10	47	—	—	—	17	64
	1974	82	7	50	15	65	15	—	15	21	101
	1975	61	24	40	17	57	6	1	7	10	74
	1976	65	11	46	33	79	1	10	11	23	113
	1977	76	10	56	36	92	4	—	4	15	111
Against public administration	1973	4,255	575	4,178	366	4,544	616	66	682	1,545	6,771
	1974	5,042	618	5,298	425	5,723	523	55	578	1,760	8,061
	1975	5,528	532	6,065	531	6,596	563	86	649	1,494	8,737
	1976	6,000	572	6,878	515	7,393	436	64	503	1,243	9,136
	1977	5,319	531	6,087	556	6,643	332	41	373	1,060	8,076
Against the public faith	1973	1,407	298	1,088	160	1,248	46	15	61	361	1,670
	1974	1,234	242	1,006	128	1,134	30	14	44	350	1,528
	1975	1,188	286	1,026	132	1,158	33	11	44	298	1,500
	1976	1,069	281	873	136	1,009	42	12	54	255	1,318
	1977	1,526	458	1,393	174	1,567	39	16	55	409	2,031

Gambling	1973	13,333	380	16,764	533	17,297	160	16	176	36	17,509
	1974	17,335	412	21,527	537	22,064	312	17	329	53	22,446
	1975	17,493	1,042	23,169	715	23,884	410	4	414	178	24,476
	1976	21,108	1,566	29,196	680	29,876	620	23	643	454	30,373
	1977	16,132	1,686	20,671	738	21,409	301	15	316	247	21,972
Special laws	1973	2,907	588	1,685	367	2,052	778	385	1,163	77	3,292
	1974	7,598	21,010	2,895	791	3,686	2,057	618	2,675	3,648	10,009
	1975	9,788	17,493	4,288	1,374	5,662	2,680	1,356	4,045	21,453	31,160
	1976	20,124	13,723	11,300	1,564	12,864	5,058	2,696	7,754	16,526	37,144
	1977	19,793	1,746	11,869	1,574	13,443	5,247	2,071	7,318	200	26,961
Total	1973	145,212	160,245	114,692	13,817	128,509	22,527	4,396	26,923	117,697	273,129
	1974	174,968	147,694	139,859	16,224	156,083	24,517	4,456	28,973	96,525	281,581
	1975	173,229	146,987	143,141	16,512	159,653	23,451	4,608	28,059	88,767	274,479
	1976	175,440	137,325	152,455	16,232	168,778	23,383	5,686	29,069	69,645	267,492
	1977	163,612	120,225	140,913	15,684	156,597	21,701	5,040	26,741	67,088	250,426

Totals from the Country 1973–77.

Classification of Crimes	Year	Quantity of Crime / Quantity of Accused Known	Quantity of Accused Unknown	Quantity of Crime 21 Years and Older			Quantity of Accused Under 21 Years			Without Identification of Sex and/or Age	General Total of Accused
				Men	Women	Subtotal	Men	Women	Subtotal		
	1973	3,111	1,899	2,621	327	2,948	278	28	306	3,425	6,679
	1974	3,791	2,559	2,849	415	3,264	387	58	445	5,164	8,873
	1975	4,729	2,643	3,533	545	4,078	422	75	497	4,477	9,052
	1976	4,257	2,588	3,259	531	3,790	346	63	409	4,789	8,988
	1977	4,353	2,506	3,556	505	4,061	244	42	286	5,167	9,514
	1973	61,601	141,731	40,953	5,649	46,602	13,929	2,227	16,156	89,633	152,391
	1974	61,620	103,720	41,098	5,521	46,619	11,990	1,914	13,904	65,071	125,594
	1975	61,975	109,544	42,553	5,473	48,026	11,125	1,750	12,875	40,550	101,451
	1976	62,827	105,385	47,276	5,889	53,165	11,058	1,683	12,741	31,780	97,686
	1977	63,319	101,655	48,010	5,490	53,500	10,125	1,575	11,700	46,281	111,481
	1973	858	1,220	680	137	817	267	26	293	5,952	7,062
	1974	1,373	1,743	1,417	269	1,686	231	60	291	826	2,803
	1975	1,278	1,546	1,287	313	1,600	204	52	256	560	2,416

Year										
1976	1,008	1,342	918	258	1,176	88	19	107	408	1,691
1977	973	1,035	816	312	1,128	73	21	94	441	1,663
1973	524	356	891	79	970	262	17	279	860	2,109
1974	1,275	1,274	2,254	261	2,515	404	45	449	2,406	5,370
1975	1,373	1,240	2,769	209	2,978	418	27	445	2,536	5,959
1976	1,358	802	3,041	152	3,193	367	21	388	2,034	5,615
1977	1,210	638	2,564	146	2,710	393	33	426	2,121	5,257
1973	5	1	7	3	10	—	—	—	—	10
1974	14	7	11	1	12	—	—	—	34	46
1975	19	13	19	1	20	—	1	1	2	23
1976	28	7	34	5	39	8	1	9	12	60
1977	18	7	19	4	23	2	—	2	—	25
1973	73	26	75	3	78	7	1	8	35	121
1974	114	54	109	7	116	—	—	—	31	147
1975	90	59	93	3	96	3	1	4	—	100
1976	39	12	62	2	64	2	—	2	3	69
1977	13	9	11	1	12	1	—	1	1	14

Annex 3
Incarcerated Population of Argentina, 1974–77

Incarcerated Population of the Country as of December 31.

	Tried						Convicted						
	Men		Women		Sub-total		Men		Women		Sub-total		Total
	Number	%	Number	%			Number	%	Number	%			
1974	14,434	92.1	1,134	7.9	15,568		7,978	96.7	254	3.3	8,232		23,800
1975	11,471	95.6	531	4.4	12,002		5,768	97.5	173	2.5	5,941		17,943
1976	12,272	86.6	1,919	13.4	14,191		5,080	82.4	1,055	17.6	6,135		20,326
1977	13,229	88.5	1,703	11.5	14,932		7,271	96.8	233	3.2	7,504		22,436

2. Venezuelan Female Criminality: The Ideology of Diversity and Marginality

L. ANIYAR DE CASTRO

Lola Aniyar de Castro is Senior Professor and Director of the Institute of Criminology. She is affiliated with the International Society of Criminology, Société Internationale de Defense Sociale, Sociedad Venezolana de Derecho Penal y Criminologia, and International Society of Victimology. Her primary interests in the field are critical criminology, sociohistorical and political studies in criminology, and epistemology. She is a member of the Scientific Commission (International Society of Criminology), Coordinator of Comparative Research in Latin America (Project: Violence and White-Collar Crime in Latin America). Her publications include: several books on criminal law subjects, victimology and criminology of the social reaction, and articles on deviance, drugs, economics, criminality, and criminological research. She has served as a member of the United Nations Meeting of experts on Criminality and the Abuse of Power, New York, 1979.

I

Methodological Aspects. As a variety of the general theory of deviant behavior, female criminality has usually been analyzed from today's dominant criminological perspectives, namely *passage à l'acte,* or the etiological approach, and interactionist or societal reaction approach. Although the latter is partially etiological, it also focuses on the problematic nature of the definition of the situation and on the mechanisms which generate so-called social expectations. We commonly see the use of positivist theories by scholars who relate female criminality with the "singular nature" of woman, with her natural passivity and with her peculiar psychology. This fact has generally prevented an understanding of female criminality, but has created a whole criminological literature, which we can call sexist, that has principally dealt with male criminality. Thus, as noted by Joseph Weis

(1976), most theories of crime refer to marginal and poor people and to male criminal behavior.[1] In general, these theories of pathological deficiency are not substantially far away from the so-called sexual reversal theories, although the latter claim their concern with social reaction. Consequently, women violate sexual role expectations rather than criminal norms. According to Chesler (1972), the female sexual role is still biologically defined. As a result, if a woman tries to change her social role, she is seen by many as an offender against her own nature. As Pitch (1975) points out, female deviance seems to be historically unrelated and might not be considered as a real danger to society. The causes are not yet determined, and their patterns of expression seem to be repeated independent of the socioeconomic context and culture.

If we understand female criminality as a violation of social-sexual role expectations, artificially formulated, we would be compelled to regard female criminal behavior as nonfeminine, and therefore female criminals as abnormal. The supposition of women's sexual role would make them be self-destructive in their own behavior, while men's role would make them be heteroaggressive. Consequently, a female criminal will be virile.[2] However, there is no pattern of expression for only one sex, nor is behavior created in a social vacuum.

In order to deal with female criminality in Venezuela, as elsewhere, it is necessary to begin with a historical analysis of women and their behavior within a socioeconomic and political context, in which we can ascertain the functionality of the roles assigned to each sex, according to the prevalent interests. One must regard women as subjects of history in a class society, dependent on the requirements of an economically active population and the profitable use of that population for the purposes of a determined system. A sociohistorical approach would require a whole account of the marginal segments of the population, including the poor, youth, the mad, the old, and women, within the actual interrelations of a socioeconomic system that is managed by a few who have the power to decide over the dominated classes.

The so-called ideology of the diversity functions, according to Basaglia and Basaglia (1973), "to sanction the most adequate form of control for a particular phase of techno-industrial development." "The old custody-punitive ideology, in fact, turns out to be inadequate for total control as correlated with the development of capitalism." Therefore, the question about how many marginals capitalism needs at any time is also valid for understanding the problems of women. Jurgen Reish (1973) estimates that in the United States the amount of ill, old, unable, and young people are around 65 percent of the whole population, that is, two thirds of the American population. If we include all women in these statistics, the figures are far greater. In Venezuela, as we will show later, more than one half of the population is female.

The proposed approach is necessarily an etiological one, in which we shall scan the determinants of an intolerable situation and where we shall analyze the functional definitions of role, sex, ideal behavior, and deviant behavior, which facilitate the maintenance of the status quo. It is also necessary to deal with the differential functioning of the entire apparatus of social control, both formal and informal, including courts, penitentiaries, and social control at its primary level, but not including the role played by "science" within the structures of the mechanisms of social consensus in relation to roles and the passive approval by women to the requirement of science.

Finally, any description of Venezuelan female criminality, its mechanisms of social control, and the theories which have tried to explain it cannot be accomplished without an accurate analysis which shows us the level of socioeconomic and cultural development of this and other Latin American countries, which is characterized by an excessively marked social stratification and by a strong external dependency. Thus, only a historical method can show us both the great complexity and the global unity of the phenomenon.

This cannot be done in states. It must be articulated within the intricate web of interactions, which are neither mechanical nor ineluctable.

II

The Latin American Woman. International data allow us to outline the common characteristics of the actual patterns of development in Latin America, although there are some local differences and variations as regards their influence on man's and woman's participation in social life. On that basis, we shall try to analyze the situation of women in this region.

1. First, we observe that at the beginning of the 1960s school enrollment increased considerably with greater increases shown for middle and upper levels, rather than to the elementary level (Wolfe, 1975).[3] This trend seems to increase intensively during the 1970s.

2. We also observe a growth of the economically active population at the upper or middle occupational levels, including employers, professionals, dealers, employees, and a decrease in the domestic agricultural labor force.

3. The unequal income distribution and the maintenance of a level of poverty below an acceptable minimum are the result of the pattern of development used, and upon its incapacity to generate equal opportunities. A capable labor force is frequently condemned to unemployment and marginalization, resulting in loss of hopes of finding a job (especially as regards women, the aged, and unskilled labor), or to underemployment or employment in jobs regarded as superfluous (Wolfe, 1975).

4. The school attendance of women has been equal to that of men. In some countries, girls who come from low-income families stay longer at school than boys because their contribution to rural work or their contribution to home spending is less useful (CEPAL-FAO). In higher education, the increase of the female population is enormous in thirteen out of fifteen Latin American countries. By contrast, their effective labor participation does not correspond to this increase. Generally, middle-class and upper-class women are only temporarily incorporated in the labor force, namely before they get married.[4] Women have lower wages than men in similar jobs, for example, in Colombia, Mexico, San Salvador, and Bolivia, according to Margaret Randall's report. Perhaps only women who graduated from universities are able to earn wages similar to those of men.

What has perhaps not been assessed is the real participation of women in Latin American development, which amounts to the provision of most of the basic family services which the state is not able to pay for or provide. All the cultural and socialization pressures on Latin American woman contribute to the maintenance of this pattern, despite the increasing modernization of these countries. As Wolfe (1975) points out, in this respect, as well as in others, Latin America opposes "modern" sexual equality through a wide range of other structures, especially that of family relationships. While female participation in the labor force in West Europe is around 43 percent, in Latin America it is around 20 percent.[5] In 1971, women participating in the labor force in Venezuela were employed mostly as houseworkers; dressmakers; and in minor services, crafts, and small industries. According to official data of the Ministry of Industry, in a period of twenty years, from 1950 to 1970, the percentage of the female labor force experienced an increase of only 6 or 7 percent.

III

The Venezuelan Woman: Roles, Expectations, and Opportunities. Over one half of the Venezuelan population is female. There is no real interest in including women in the active economic structure of the nation because there is a reluctance to expand the employment opportunities for half of the population, a task the national state is not able to accomplish. Thus, all models of development—social, cultural, and economic—continue to make women dependent on a matriarchal family structure and even to push them into a secondary and dependent role at home. Despite the apparently great and aggressive development of Venezuela during the last six years, the "primary values" of womanhood are still being exalted: on the one hand, the importance of women as an object (femininity as decoration), and on the other hand, the maternal responsibility and a particular sexual virtue (instrumental femininity). Although this seems to be contradictory, it is not so if we analyze these values from a social class viewpont. For marginal women, the patterns of maternal responsibility have been established as follows:

1. The maintenance of their children who live with them, but without a responsible father. These women, in order to maintain their children, have to work at home or outside as housekeepers, or in other low-paying jobs which do not require professional training. Nor does the state provide it.

2. A particular conception about sexual morality which accepts a diversity of relationships within a temporary but frightening "concubinary" marriage established in order to provide the vital needs to the children, who have been procreated as a result of successive extralegal unions. On the other hand, there are some cultural and occupational possibilities for middle- and upper-class women, who thus can improve their standard of living. For example, in Venezuela, as in other Latin American countries, we observe a high university assistant rate which is sometimes even higher for female students. Nevertheless, we also observe that this female population flocking to the free university centers is largely composed of students coming from the middle and upper classes.

In 1966, of 21,000 female university students, only 6,000 were working (28 percent) (Colomina, 1975). For these women expectations are different, namely a decorative femininity. Because of their high buying power, perfume and cosmetic shops have been created in the last few years, as well as sophisticated boutiques, with abundant selections of dresses imported from the most famous international fashion centers. Commercial advertising relies on this kind of woman to increase sales. North American magazines, such as *Cosmopolitan* and others, convey a false image of women's liberation by depicting sexual daring, thus confirming women in their role as geisha, existing to satisfy male pleasures. The interests of women are thus directed by this capitalist system in which we live. Although there are more women occupying important jobs, both private and public, as Colomina says (1975), they are the superstars who mask the social and economic marginalization of all other women.

These quick changes derived from the new oil incomes. The middle class has expanded, but it is necessary to note the slowness of institutional transformations and implementation of basic services for an increasingly consumer-oriented, exigent, and problematic population. As a result, health and education services, professional skills, citizen security, detention and repressive facilities, and official registration centers are chaotic and insufficient. This explains, for example, the difficulty of obtaining sensitive data needed in order to undertake a serious analysis of female deviance and its control.

IV

Official Data on Venezuelan Female Delinquency. As elsewhere, the registered female criminality rate is very low. By 1959, out of 2,396 sentenced inmates, 68 were women (2.84 percent). By 1976 there are 16,005 sentenced male inmates and only 282 sentenced female inmates (1.76 percent). From 1969 to 1971, the percentage of female inmates, including those processed and sentenced, was 2.58, 2.84, and 2.56 percent, respectively. For the same years, the percentage of sentenced women was 1.64, 1.89, and 1.50 percent, respectively. Contrary to developed countries,[6] in Venezuela the mechanisms of social control still seem to be sexist. Yet it is also possible that the kind of criminality more frequently prosecuted in this country (homicide, assaults, and larceny) has actually remained lower—partly because of the great protection of women at home, and partly because of the minimal social participation of women in this country. We must not forget that the social control applied to Venezuelan women begins at home, carried out by their fathers, husbands, and children, due to traditional family limitations. Consequently, we can assert that in Venezuela the home acts as a confinement or a closed institution, or as a total institution of control, which functions as such even before female behavior becomes public, and serves the primary and secondary socialization functions. Certainly, women's liberation movements create increasing and frustrating expectations, but had there been a real participation, there should have been increased stress, conflict, and deviance as in some other countries.

This is not yet the case in Venezuela. Here, the actual situation is primarily one of class differences, as we shall see in our analysis of the composition of inmate populations. Social class determines not only needs and situations to which individuals respond with criminal behavior but also the repressive activities of the criminal justice system.

On the basis of the statistics cited above, it appears that: (1) Venezuela has one of the lowest rates of recorded female criminality. (2) This percentage is even smaller with regard to sentenced women. Perhaps this fact confirms Freda Adler's assertion that the low incidence of female criminality is related, in part, to a chivalry posture. Nevertheless, there is not a single fact that leads us to assert that the mentioned variable is the only one which would explain the low number of female inmates. It is possible that, in this case, the increase of the dark number of criminality plays a significant role, especially as regards crimes called "typically feminine": larcency committed by housekeepers, larceny at department stores, because of the small economic damage involved. We can say the same for other crimes committed by women—abortion, infanticide, and adultery—because it is difficult to prove or detect them. Sometimes the nature of female jobs (housekeepers, secretaries, nurses) makes the criminal act less visible (Pollack, 1959). This circumstance, on the other hand, reduces the risks of criminalization, since it excludes the possibility of affecting the interests of the most powerful sectors in society.

Likewise, it is difficult to estimate accurately the so-called golden figures. Nevertheless, we would presume that this figure is not relevant, except for criminal acts committed by middle- and upper-class persons, because the most important economic tasks are rarely in the hands of women. From time to time, a public official is accused of corruption; yet this does not happen frequently, and the accusation generally is due to concrete political reasons. Political female criminality has lately increased, generated by the appearance of new forms of total liberation.

As in all criminal matters, the economic reality of social control directs its attention to catching "easier fish." It also directs its attention to events which have caused social disapproval, therefore justifying the existence of repressive mechanisms of social control. In 1971 in Venezuela, for instance, of 54 sentenced women, 15 were sentenced for homicide, 6 for damages, and only 5 for larceny and 2 for robbery. The largest category is "vagrants and rogues," composed of 18 women, including those cases which positivists categorize as "predelictual danger," such as prostitution. Since the dangers never come to fruition, we can only suppose that such typical transgressions are simply conceived as running counter to "sexual role expectations."

Some types of crimes, such as fraud and drug traffic, have increased within the narrow limits of registered criminality.

The selectivity of social control is more evident in sentences than in arrests. The latter indicate a similar situation with offenses against property, according to recent statistics.[7]

In research done by us (Aniyar and Santos, 1974) in Maracaibo, the second-largest city of Venezuela, and therefore a good sample of the whole universe, we found that for 29 processed women, 3 were processed for political offenses. This statistic does not show up, of course, in the official criminal statistics in a country which proclaims itself to be one of the strongest democratic systems on this continent. The most current offenses are injuries (32 percent), homicides (28 percent), and larcenies (2 percent). Infanticide and drug sales reach only 8 percent and concealment 4 percent. Although abortion still remains in our criminal code, and is frequently committed, no woman has been sentenced for this criminal behavior. From the sample of 29 processed women, 77 percent were housekeepers, 16 percent were housewives, and 4 percent were working as dressmakers or attending small stores. Their wage was $46.50 monthly, which was supposed to maintain an average family composed of seven children. Their educational level corresponded with the social class they represented: 60 percent of these women had reached only the fourth and sixth grades of elementary school; 24 percent were illiterate; and 16 percent had between a first- and fourth-grade elementary school education. A comparative analysis of male inmates showed us that female educational and economic levels were even lower than male educational and economic levels, even though 99 percent of male inmates also belong to the marginal classes. We can, then, conclude that the known female criminal is marginal in many areas by science, by law and its institutions, by class, and by being a woman.

Age and Civil Status. A study based on the proceedings from the juvenile courts of Zulia State (Alcala, Silva, Garcia *et al.,* 1975) on female youth under legal age (18 years according to our civil code) shows that interventions of juvenile courts are more frequent than those of criminal courts in relation to female adults. In fact, for a total of 1,572 boys (85.25 percent) there are 272 girls (14.75 percent). This differs from the relationship of men to women offenders. Even though in Venezuela we do not have the situation where girls are three times more frequently institutionalized than boys, as in the United States (Chesney-Lind, 1973), our situation leans toward the same direction. The explanation might lie in the legal criteria which generate the intervention of juvenile court judges: the status definitions, such as "minors in need of supervision," are broader and looser than the criteria followed by criminal court judges in the case of adults. In addition, we may tentatively assert that it is possible for typically sexist variables concerning sexual roles to be significant, together with the guardian and protector function of juvenile court judges. The category of "minor in need of supervision" (13.66 percent of the sample) traditionally includes the following: (1) nuisance-type behavior, including truancy, sleeping in the streets, roaming in the streets late at night, activities inappropriate to the age, offenses to parents and teachers, and so on; (2) victims of crime; (3) consumption of drugs and prostitution (which are not crimes for adults); and (4) begging.

Girls show a higher average of irregular situations between 13 and 15 years of age, an age in which the imposed stability of their sexual role becomes more pronounced, while for boys the critical age is between 17 and 18. Unfortunately, there is a lack of academic or official data differentiated by sex.

Among 154 processed women, 109 were single. This category includes, of course, women involved in concubinage and in families without a man, a characteristic of the great majority of marginal homes in Venezuela. Sixty-five percent were housewives and 35 percent housekeepers.

It is not difficult, then, to perceive the relationship of the socioeconomic deprivation which precedes the act, and the lack of protection which is always present at the moment when the administration of justice intervenes.

The majority of female inmates are between 20 and 30 years old (75 cases), which is an age of great responsibility for a premature maternity; followed by female inmates whose age is between 30 and 40 (19 cases). Between 50 and 60 years of age there are 12 cases, but only 9 between 18 and 20.

There are no studies on the differential amount of the sanction by sex. Doubtless, this type of study would shed some light on the dark aspect of the formalized societal reactions. So far, these are only hypotheses. Neither are there studies on prostitution and its relation to female arrests. The Venezuelan prostitute has a vastly inferior status. It is so evident that when a prostitute is raped, the penalty against the rapist is reduced to one fifth of the normal sentence. In any case, prostitution is not generally the legal reason for intervention. Therefore, it does not appear in official registers, and thus interviewed women generally hide this fact. But what is absolutely true is that the lower the degree of respectability of a prostitute, the greater is the victimization.[8] This assertion is also valid for other Latin American countries. A study from the Feminine Center of Rehabilitation in Panama reports that the great majority of female inmates are declared prostitutes.

V

Societal Reaction: Laws and Institutions. The penal legislative structure best reflects the structure of values and interests of a socioeconomic system.

It represents the acme of social control as regards these values and interests. For women this societal control begins with birth and is maintained by the family, the school, and the values and attitudes these institutions preserve.

From a perspective of economic interest in which women are marginated to secondary home labor, which is neither remunerated nor respected, the whole perspective finds a coherence within a framework in which all parts serve total control. Not surprisingly, the repressive laws and institutions in Venezuela are clearly sexist. Men are not only the ones who legislate, but also, as Price (1977) says, "they manage our spiritual needs, orientate our physical and emotional problems and also interpret all this for the use of mass media. . . . Perhaps the most exclusively male dominant part of this system is the Administration of Criminal Justice." Men make the laws and enforce them (police, correctional personnel, and programs of rehabilitation). They also interpret the laws (judges). However, as we can see, if we simply qualify a legislative organization as sexist, we are then losing the hidden aims served by sexism.

The Venezuelan criminal code of 1926 makes a clear discrimination by sex, ratifying the sexual role attached to woman. There are some crimes, such as adultery, in which, if the offender is a woman, the simple fact of having an affair is enough to constitute the crime. But if the offender is a man, he must "maintain publicly and notoriously a concubine" in order to be guilty of adultery. Also, there are considerable attenuating circumstances for a husband who finds his wife in an adulterous act and "kills or wounds one of them or both." It must be noted in this connection that the value assigned to honor arising from woman's sexual behavior is so significant that the punishment is the same if the result is 2 deaths, 1 death, 2 wounds, or 1 wound. A similar attenuating circumstance exists for a father or grand-father who kills or wounds the person whom he finds lying at their home with his single daughter or granddaughter. Not surprisingly, these crimes are called "privileged homicides." Seduction, a carnal act obtained by a promise of marriage, is punished only if the "woman is known as an honest one." Other privileged crimes are infanticide, abortion, and minor child abandonment "to safeguard the mother's honor." The criminal code also takes into account the passive and secondary role assigned to woman within the society when it allows for the punishment of a woman sentenced to prison (if the total penalty does not exceed six months), to be commuted to service of a jail sentence for the same period. Moreover, this penalty can also be commuted to "local banishment." It is the usual practice that "honest" women (read: high- and middle-class women) fulfill their punishment with domiciliary detention and do not go to jail.

There are also instances in which the legislation and also the practice of correctional facilities correspond totally to society's expectation of women. Penitentiaries for women are generally built with greater rationality and are less like ordinary prisons. Perhaps, due to the small number of inmates, promiscuousness is not so visible. Jail laws and regulations provide for differential treatment for women: they can live with children, and the state provides them a financial assistance until these children are 3 years old. There exist rigorous rules on the segregation of inmates by sex. The internal guards are women. Male guards are not readily permitted inside the prison.

Although conjugal visits are not prohibited by law for any of the two sexes, this practice is permitted only to men and not to women. This has led to a serious problem of female homosexuality in our jails.

The maintenance of sexual roles, reflected in the protection of womanhood, in their discriminatory treatment, and in the search for sexual virtue, even when a woman is already a subject of law, all combine to create a complex mechanism that was meant to socialize and transmit dependency and secondary values and attitudes. All this is necessary so that women will be denied their own place in socioeconomic development.

Summary

The theories which generally explain female criminality attempt to remove women from the historical role they play. However, in order to fully explain the problem, it is necessary to understand the subject in the context of social order and change. Consequently, this paper defines the socioeconomic functions that the marginality of Latin American women play in the labor market and economic opportunities. Her role has been interpreted in the context of the sexual patterns which have been planned for her in a class-oriented, underdeveloped, and dependent society. The legal definitions, the differential opportunities to commit criminal acts, the special treatment granted at all levels of social control, from police to penitentiary—all these ratify her role as propitious victim in order that the system of exploitation, segregation, and management of public and social interests for a few will be stable.

Notes

1. Weis, (1976) says: "When pressed to account for other-than lower class, male criminal behavior, criminologists tend to rely on psychologistic theories that impute some pathological

difference to the criminal, such as some abnormality of sex-role socialization, identification, or performance'' (p. 17).

2. Lombroso said that female criminals had a virile cranium, an excess of hair on their body, and a cerebral capacity similar to men's. According to the psychoanalytical school (Klein, 1973), a woman could overcome her frustration of not having a penis by symbolically obtaining manhood through aggressivity. A female criminal will try to be a man. For liberationists (Adler, 1975), ''the social revolution of the sixties has virilized its previously or presumably docile female segment.'' Adler points out that women actually commit more crimes than before, and these crimes are much more violent (an active participation in criminal gangs, in robberies, etc.), noting a lesser frequency of larceny at big stores. Weis (1976) says that this behavior is more frequently evident among middle-class women because expectations of equal sexual roles are bigger, both at the school and the family, and also in the particular cultural patterns of this social class. Consequently, middle-class male criminality would be more ''feminine'' than lower-class criminality, which is more violent. Other authors, such as Thomas (1923), argued otherwise. He said that what female criminals do is to confirm their womanhood ''illegally,'' especially through robberies in big stores, sexual malpractices, and so on.

3. Between 1960 and 1972 or 1973 elementary school enrollment increased from 25 million to 44 million in 20 countries; high school tuition from 3.7 million to 12.3 million; and university from 50,000 to 2.1 million; cited by Marshall Wolfe, ''La Participacion de la Mujer en el Desarrollo de America Latina,'' in *Mujeres en America Latina, Aportes para una discusion* (CEPAL, Mexico: Fondo de Cultura Economica, 1975), p. 13.

4. ''In the industrial labor market, which is slowly developing, woman has lost opportunities in relation to man, and an important number of women, who have to look for a job to complete the insufficient salary of their husbands or because the family has no man to support it, are still limited to be working as housekeepers or having other marginal jobs with a minimum salary.'' Wolfe, *ibid.,* p. 19.

5. For 1970, in Argentina only 24.5 percent of women older than 10 years were working; in Brazil, 18.5 percent; in Chile, 18.2 percent; in Mexico, 16.4 percent; in Panama, 25.7 percent. In Venezuela only around 22.5 percent of women older than 15 years were working in that same year. Henry Kirsh; *Participacion de la mujer en los mercados laborales* (CEPAL: Division de Desarrollo Social, 1975).

6. Price informs us that in the United States women's arrests increased two thirds between 1968 and 1973. Detentions for serious crimes increased 52 percent. While men's detentions duplicated their arrests between 1969 and 1974, women's detentions increased two thirds. Also, men go to prison more often than women (85 percent in the last years). Ray Price, ''The Forgotten Female Offender,'' *Crime and Delinquency* (April 1977), vol. 3, no. 2.

7. Of 154 processed women, 55 are in prison for crimes against the person (26 homicides, 15 infanticides, 10 damages, 4 abortions); 49 for property crimes (larceny, 21; fraud, 13; robbery, 10; seizure of things for lucrative purpose, 2; illegal appropriation, 1; receiving, 2). The category which shows the highest incidence is drug traffic (44), according to a study done by Helena Fierro; ''Delincuencia femenina y maternidad,'' presented to the Ninth International Congress on Social Defense in 1976.

8. As a phenomenon itself, prostitution in Venezuela is highly represented by foreign women. A study of the Commission of Crime Prevention found 61 percent foreign prostitutes among 1,000 prostitutes in 1960. In Caracas, Mayorca, it was found that 52.7 percent of prostitutes are illegally living in this city—36 percent Colombians, 14.5 percent Italians, 10.2 percent Cubans, 5.2 percent Argentinians, and 20 percent Central-American and other South Americans. Doubtless, this phenomenon has emerged due to Venezuela's strong currency and

an "economic development faster than that of other Latin American countries." Juan Manuel Mayorca, "Introduccion al Estudio de la Prostitucion," Caracas, *Grafica Orellana*, s.f.

References

Adler, Freda. *Sisters in Crime*. New York: McGraw-Hill Book Company, 1975.

Alcalá, Carmen Celinda, Silva de Ramírez, Virtud, García de Peña, Ydamys, Ortega Alvarez, Lourdes. "Estudio de Casos de menores sometidos a protección correccional." *Capítulo Criminológico*. No. 3. Organo del Instituto de Criminologia de la Universidad del Zulia, 1975.

Aniyar de C, Lola y Santos, Thamara. "Prisión y Clase Social." Capítulo Criminológico. No. 2. Organo del Instituto de Criminologia de la Universidad del Zulia. Maracaibo, 1974.

Basaglia, Franco y Basaglia Franca. *La Mayoría Marginada*. Barcelona: Ed. Laia, 1977. P. 33.

Colomina, Marta. *La Celestina Mecánica*. México, siglo 21, 1975.

Chesney-Lind, Meda. "Judicial Enforcement of the Female Sex Role." Social Problems. Vol. 8, No. 2 (1973) 11: 131–139.

Fierro, Helena. "Delincuencia femenina y Maternidad." Paper presented at the International Congress of Social Defense, Caracas, 1976.

Kirsh, Henry. *Participacion de la mujer en los mercados laborales latinoamericanos*. CEPAL. División de Desarrollo Social, 1975.

Klein, Dorie. "The Ethiology of Female Crime: a Review of the Literature," *Issues in Criminology*, 8 (Fall 1973): 3–30.

Mayorca, Juan Manuel. Introducción al Estudio de la Prostitución. Caracas: Gráfica Orellana, s.f.

Pitch, Tamav. "Prostituzione e malattia mentale, Due aspetté della devianza nella condizione femminile." *La Questione Criminale*. Anno 1. Maggio–Agosto 1975.

Price, Ray. "The Forgotten Female Offender." Crime and Delinquency (April 1977). Vol. 3, no. 2.

Thomas, W. I. *The Unadjusted Girl*. New York: Harper and Row, 1923.

Weis, Joseph. "Liberation and Crime. The Invention of the New Female Criminal." Crime and Social Justice (Fall-Winter, 1976), 6.

Wolfe, Marshall. "La participación de la mujer en el Desarrollo de America, Latina." *Mujeres en América Latina. Aportes para una discución*. CEPAL, Mexico: Fondo de Cultura Económica, 1975.

CHAPTER SIX

ASIAN AND PACIFIC REGION

1. Criminality Amongst Women in India:
A Study on Female Offenders and Female Convicts

M.L. BHANOT AND SURAT MISRA

M. L. Bhanot is Deputy Director of the Bureau of Police Research and Development, Ministry of Home Affairs, Government of India.

Surat Misra is Research Officer of the Bureau of Police Research and Development, Ministry of Home Affairs, Government of India.

I. Introduction

1. It is generally believed that the female is not much of a risk for crime, especially so in India where she is brought up in a spirit of modesty and the general attitude towards her is that of "protection." However, rapid urbanization, new socio-economic stresses, and the gradual break-up of the age-old institution of the joint family have exposed her lately and increasingly to a process of readjustment of social values. Additionally, she has started participating in numerous fields of activity which were formerly considered

to be the exclusive domain of men. It is now a familiar sight to see her not merely in the traditional role of a school teacher, or nurse but also as a business executive, sales executive, secretary, factory worker, shopper, or police officer. One result of all this has been some evidence of greater deviant behaviour amongst women in India.

2. The object of the present study is to throw light on the nature and pattern of female criminality. This should, in our view, help the criminologist, the social reformer, and the policeman to reorient policies and programs with a view to handle problems which are likely to be created by increased criminality amongst women, because, hitherto, such policies were designed to deal mainly with a situation in which the basic assumption was that many crimes would be committed by the female.

3. It is difficult to determine the extent of criminality amongst women accurately on the basis of published and related statistics for two reasons. First, crimes by women are grossly under-reported. There is a tendency even on the part of the victims to protect women offenders. In India, the society does not look approvingly of efforts on the part of individuals to bring women to face the process of law for certain crimes reportedly committed by them. Second, statistics are not available to show the number of crimes committed by women: only figures of their total arrest under various offences are available. The extent of criminality amongst them is, therefore, thought to be reflected through the number of women arrested. This has obvious limitations because there might be a situation in which crimes committed by women may have gone up. For example, arrest of scores of women in a single case of violation of prohibitory orders during an agitation might push up the total number of women arrested substantially although only one case of rioting would be registered by the police. Notwithstanding these limitations, we believe that the published and related statistics should help generally to indicate the trend and the nature of the problem for stimulating further research and for formulating preventive, correctional and rehabilitational programs.

4. The study has taken into account two sets of statistics: those of women offenders from police records and those reflected by a sample survey of 641 women convicts. The former data should help to throw light on the extent and nature of criminality amongst women as indicated by their arrest under Indian Penal Code crimes. Data obtained from some other countries through the Interpol have also been shown. We have limited the scope of statistics (obtained from police records) to cover only I.P.C. crimes because the involvement of women in this category of crimes should offer a better index of the nature of the emerging problem. The data on women convicts are

based on the sample survey of 641 female convicts taken from the Central Jail of Delhi, Nari Bandi Niketan of Lucknow, Naini Central Jail of Allahabad, and district jails of Fatehgarh, Mathura, and Kanpur. The analysis of these data should help to understand the nature of the problem arising out of criminality amongst women by providing information on the socioeconomic background of female convicts, their age, education, and marital status. Incidentally, this information is not available on women offenders who are not incarcerated.

5. It is hoped that a combined study of the two sets of data should help to provide a better insight into some of the problems posed by criminality amongst women in India.

II. Women Offenders

The Trends. 1. Published statistics indicate that more women were arrested by the police in India under I.P.C. crimes during 1975 as compared to the figures of arrests made in 1971. Table 1 presents arrest statistics for women involved in I.P.C. crimes in the period from 1971 to 1975 with comparative figures of male offenders, together with the male and female population and arrests per one lakh of population of either category.

Table 1. Population and Arrests.

Year	Population (000)		Number of Arrests under the Indian Penal Code		Arrests per Lakh of Population	
	Male	Female	Male	Female	Male	Female
1971	283,503	263,634	958,950	16,303	338.25	6.18
1972	289,830	269,587	1,170,154	27,891	403.74	10.35
1973	296,188	275,568	1,211,825	30,677	409.14	11.13
1974	302,574	281,576	1,448,451	25,766	478.71	9.15
1975*	308,988	287,609	1,412,692	23,939	457.20	8.32

*Figures for 1975 in this and Table 2 are provisional.

2. A perusal of the statistics in Table 1 reveals that women constitute a small proportion of the total arrests made by the police. For every 59 males arrested by the police in 1975, there was only one female. However, the statistics in this regard need closer analysis.

3. The number of women arrested has shown an erratic trend in the period from 1971 to 1975. It increased from 16,303 in 1971 to 27,891 in 1972

and touched the peak figure of 30,677 in 1973. In 1974, however, the number fell to 25,766. There was a further decline in 1975 when it stood at 23,939. But the absence of a trend appears to be misleading. Take 1971 as the base year. The number of women arrested jumped from 16,303 in 1971 to 23,939 in 1975, an increase of 46.8 percent. In the same period, the crime per lakh of female population rose from 6.18 in 1971 to 8.32 in 1975 (although it had touched 11.13 in 1973).

Male and Female Criminality. 4. When compared with male criminality, the extent of the female criminality denotes a perceptible movement. The total number of males arrested increased from 958,950 in 1971 to 1,412,692 in 1975, a rise of 47.3 percent. In the same period, female arrests increased by 46.8 percent. Thus, female arrests increased more or less at the same rate as male arrests. In other words, taking I.P.C. arrests as the index of criminality, the rate of rise of criminality amongst the males was not materially faster as compared with that of the female. This is against the popular belief that the rise in crime in India is primarily due to more men committing crimes on account of unemployment, economic hardship, and such other factors.

5. In short, female criminality has gone up in India in recent years. It may not be unreasonable to infer that, in the years to come, a larger number of women are likely to be involved in crimes and arrested by the police unless steps are taken to deal with the problem.

Juvenile Offenders. 6. Statistics on the female arrests given in Table I include juvenile arrests too. It may be interesting to note that the trend of criminality revealed from these statistics does not materially change if figures on females up to the age of 21 years are excluded from the total arrests made. This should be evident from Table 2.

7. It can be seen that the number of female juveniles arrested rose from 1,329 in 1971 to 1,750 in 1975, an increase of 31.6 percent, whereas the number of women offenders arrested by the police in the age group of 21

Table 2. Number of Female Arrests.

Year	Women	Juveniles (Up to the Age of 21)	21 Years and Above
1971	16,303	1,329	14,947
1972	27,891	2,473	25,418
1973	30,677	1,508	29,169
1974	25,766	2,309	23,457
1975	23,959	1,750	22,209

years and over increased from 14,947 to 22,209 in the same period, an increase of 48.5 percent. This means that criminality amongst female offenders increased more on account of a greater number of arrests of women of and above the age of 21 years and not necessarily and entirely on account of a higher incidence of juvenile arrests. Unfortunately, arrest statistics broken down by age after 21 years are not maintained by the police and, therefore, it is not possible to say which particular age group amongst women is particularly affected by the increasing criminality. Some idea, however, can be gleaned from the age groups of 'women convicts' given in the following chapter.

Trend in Other Countries. 8. Statistics on the arrests of women were obtained through Interpol from some other countries. These are presented in Table III.

Table 3.   Female Arrests per Lakh of Population in Some Countries.

	1971	*1972*	*1973*	*1974*	*1975*
1. India	6.18	10.35	11.13	9.15	8.32
2. U.S.A.	987.0	990.1	927.3	916.9	1,154.5
3. West Germany	546.5	563.8	558.0	573.1	604.0
4. France	n.a.	558.	561	445	n.a.
5. Japan	115.3	110.8	118.2	133.2	138.6
6. Ireland	65	57	59	67	73
7. Thailand	400.43	385.40	321.28	321.44	316.65
8. Scotland	.40	.40	.44	.45	.47

9. Before any comparison is drawn, it seems necessary to point out that these figures may be used only to make intra-country and not inter-country comparison. One reason is that, except for crimes like murder, house-breaking and theft, definitions of numerous crimes included in the national crime reporting systems of various countries are not uniform. Second, the process of criminalization and, to some extent, decriminalization makes inter-country comparisons a grope in the dark. It would, therefore, be advisable to use the data above to form an idea about the trend of criminality in different countries.

10. Taking 1971 as the base year, we see that in India, as already mentioned, the female crime per lakh of population increased from 6.18 in 1971 to 8.32 in 1975. It is interesting to note that, in the same period, the female crime per lakh of population increased from 0.40 to 0.47 in Scotland; from 65 to 73 in Ireland; from 115.3 to 138.6 in Japan, from 546.5 to 604.0 in West Germany; and from 987.0 to 1154.5 in the United States of America.

As regards France, figures for the years 1971 and 1975 are not available. The available data reveal that the rate of crime by the female fell from 558 in 1972 to 446 in 1974. It would thus appear that the rate of criminality amongst women has been showing an upward trend in many other countries like India.

Constant Increase in Some Countries. 11. Another point which emerges from these figures is that, in some countries, the rate of criminality amongst women has been on the increase for the last several years. This is unlike India where after the peak was reached in the year 1973 when 11.13 crimes per lakh of population were reported, there was a decline to 9.15 in 1974 and to 8.32 in 1975. In Japan, criminality amongst women has been constantly on the increase since 1972. It increased from 110.8 in 1972 to 118.2 in 1973, to 133.2 in 1974, and to 138.6 in 1975. In Ireland, it increased from 57 in 1972 to 59 in 1973, to 67 in 1974 and to 73 in 1975. West Germany reported an erratic trend but the rate has been constantly on the increase since 1973 when it stood at 558.0. Thereafter, it rose to 573.1 in 1974 and to 604.0 in 1975. Scotland has also reported a gradual increase from 0.40 in 1972 to 0.47 in 1975. The U.S. has shown a substantial jump from 916.9 in 1974 to 1,154.5 in 1975, the trend being erratic before this. Thailand is the only country which has reported a decline from 400.43 in 1971 to 316.65 in 1975. Thus, while the rate of female criminality has shown an upward trend in India, it has not shown as constant and gradual an increase as in some other countries like Japan, Ireland, West Germany, Scotland and the U.S.A.

The Nature of Criminality. 12. The nature of criminality amongst women may be partly demonstrated by statistics given in Table 4 below.

13. It can be seen that the maximum percentage of arrests in 1975 is for the offence of theft, followed by rioting. In 1975, 21.8 percent of the arrests for theft were women. This means that women are more prone to commit crimes like shoplifting, petty pilferage and even pick-pocketing. Similar trends have been noticed in some other countries. In Japan, 84.2 percent of total arrests amongst women in 1975 were for theft. In Ireland, this figure was 76 percent. It was 54.7 percent in West Germany and 30.8 percent in France. One reason for this could be the irresistible human temptation coupled with the fact that women have more opportunities than men to come into contact with shopping areas and other such places where thefts are easy to commit. Also perhaps is the fact that women are less suspicious in such places.

14. As regards cases of rioting, 19.34 percent were arrested for this offence in 1975. This figure was higher in 1973 (23.65) and in 1974 (27.42).

Table 4. Involvement of Women in I.P.C. Crimes (1971-75)

Crime	1971		1972		1973		1974		1975	
	a	b	a	b	a	b	a	b	a	b
Murder	769	4.72	908	3.26	772	2.52	927	3.60	1053	4.40
Culpable homicide not amounting to murder	59	0.36	77	0.28	73	0.24	66	0.26	70	0.29
Rape	7	0.04	47	0.17	21	0.07	35	0.14	21	0.09
Kidnapping and abduction	429	2.63	526	1.88	460	1.50	501	1.94	478	2.00
Dacoity	103	0.63	131	0.47	211	0.69	144	0.56	133	0.55
Robbery	83	0.51	65	0.23	177	0.58	125	0.49	124	0.52
Burglary	972	5.96	872	3.13	1,747	5.69	1,468	5.70	1,419	5.93
Theft	4,198	25.75	4,177	14.98	5,013	16.34	5,144	19.96	5,218	21.80
Riots	2,580	15.83	5,977	21.43	7,255	23.65	7,065	27.42	4,631	19.34
Criminal breach of trust	65	0.40	61	0.22	100	0.32	91	0.35	119	0.50
Cheating	85	0.40	124	0.44	168	0.55	130	0.50	213	0.89
Counterfeiting	1	0.01	4	0.01	3	0.01	—	—	4	0.02
Misc. I.P.C.	6,952	42.64	14,922	53.50	14,677	47.84	10,070	39.08	10,456	43.67
Total I.P.C.	16,303	100.00	27,891	100.00	30,677	100.00	25,766	100.00	23,939	100.00

a denotes numbers arrested.
b denotes percentage to total arrests.

This seems to be due to a series of agitations and demonstrations in the country due to political turmoil during 1973 and 1974. Comparable figures for other countries are not available because of the difficulty in classifying this type of crime.

15. The involvement of women in burglaries is also perceptible. Of all arrests of women in 1975 5.93 percent were for burglaries. In Ireland, the only country for which figures are available, it was 4.1 percent in 1971 and rose to 6.1 percent in 1975.

16. Murders come next. Out of total arrests, the percentage of arrests in murder cases in India was 4.40 in 1975. It was as low as 2.52 in 1973, although in 1971 it was 4.62. In Japan, where this crime is shown under the heading "homicide," the figure varied between .8 percent in 1971 to .6 percent in 1975. In Ireland, where it comes under the head "manslaughter and infanticide," the figure rose from .2 percent in 1971 to .4 percent in 1975. In Thailand, the figure was .1 percent in 1975 compared with .2 percent in 1974. In West Germany, the figure ranged between .1 and .2 in the period 1971 and 1975. In the U.S.A., the figure rose from .23 in 1974 to .24 in 1975. This means that the percentage of arrests for involvement of

women in murders is higher in India than in other countries for which figures are available. It is difficult to explain this phenomenon unless further studies are made.

17. Another feature is that the involvement of women in white collar crimes, namely, criminal breach of trust and cheating, has shown an upward trend in India. In criminal breach of trust, the percentage of arrest of women to total arrests was .4 in 1971. It rose to .5 in 1975. In cheating, the percentage rose from .52 in 1971 to .89 in 1975. This variation cannot be ignored as fortuitous. Perhaps more and more women are being utilized as decoys and accomplices to commit white-collar crimes.

18. Two percent of arrests in 1975 were made for the offence of kidnapping and abduction. The figure was 2.63 in 1971. While some incidents of kidnapping and abduction might be of a technical nature, a large number might be those in which women are used as accomplices.

19. Women have also been arrested in heinous crimes, like dacoity and robbery. .55 percent of arrests in 1975 were made for dacoity and another .52 percent for robbery. Involvement of women in heinous crime against property is a serious matter for the police.

The following diagram will demonstrate the percentage of women arrested under some important I.P.C. crimes during 1975.

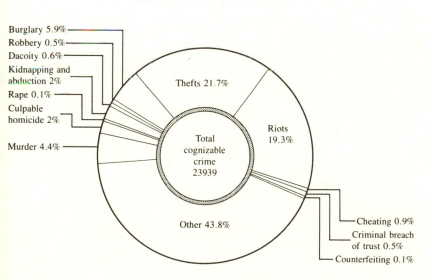

Females arrested under I.P.C. 1975

Trend in States and Union Territories. 20. It also would be worthwhile to analyze data with a view to finding out the extent and nature of involvement of women in I.P.C. crimes in different states and Union territories. For this purpose, certain categories of crime have been used. These are murder, burglary, theft, dacoity, robbery, kidnapping and abduction, cheating, and criminal breach of trust and total I.P.C.

Murder 21. Table 5 presents statistics on women arrested for murder in the period from 1971 to 1975 in States and Union Territories.

Table 5. Murder: Number of Women Arrested

S. No.	States	1971	1972	1973	1974	1975	Average
1.	Andhra Pradesh	81	54	57	69	70	66.2
2.	Assam	16	8	26	11	n.a.	15.2
3.	Bihar	32	28	30	51	34	35.0
4.	Gujarat	61	26	46	66	74	54.6
5.	Haryana	—	—	4	1	21	5.4
6.	Himachal Pradesh	—	11	11	3	7	6.8
7.	Jammu & Kashmir	4	4	5	6	8	5.4
8.	Kerala	44	40	31	43	45	40.6
9.	Karnataka	85	76	74	51	89	75.0
10.	Madhya Pradesh	62	173	12	77	103	85.4
11.	Maharashtra	139	193	140	178	208	171.6
12.	Manipur	—	1	—	—	—	0.2
13.	Meghalaya	—	1	6	2	2	2.2
14.	Nagaland	—	—	—	1	2	0.6
15.	Orissa	27	12	25	43	35	28.4
16.	Punjab	14	22	38	28	41	28.6
17.	Rajasthan	26	28	26	58	52	38.0
18.	Tamil Nadu	79	73	61	59	101	74.6
19.	Tripura	3	1	2	—	1	1.4
20.	Uttar Pradesh	89	127	145	127	155	128.6
21.	West Bengal	n.a.	30	32	38	n.a.	31.7
22.	Sikkim	—	—	—	—	—	—
	Union Territories						
1.	Andaman & Nicobar Islands	—	—	—	—	—	—
2.	Arunachal Pradesh	—	—	n.a.	2	—	0.5
3.	Chandigarh	—	—	—	—	—	—
4.	Dadra & Nagar Haveli	—	—	—	—	—	—
5.	Delhi	—	—	n.a.	14	5	4.8
6.	Goa	2	—	—	1	—	0.6
7.	Lakshadweep	—	—	—	—	—	—
8.	Mizoram	—	—	n.a.	—	—	—
9.	Pondicherry	2	—	—	3	—	1.0

22. These statistics show that the highest number of arrests for murder was made in Maharashtra in 1971 (139), 1972 (193), 1974 (178), and 1975 (208). In the year 1973, the highest number of arrests was made in U.P. (145) followed by Maharashtra (140). U.P. came next to Maharashtra in 1971, 1974, and 1975 with the arrest figure of 89, 127, and 155. In 1972, Madhya Pradesh ranked next to Maharashtra with 173 arrests. The third and fourth places were occupied by Karnataka (85) and Andhra Pradesh (81) in 1971, U.P. (127) and Karnataka (76) in 1972, Karnataka (74) and Tamil Nadu (61) in 1973, Madhya Pradesh (77) and Andhra Pradesh (69) in 1974, and Madhya Pradesh (103) and Tamil Nadu (101) in 1975. No arrest for murder was reported from Manipur, Nagaland, and Meghalaya in 1971, from Haryana and Nagaland in 1972, from Manipur and Nagaland in 1973, from Manipur and Tripura in 1974, and from Manipur and Sikkim in 1975.

23. In the Union Territories, the number of arrests of women for the crime of murder had been negligible. In the year 1975, Delhi was the only Union Territory where 5 women were arrested for murder, there being no arrest in any other Union Territory. The Union Territories of Andaman and Nicobar Islands, Chandigarh, Dadra and Nagar Haveli, Lakshadweep and Mizoram did not report any arrest, in the entire period from 1971 to 1975.

24. Taking the five year average, it can be seen that the States where murders by women are reported in sizable number are Maharashtra, Uttar Pradesh, Madhya Pradesh, Karnataka, and Tamil Nadu, in that order. Amongst the Union Territories, Delhi has the highest five year average of 4.8.

Burglary. 25. The number of women arrested in burglary cases in States and Union Territories is given in Table 6. Since no trend is visible in respect to these arrests in the period from 1971 to 1975, it would be advisable to make a comparison on the basis of the five year average. Maharashtra tops the list with the average arrest figure of 421.8, followed by Madhya Pradesh where the average annual arrest rate of women in burglaries is 225.6. The average figure for Gujarat, Uttar Pradesh, Tamil Nadu, Orissa, Rajasthan, and Andhra Pradesh is 95.2, 90.2, 87.6, 75.8, 60,2, and 55.2, respectively. In other states, the average annual figure of arrests of women in burglary cases is below 50. As regards the Union Territories, only Goa and Delhi reported 10 and 9 arrests respectively in 1975. Elsewhere, burglary by women is not much of a problem.

Theft. 26. The arrest figure of women for theft, which includes shoplifting, pickpocketing, and petty pilferages, may be found in Table 7. Maharashtra tops the list with the average annual arrest figure of 1,437.4. It may be of interest to note that in Maharashtra, the trend of criminality amongst

Table 6.   Burglary: Number of Women Arrested

S. No.	States	1971	1972	1973	1974	1975	Average
1.	Andhra Pradesh	13	32	66	95	70	55.2
2.	Assam	16	—	35	11	n.a.	15.5
3.	Bihar	22	12	64	75	29	40.4
4.	Gujarat	16	96	93	96	75	95.2
5.	Haryana	7	6	4	5	36	11.6
6.	Himachal Pradesh	2	19	34	17	7	15.8
7.	Jammu & Kashmir	—	4	—	—	—	0.8
8.	Karnataka	55	26	32	49	82	48.8
9.	Kerala	22	20	37	7	11	19.4
10.	Madhya Pradesh	128	117	446	202	235	225.6
11.	Maharashtra	328	273	596	428	484	421.8
12.	Manipur	—	—	—	—	—	—
13.	Meghalaya	—	—	—	4	8	2.4
14.	Nagaland	5	2	—	—	—	1.4
15.	Orissa	60	29	110	104	76	75.8
16.	Punjab	5	5	7	2	5	4.8
17.	Rajasthan	27	55	51	71	97	60.2
18.	Tamil Nadu	64	57	62	153	102	87.6
19.	Tripura	14	—	2	—	—	3.2
20.	Uttar Pradesh	85	114	97	79	76	90.2
21.	West Bengal	n.a.	6	10	53	n.a.	22.7
22.	Sikkim	—	—	—	—	—	—
	Union Territories						
1.	Andaman & Nicobar Islands	1	—	—	—	5	1.2
2.	Arunachal Pradesh	—	—	—	—	—	—
3.	Chandigarh	—	—	—	—	2	0.4
4.	Dadra & Nagar Haveli	—	—	—	3	—	0.6
5.	Delhi	—	—	n.a.	2	9	2.8
6.	Goa	1	—	1	12	10	4.8
7.	Lakshadweep	—	—	—	—	—	—
8.	Mizoram	—	—	n.a.	—	—	—
9.	Pondicherry	1	—	—	—	—	0.2

women with respect to theft has been on the increase since 1971. Against 1,210 arrests made in 1971, as many as 1,655 women were arrested in 1975, showing an increase of 36.8 percent. Madhya Pradesh ranks next with an average of 659.4 arrests per annum. However, there the trend in the period from 1971 to 1975 was erratic. The number of arrests was 604 in 1971, 599 in 1972, 879 in 1973, 623 in 1974, and again 592 in 1975. Tamil Nadu rates third with an annual average of 535.2 arrests. The highest num-

Table 7. Theft: Number of Women Arrested

S. No.	States	1971	1972	1973	1974	1975	Average
1.	Andhra Pradesh	99	148	47	248	216	151.6
2.	Assam	20	37	134	55	n.a.	61.50
3.	Bihar	169	225	507	325	303	305.8
4.	Gujarat	318	331	381	327	702	411.8
5.	Haryana	12	13	15	17	66	24.6
6.	Himachal Pradesh	3	68	46	67	36	44.0
7.	Jammu & Kashmir	7	12	—	—	21	8.0
8.	Karnataka	188	142	185	188	230	186.6
9.	Kerala	118	145	101	136	130	126.0
10.	Madhya Pradesh	604	599	879	623	592	659.4
11.	Maharashtra	1,210	1,321	1,392	1,609	1,655	1,437.4
12.	Manipur	—	—	—	—	—	—
13.	Meghalaya	n.a.	—	4	5	—	2.2
14.	Nagaland	10	10	7	20	—	9.4
15.	Orissa	152	172	433	274	195	245.2
16.	Punjab	18	26	23	12	19	19.6
17.	Rajasthan	49	169	168	95	216	139.4
18.	Tamil Nadu	833	363	311	616	553	535.2
19.	Tripura	20	—	1	15	9	9.0
20.	Uttar Pradesh	348	266	173	145	201	226.6
21.	West Bengal	n.a.	92	168	302	n.a.	187.3
22.	Sikkim	—	—	—	—	3	3.0
	Union Territories						
1.	Andaman & Nicobar Islands	—	1	1	—	—	0.4
2.	Arunachal Pradesh	—	—	n.a.	—	—	—
3.	Chandigarh	8	5	2	1	6	4.4
4.	Dadra & Nagar Haveli	—	—	1	—	1	0.4
5.	Delhi	—	—	n.a.	40	28	17.0
6.	Goa	7	19	11	22	30	17.8
7.	Lakshadweep	—	—	—	—	—	—
8.	Mizoram	—	—	n.a.	1	2	0.8
9.	Pondicherry	5	13	23	1	4	9.2

ber of arrests, 833, in Tamil Nadu was reported in 1971. It dropped to 311 in 1973 but rose again to 553 in 1975. Fourth in the order of arrests is Gujarat which reported an annual average of 411.8. Bihar had an annual average figure of 305.8 arrests, followed by Orissa for which the average stood at 245.2 arrests. In Uttar Pradesh, the incidence of theft by women is comparatively small, the figure being 226.6. In all other states, the incidence is below 200 arrests per annum.

27. Amongst the Union Territories, Delhi reported the highest average arrest figure of 17, followed by Pondicherry, where this figure stood at 9.2. Arunachal Pradesh and Lakshadweep did not report any arrest since 1971.

28. It would thus be seen that the States where special attention is required to deal with the problem of theft by women are Maharashtra, Madhya Pradesh, Tamil Nadu, Gujarat, Bihar, Orissa, and Uttar Pradesh.

Dacoity. 29. As regards dacoity, statistics on women arrested for this offence may be found in Table 8. There are some States where no arrest for

Table 8.   Dacoity: Number of Women Arrested

S. No.	States	1971	1972	1973	1974	1975	Average
1.	Andhra Pradesh	20	1	2	6	1	6.0
2.	Assam	1	1	1	—	n.a.	0.8
3.	Bihar	—	4	—	6	5	3.0
4.	Gujarat	1	2	3	6	2	2.8
5.	Haryana	—	—	—	—	—	—
6.	Himachal Pradesh	—	—	—	5	—	1.0
7.	Jammu & Kashmir	—	—	—	—	—	—
8.	Karnataka	—	2	2	3	7	2.8
9.	Kerala	—	—	8	—	—	1.6
10.	Madhya Pradesh	—	3	—	7	1	2.2
11.	Maharashtra	30	38	148	56	71	54.4
12.	Manipur	—	—	—	—	—	—
13.	Meghalaya	—	—	—	—	—	—
14.	Nagaland	—	—	—	—	—	—
15.	Orissa	—	—	1	—	13	2.8
16.	Punjab	—	—	—	—	—	—
17.	Rajasthan	—	3	—	—	9	1.4
18.	Tamil Nadu	—	—	—	—	—	—
19.	Tripura	—	—	—	—	—	—
20.	Uttar Pradesh	51	68	26	22	24	38.2
21.	West Bengal	—	9	20	33	n.a.	15.5
22.	Sikkim	—	—	—	—	—	—
	Union Territories						
1.	Andaman & Nicobar Islands	—	—	—	—	—	—
2.	Arunachal Pradesh	—	—	n.a.	—	—	—
3.	Chandigarh	—	—	—	—	—	—
4.	Dadra & Nagar Haveli	—	—	—	—	—	—
5.	Delhi	—	—	na.	—	—	—
6.	Goa	—	—	—	—	—	—
7.	Lakshadweep	—	—	—	—	—	—
8.	Mizoram	—	—	n.a.	—	—	—
9.	Pondicherry	—	—	n.a.	—	n.a.	—

this offence was made in the period from 1971 to 1975. These are Assam, Haryana, Jammu and Kashmir, Manipur, Meghalaya, Nagaland, Punjab, Tamil Nadu, and Assam. In the Union Territories, no arrest was made anywhere. The maximum average number of arrests was in Maharashtra (54.4), followed by Uttar Pradesh (38.2) and West Bengal (15.5). In other States, the incidence of this crime was negligible.

Robbery. 30. Coming to robbery, statistics of arrests of women are contained in Table 9. No arrest was reported from Assam, Jammu and Kashmir,

Table 9.   Robbery: Number of Women Arrested

S. No.	States	1971	1972	1973	1974	1975	Average
1.	Andhra Pradesh	—	—	—	1	2	0.6
2.	Assam	—	—	—	—	n.a.	—
3.	Bihar	—	—	—	2	—	0.4
4.	Gujarat	13	5	3	14	8	8.6
5.	Haryana	—	—	—	—	1	0.2
6.	Himachal Pradesh	—	1	3	—	—	0.8
7.	Jammu & Kashmir	—	—	—	—	—	—
8.	Karnataka	3	—	3	—	5	2.2
9.	Kerala	2	7	3	1	1	2.8
10.	Madhya Pradesh	1	4	42	3	2	10.4
11.	Maharashtra	39	28	83	55	47	50.4
12.	Manipur	—	—	—	—	—	—
13.	Meghalaya	—	—	—	—	—	—
14.	Nagaland	—	—	—	—	—	—
15.	Orissa	—	—	21	—	—	4.2
16.	Punjab	—	—	—	—	—	—
17.	Rajasthan	1	10	9	41	49	22.0
18.	Tamil Nadu	1	—	3	3	1	1.6
19.	Tripura	1	—	—	—	—	0.2
20.	Uttar Pradesh	20	8	5	4	6	8.6
21.	West Bengal	—	—	—	—	n.a.	—
22.	Sikkam	—	—	—	—	—	—
	Union Territories						
1.	Andaman & Nicobar Islands	—	1	2	—	2	1.0
2.	Arunachal Pradesh	—	—	n.a.	—	—	—
3.	Chandigarh	—	—	—	—	—	—
4.	Dadra & Nagar Haveli	—	—	—	—	—	—
5.	Delhi	—	—	n.a.	—	—	—
6.	Goa	2	1	—	1	—	0.8
7.	Lakshadweep	—	—	—	—	—	—
8.	Mizoram	—	—	—	—	—	—
9.	Pondicherry	—	—	—	—	—	—

Manipur, Meghalaya, Nagaland, Punjab, and West Bengal. Except in Andaman and Nicobar Islands and Goa, no arrest for robbery was made in any other Union Territory.

31. The maximum average arrest for this crime was reported from Maharashtra (50.4), followed by Rajasthan (22). Uttar Pradesh reported 8.6 and Gujarat also reported 8.6 arrests in a year.

Kidnapping and Abduction. 32. Statistics of kidnapping and abduction may be found in Table 10. As already mentioned, women are mostly used as accomplices in this crime, and, in many cases, the offence is purely of a

Table 10.   Kidnapping and Abduction: Number of Women Arrested

S. No.	States	1971	1972	1973	1974	1975	Average
1.	Andhra Pradesh	14	2	9	14	19	11.6
2.	Assam	10	7	11	2	n.a.	7.5
3.	Bihar	47	16	69	64	73	53.8
4.	Gujarat	16	12	8	21	19	15.2
5.	Haryana	1	3	7	5	3	3.8
6.	Himachal Pradesh	1	30	30	4	20	17.0
7.	Jammu & Kashmir	—	21	8	7	5	8.2
8.	Karnataka	8	2	2	14	2	5.6
9.	Kerala	1	9	—	—	1	2.2
10.	Madhya Pradesh	18	23	—	32	44	23.4
11.	Maharashtra	30	52	62	66	76	57.2
12.	Manipur	—	—	—	—	—	—
13.	Meghalaya	—	3	—	3	3	1.8
14.	Nagaland	—	—	—	5	—	1.0
15.	Orissa	—	6	2	—	—	1.6
16.	Punjab	35	36	24	26	18	27.8
17.	Rajasthan	31	36	33	62	57	43.8
18.	Tamil Nadu	12	15	9	11	7	10.8
19.	Tripura	—	—	—	5	—	1.0
20.	Uttar Pradesh	205	179	163	91	101	147.8
21.	West Bengal	—	27	18	47	n.a.	23.0
22.	Sikkim	—	—	—	—	—	—
	Union Territories						
1.	Andaman & Nicobar Islands	—	—	2	—	—	0.4
2.	Arunachal Pradesh	—	—	n.a.	—	—	—
3.	Chandigarh	—	1	3	1	1	1.2
4.	Dadra & Nagar Haveli	—	2	—	—	—	0.4
5.	Delhi	—	—	n.a.	12	22	8.5
6.	Goa	—	—	—	—	2	0.4
7.	Lakshadweep	—	—	—	—	—	—
8.	Mizoram	—	—	n.a.	—	—	—
9.	Pondicherry	—	—	—	9	5	2.8

technical nature. The incidence of this crime was the highest in Uttar Pradesh (147.8), followed by Maharashtra (57.2), Bihar (53.8), Rajasthan (43.8), and Punjab (27.8). In Madhya Pradesh, and West Bengal also, the incidence was high with the average annual arrest figure of 23.4, and 23. In other States, the incidence was below 20 arrests per annum.

33. As regards the Union Territories, Delhi topped with 8.5 arrests per annum, followed by Pondicherry with the figure of 2.8. Arunachal Pradesh, Lakshadweep, and Mizoram did not report any arrest in the last five years.

White-collar Crimes. 34. As regards the involvement of women in the white-collar crime of cheating and criminal breach of trust, the statistics are set forth in Table 11. There are a few states where no such case was reported in the period from 1971 to 1975. These are Meghalaya, Nagaland, Manipur, and Tripura. In the Union Territories, no case was reported from Andaman and Nicobar Islands, Arunachal Pradesh, Chandigarh, Dadra and Nagar Haveli, and Lakshadweep.

35. In Maharashtra, the incidence of this crime seems to be high. On an average, 58.8 arrests were made per annum between 1971 and 1975. This could be due to a large concentration of urban population in some big cities of Maharashtra like Bombay, Poona, and Nagpur. Madhya Pradesh reported an average figure of 22.6 arrests in a year followed by Karnataka (19), Gujarat (18.6), and Andhra Pradesh (18.4). Tamil Nadu and Uttar Pradesh reported 17.8 and 16 arrests per annum, respectively. Kerala also reported a high incidence with an annual average figure of 16.8. In other areas, the incidence of this crime was small.

Total I.P.C. crimes. 36. The distribution of total I.P.C. crimes amongst States and Union Territories may be seen in Table 12. In the absence of a definite trend, it would be worthwhile to rely on the average annual figure of arrests. Maharashtra has reported the highest incidence of I.P.C. crimes amongst women with an average annual figure of 4,255 arrests. West Bengal comes next with 3,779 arrests, followed by Kerala (2,678), Tamil Nadu (2,168.80), and Andhra Pradesh (2,048.20). Gujarat (1,606.60), Madhya Pradesh (1,580), Uttar Pradesh (1,580), Karnataka (1,469), Rajasthan (1,-344), and Bihar (1,245.80) also reported a high incidence of I.P.C. crimes by women.

37. Coming to the Union Territories, Pondicherry topped the list with the average figure of 339.20 arrests per year, followed by Delhi with a figure of 134.66.

38. To sum up, it would appear that the highest incidence of I.P.C. crimes amongst women was in Maharashtra, followed by West Bengal, Kerala, Tamil Nadu, and Andhra Pradesh, in that order. In the Union Territories, Pondicherry reported a high incidence followed by Delhi.

Table 11. Cheating and Criminal Breach of Trust: Number of Women Arrested

S. No.	States	1971	1972	1973	1974	1975	Average
1.	Andhra Pradesh	6	2	54	9	21	18.4
2.	Assam	—	—	3	—	n.a.	0.7
3.	Bihar	16	1	7	16	25	13.0
4.	Gujarat	18	5	16	21	33	18.6
5.	Haryana	—	3	3	3	1	2.0
6.	Himachal Pradesh	—	14	3	3	3	4.6
7.	Jammu & Kashmir	—	2	1	—	—	0.6
8.	Karnataka	12	16	41	10	16	19.0
9.	Kerala	8	23	19	20	14	16.8
10.	Madhya Pradesh	12	13	21	45	22	22.6
11.	Maharashtra	27	46	54	30	137	58.8
12.	Manipur	—	—	—	—	—	—
13.	Meghalaya	—	—	—	—	—	—
14.	Nagaland	—	—	—	—	—	—
15.	Orissa	1	—	13	—	—	2.8
16.	Punjab	1	4	5	—	7	3.4
17.	Rajasthan	4	13	7	4	6	6.8
18.	Tamil Nadu	12	15	12	26	24	17.8
19.	Tripura	—	—	—	—	—	—
20.	Uttar Pradesh	28	18	6	12	16	16.0
21.	West Bengal	—	11	3	7	n.a.	5.2
22.	Sikkim	—	—	—	—	1	1.0
	Union Territories						
1.	Andaman & Nicobar Islands	—	—	—	—	—	—
2.	Arunachal Pradesh	—	—	—	—	—	—
3.	Chandigarh	—	—	—	—	—	—
4.	Dadra & Nagar Haveli	—	—	—	—	—	—
5.	Delhi	—	—	n.a.	7	2	2.2
6.	Goa	2	1	—	6	4	2.6
7.	Lakshadweep	—	—	—	—	—	—
8.	Mizoram	—	—	—	2	2	1.0
9.	Pondicherry	3	1	—	—	—	—

39. The breakdown of arrest figures according to age, occupation, marital status, education, and religion was not available.

III. Female Convicts

A sample of 641 female convicts was taken for this study. Detailed information about the age, occupation, marital status, education, rural and urban

Table 12.   Total I.P.C. Crimes: Number of Women Arrested

S. No.	States	1971	1972	1973	1974	1975	Average
1.	Andhra Pradesh	596	3,689	3,346	1,098	2,108	2,048.20
2.	Assam	166	1,807	628	798	n.a.	849.75
3.	Bihar	682	1,772	1,279	1,726	770	1,245.80
4.	Gujarat	1,026	1,398	1,419	1,596	2,594	1,606.60
5.	Haryana	50	44	155	41	206	99.2
6.	Himachal Pradesh	54	533	659	538	854	527.60
7.	Jammu & Kashmir	43	458	849	121	174	329.00
8.	Karnataka	2,031	1,262	1,206	1,499	1,347	1,469.00
9.	Kerala	1,284	3,433	n.a.	3,371	2,624	2,678.00
10.	Madhya Pradesh	1,409	1,742	463	1,968	2,320	1,580.00
11.	Maharashtra	3,792	3,920	4,484	4,416	4,663	4,255.00
12.	Manipur	n.a.	1	—	—	—	0.25
13.	Meghalaya	—	10	21	21	38	18.00
14.	Nagaland	n.a.	17	7	30	2	14.00
15.	Orissa	441	456	783	835	403	583.60
16.	Punjab	263	454	390	235	202	308.80
17.	Rajasthan	697	1,421	1,464	1,291	1,847	1,344.00
18.	Tamil Nadu	1,341	2,246	3,125	2,559	1,573	2,168.80
19.	Tripura	48	1	5	23	10	17.40
20.	Uttar Pradesh	2,040	1,634	1,145	1,446	1,635	1,580.00
21.	West Bengal	n.a.	1,349	8,622	1,366	n.a.	3,779.00
22.	Sikkim	—	—	—	—	14	14.00
	Union Territories						
1.	Andaman & Nicobar Islands	10	4	17	18	29	15.60
2.	Arunachal Pradesh	—	—	n.a.	2	—	.50
3.	Chandigarh	1	8	32	6	9	11.20
4.	Dadra & Nagar Haveli	15	2	3	6	2	5.60
5.	Delhi	n.a.	—	n.a.	253	151	134.66
6.	Goa	19	36	32	77	79	48.60
7.	Lakshadweep	—	—	—	—	—	—
8.	Mizoram	—	—	—	3	8	2.20
9.	Pondicherry	259	194	543	423	277	339.20

background, length of sentence, and socioeconomic background of female convicts who had been lodged in jail between 1968 and 1975 was collected. The sample was chosen from the Central Jail of Delhi, Nari Bandi Niketan of Lucknow, Naini Central Jail, Allahabad and District Jails of Fatehgarh, Mathura and Kanpur. The actual sample was determined in consultation with the Jail Administration, keeping in view the number of female convicts lodged in a particular jail. Unlike women offenders where analysis of their arrest (only) under I.P.C. offences was made, this sample of female convicts was selected at random, from all types of offences including local and special laws, vagrancy, among others.

2. An important factor which should be borne in mind is that the female suspect/criminal receives differential treatment at all levels of the criminal justice system. First, there is the reluctance on the part of the victim to report her. Then, there is the informal advice of the police officer to the complainant to "think twice" before reporting her. If the victim insists on a report, in many cases the offence is diluted in favour of the women. At the trial stage, some consideration is shown to her at least in the sentencing tariff. It follows that trends revealed by the study of 641 convicts can only be relied upon unreservedly to draw broad conclusions about the extent and nature of criminality amongst women. In any case, the results of the survey can be safely used to formulate policies in regard to prevention, correction and rehabilitation of women criminals because the only women who are incarcerated are those whose behaviour is so patently undesirable or socially dysfunctional so as to escape compassion at the various levels up to and inclusive of sentencing.

3. Table 13 will highlight the nature of offences committed by the female convicts in our sample.

4. The figures in Table 13 show that out of 641 female convicts, as many as 24.5 percent were responsible for murder and or murderous assault. Fifteen percent were undergoing sentences for theft/house breaking. Travelling

Table 13.   Classification of Female Convicts by Offence

1. Murder and/or murderous assault	157(24.5%)
2. Kidnapping/abduction	52(8.1%)
3. Theft/house breaking	96(15.0%)
4. Cheating	12(1.8%)
5. Trespassing	5(0.8%)
6. Forming unlawful assemblies (rioting)	15(2.3%)
7. Miscellaneous offenses under I.P.C. (including 28 hurt cases)	59(9.2%)
8. Illicit distillation and sales	62(9.7%)
9. Begging (under Bombay Police Act and Police Act)	44(6.9%)
10. Immoral traffic	16(2.5%)
11. Travelling without a ticket in trains	51(8.0%)
12. Unauthorized possession of arms	11(1.7%)
13. Miscellaneous offenses under local and special laws	17(2.7%)
14. Arrest under breach of peace	12(1.8%)
15. Arrest under vagrancy and habitual offenders	32(5.3%)
Total	641(100.0%)

without ticket in trains accounted for 8 percent, while another 8.1 percent were undergoing sentence for the offence of kidnapping and abduction. As many as 5 percent were there on account of vagrancy and repeat offence and 6.9 percent for begging. This means that begging and vagrancy were responsible for 11.9 percent of the cases, and 9.7% of the female convicts were sentenced for distilling or selling illicit liquor. Cheating and criminal breach of peace accounted for 2.6 percent, and 2.3 percent of the convicts had been sentenced in rioting cases. Sentences in murder and murderous assault cases are necessarily of a longer duration. That is why the largest number of female convicts (24.5 percent) belongs to this category. Otherwise, theft and house breaking, which constitute 15 percent of the convicts should be construed to occupy the first place. This is in conformity with the trend over all of India noted for female offenders in the foregoing section when we pointed out that thefts and burglaries are responsible for the highest number of arrest of women in India (27.93 percent in 1975).

5. Female convicts were also divided by age. Table 14 contains statistics to highlight age groups.

Table 14. Classification of Female Convicts by Age Group

20 Years and Under	21–24 Years	25–29 Years	30–39 Years	40–49 Years	50–59 Years	60 Years and Above	Age Not Known	Total
55	50	57	155	142	66	40	76	641
8.58	7.80	8.89	24.18	22.15	10.30	6.24	11.86	100.0

6. The figures in Table 14 show that the highest number of convicts, 24.18 percent, were in the age group of 30 to 39 years, followed by 22.15 percent in the age group of 40 to 49 years. In the age group of 50 to 59 years, there were 10.30 percent of the convicts. The lowest percentage of convicts, 6.24 percent, was in the age group of 60 years and above. Juveniles in the age group of 20 years and under accounted for 8.58 percent. Women in the age group of 21 to 24 years and in the age group of 25 to 29 years were 7.80 and 8.89 percent, respectively. It may be noted that 11.86 percent of women convicts did not state their age.

The statistics also reveal that young women in the age group of 21 to 24, 25 to 29 and 30 to 39 together accounted for 40.8 percent of the convicts. It shows that correctional and rehabilitational programmes should be undertaken by the government and the social reformer with a view to ensuring that such a large number of youthful offenders do not take to vagrancy or repeat offence after release from jail. The problem of reintegrating them with their children and other family members and relatives also needs attention.

7. Female convicts were further classified to relate age of the convicts with the type of offence committed. The statistics in this regard are presented in Table 15.

8. It can be seen that women in the age group of 30 to 39 years were responsible for the highest number of murder/murderous assaults, kidnapping and abduction, illicit distillation, and travelling without a ticket in a

Table 15. Classification of Female Convicts by Offence and Age

	Under 20 Years	21–24 Years	25–29 Years	30–39 Years	40–49 Years	50–59 Years	60 Years and Above	Age Not Known	Total
Murder and murderous assault	12	14	20	46	29	16	3	17	157
Kidnapping/abduction	2	1	3	16	10	5	7	8	52
Theft/house breaking	8	8	9	24	27	13	3	4	96
Cheating	1	—	2	2	1	—	4	2	12
Trespassing	—	—	—	2	2	1	—	—	5
Forming unlawful assemblies	—	—	—	1	—	—	—	14	15
Misc. offences under I.P.C.	2	6	7	15	8	8	7	6	59
Illicit distillation and sales	2	3	2	19	13	8	4	11	62
Begging under Bombay Police Act	4	1	3	8	18	3	—	7	44
Immoral traffic	1	4	3	1	3	1	1	2	16
Travelling without a ticket in railways	8	3	5	13	11	6	5	—	51
Unauthorized possession of arms	1	2	—	—	4	—	3	1	11
Misc. offences under local and special laws	—	1	2	3	4	4	2	1	17
Arrests under breach of peace	3	2	—	3	4	—	—	—	12
Arrest under vagrancy and habitual offenders	11	5	1	2	8	1	1	3	32
Total	55	50	57	155	142	66	40	76	641

train. Further, out of a total of 157 convicts sentenced for murder and/or for murderous assaults, as many as 46 (29.2 percent) belonged to the age group between 30 and 39 years, followed by 29 (18.4 percent) in the age group of 40 to 49 years. The age group of 25 to 29 years came next with 20 (12.7 percent) convicts. Regarding kidnapping and abduction, as many as 16 (30.7 percent) convicts belonged to the age group of 30 to 39 years, followed by 10 (19.2 percent) in the age group of 40 to 49 years and 7 (13.4 percent) in the age group of 60 years and above. For theft and house breaking, the first place was occupied by the age group of 40 to 49 years with 27 convicts (28.1 percent), followed by 24 convicts (25 percent) in the age group of 30 to 39 years and 13 convicts (13.5 percent) in the age group of 50 to 59 years. For the offences of illicit distillation and sale of liquor, the maximum number 19 (30.6 percent) was in the age group of 30 to 39 years. This was followed by 13 convicts (20.9 percent) in the age group of 40 to 49 years and 8 (12.9 percent) in the age group of 50 to 59 years. For begging, the maximum number (18) was in the age group of 40 to 49, followed by 8 in the age group 30 to 39 years. In immoral traffic offences, the maximum number, 4, was in the age group of 21 to 24, followed by the age group of 25 to 29 years with 3 convicts.

9. The statistics also reveal that the preponderance of convicts for offences against property, namely, thefts and house breakings, belong to the age group of 30 to 49 years (51 convicts out of 96 were undergoing sentence for these offenses. (53.6 percent).

10. The data on the 641 female convicts were also classified to show age by length of sentence. These statistics are presented in Table 16.

11. It can be seen that the maximum number of female convicts undergoing life imprisonment were in the age group of 30 to 39 years, followed by convicts in the age group of 40 to 49 years and 25 to 29 years, the number being 36 (30.3 percent), 22 (18.5 percent) and 15 (12.6 percent), respectively.

12. Statistics with respect to the 641 convicts according to the length of sentence are presented in Table 17.

13. It can be seen that as many as 25.74 percent of the convicts were undergoing imprisonment of up to one month, followed by those undergoing life imprisonment, 18.56 percent, 13.10 percent were sentenced to undergo imprisonment between 6 and 12 months, 12.64 percent imprisonment between 3 to 6 months, 9.52 percent to imprisonment of one to two years and 8.42 percent to imprisonment of 1 to 3 months. Those undergoing imprisonment of three to five years constituted 5.46 percent, 3.59% for two to three years and .94 percent for five to seven years. Details of the sentence of ten convicts could not be ascertained at the time of visit.

Table 16. Classification of Female Convicts by Age and Length of Sentence

Length of Sentence	20 Years and Under	21–24 Years	25–29 Years	30–39 Years	40–49 Years	50–59 Years	60 Years and Above	Age Not Known	Tota
0–1 month	15	10	12	34	36	18	10	30	16?
1–2 months	3	6	5	14	11	2	4	9	5?
3–6 months	13	7	5	22	21	4	6	3	8?
6–12 months	7	9	4	20	19	9	5	11	84
1–2 years	2	4	9	10	15	11	5	5	6?
2–3 years	4	1	1	4	7	3	3	—	2?
3–5 years	1	2	4	8	8	5	6	1	3?
5–7 years	1	—	—	3	1	—	—	1	?
7–10 years	—	1	1	1	—	—	—	—	?
Over 10 years	—	—	—	—	—	—	—	—	—
Life Imprisonment	8	10	15	36	22	12	1	15	11?
Unknown	1	—	1	3	2	2	—	1	1C
Total	55	50	57	155	142	66	40	76	64?

Table 17. Classification of Female Convicts by Length of Sentence

Length of Sentence	Number of Convicts	Percentage
0–1 months	165	25.74
1–3 months	54	8.42
3–6 months	81	12.64
6–12 months	84	13.10
1–2 years	61	9.52
2–3 years	23	3.59
3–5 years	35	5.46
5–7 years	6	0.94
7–10 years	3	0.47
Over 10 years	—	—
Life imprisonment	119	18.56
Sentence not known	10	1.56
Total	641	100.0

It can be seen that as many as 60 percent of the convicts were found to be undergoing imprisonment of up to 12 months. This supports the findings of many criminologists that, in the matter of sentencing, women suspects are treated leniently by the courts.

14. Figures were also analyzed to highlight offences vis-à-vis length of sentence. The relevant statistics may be found in Table 18.

Table 18. Offense by Length of Sentence

Offense	0–1 Months	1–3 Months	3–6 Months	6–12 Months	1–2 Years	2–3 Years	3–5 Years	5–7 Years	7–10 Years	10 Years and Above	Life	Unknown	Total
Under I.P.C.													
1. Murder and murderous assault	—	—	1	2	5	5	10	3	3	—	119	9	157
2. Kidnapping/abduction	—	2	1	15	8	11	14	1	—	—	—	—	52
3. Theft/house breaking	5	13	28	25	18	1	5	1	—	—	—	—	96
4. Cheating	—	—	1	5	4	1	1	—	—	—	—	—	12
5. Trespassing	3	2	—	—	—	—	—	—	—	—	—	—	5
6. Forming unlawful assemblies	15	—	—	—	—	—	—	—	—	—	—	—	15
7. Misc. offenses under I.P.C.	15	2	10	8	14	4	4	1	—	—	—	1	59
Under Local and Special Laws													
1. Illicit Distillation and sale etc.	20	15	17	9	1	—	—	—	—	—	—	—	62
2. Begging (under Bombay Police Act)	31	—	—	2	11	—	—	—	—	—	—	—	44
3. Immoral traffic	7	7	—	—	—	1	1	—	—	—	—	—	16
4. Travelling without a ticket in railways	51	—	—	—	—	—	—	—	—	—	—	—	51
5. Unauthorized possession of arms	4	6	—	1	—	—	—	—	—	—	—	—	11
6. Misc. offenses under local and special laws	11	2	3	1	—	—	—	—	—	—	—	—	17
Under Cr. P.C.													
1. Breach of peace	2	—	5	5	—	—	—	—	—	—	—	—	12
2. Vagrancy and habitual offenders	1	5	15	11	—	—	—	—	—	—	—	—	32
Total	165	54	81	84	61	23	35	6	3	—	119	10	641

The figures show that the maximum number of female convicts to be given a short sentence of between three to six months was for the offences of theft and house breaking (28), followed by excise offences (17), vagrancy and repeat offences (15), and miscellaneous I.P.C. offences (10). The sentence of five to seven years was given in one case of kidnapping, one case of theft/house breaking and one case under miscellaneous I.P.C., apart from three cases of murder and murderous assault. The sentence of three to five years was given in as many as 14 cases of kidnapping/abduction, 10 cases of murder/murderous assault, five cases of theft/house breaking, one case of cheating, four cases under miscellaneous I.P.C. and one case under immoral traffic. The sentence of two to three years was given in five cases of murder/murderous assault, 11 cases of kidnapping/abduction, four cases of miscellaneous I.P.C., one case of theft/house breaking, one case of cheating, and one case of immoral traffic. The sentence of one to two years was given in five cases of murder/murderous assault, eight cases of kidnapping/abduction, 18 cases of theft/house breaking, four cases of cheating, 14 cases under miscellaneous I.P.C., one case under the Excise Act and 11 cases of begging. The sentence of 6 to 12 months was given in two cases of murder/murderous assaults, 15 cases of kidnapping and abduction, 25 cases of theft/burglary, five cases of cheating, eight cases under miscellaneous I.P.C., nine cases under the Excise Act, two cases of begging, two cases under the Arms and other acts, five cases of breach of peace and 11 cases of vagrancy/repeat offence. The sentence of three to six months was given in one case of murderous assault, one case of kidnapping/abduction, 28 cases of theft and house breaking, one case of cheating, 10 cases under miscellaneous I.P.C., 18 cases under the Excise Act, five cases of breach of peace, 15 cases of vagrancy and repeat offence and three other cases.

15. For the offence of theft/house breaking, 28 of the 96 convicts (29.1 percent) were sentenced to a term of three to six months and 25 (26.04 percent) were sentenced to undergo imprisonment between 6 to 12 months. For murder/murderous assault, 119 convicts out of a total of 157 (25.8 percent) were sentenced to life imprisonment. For kidnapping and abduction, the maximum number, 15 out of 52 (28.8 percent), were sentenced to undergo imprisonment of 6 to 12 months. For illicit distillation and sale of illicit liquor, the highest number was 20 out of 62 (32.2 percent) sentenced to undergo imprisonment of up to one month. This was also true for the offence of begging where 31 out of 44 (70.4 percent) convicts were undergoing imprisonment of one month. For the offence of travelling without ticket in train, all the 51 convicts were undergoing imprisonment of up to one month.

16. It can be seen that short sentences of up to one month were given to 165 out of 641 convicts, that is, 25.7 percent. This fact cannot be ignored by those interested in tackling the problem of criminality amongst women because steps must be taken by the police, the Social Welfare Department and other agencies to ensure that women released from jail after undergoing short sentences are reunited with their families and do not fall into the bad habit of repeating crimes. It is this category of offenders whose repeat offence habits can lead to increased criminality in the years to come.

17. Efforts were also made to find out, as far as possible, the occupation, rural and urban background, marital status and education of the female convicts. Statistics in this regard are contained in Tables 19, 20, 21, and 22.

Table 19. Classification of Female Convicts by Occupation

Total	Housewife	Service	Domestic Work	Student	Laborer	Vendor	Prostitute	Agriculture
641	231	27	38	1	119	19	3	203
100	36	4.2	5.9	0.1	18.5	3.0	0.5	31.7

Table 20. Classification of Female Convicts by Rural and Urban Background

Total	Rural	Urban	Not Given
641	267	367	7
100.0	41.6	57.3	1.1

Table 21. Classification of Female Convicts by Marital Status

Total	Married	Unmarried	Widow	Divorcee
641	590	48	2	1
100.0	92	7.5	0.3	0.2

Table 22. Classification of Female Convicts by Education

Total	Literate	Illiterate
641	24	617
100.0	3.7	96.3

It can be seen that 36 percent of the convicts were housewives, 31.7 percent were engaged in agriculture, 18.5 percent were working as laborers, 5.9 percent were engaged in domestic work, 4.2 percent were in service, 3 percent were vendors, .5 percent were prostitutes and .2 percent were students. This reveals that a majority of the female convicts were housewives, agriculturists, and laborers (86.2 percent of the total).

18. It can be seen that 57.3 percent of the convicts came from urban areas, whereas 41.6 percent lived in rural areas (1.1 percent did not disclose their residential address). This confirms the belief that more women are subject to deviant behavior in urban areas on account of the concentration of heterogenous communities & more tensions.

19. It can be seen that out of 641 female convicts, 92 percent were married and 7.5 percent were unmarried (.3 percent were widows and .2 percent were divorcees). Married women may have committed more crimes on account of the operation of factors like strained family relations, temperamental incompatibility, domestic quarrels, and property disputes.

20. It can be seen that 96.3 percent of the convicts were illiterate and only 3.7 percent were educated. There is need for further research to find out the causes which have led to more criminality amongst illiterate women. The basic reason seems to be the lack of social & other opportunities among the illiterate for attaining the desirable level of integration with the family and the society in general.

21. An attempt was also made to collect data to determine the mode of committing the offence of murder by the female convicts. This information was collected for 56 murder cases and is contained in Table 23.

Table 23. Mode of Committing Murder

Sharp Weapon	Strangu- lation	Poison	Firearms	Burning	Total
43	6	4	1	2	56

It can be seen that as many as 43 murders (76.7 percent) were committed using sharp-edged weapons. In six cases, the victims were strangled; in four cases, the victims were poisoned; in one case the victim was shot; and two victims were burned.

IV. Conclusions

1. It is time that female crime was treated as a topic in its own right by the police, the social welfare organizations, and the jail authorities. Notwithstanding the fact that crimes committed by females are usually screened and are, therefore, grossly underreported, there is evidence to show that more and more female arrests have been reported and dealt with by the police since 1971. There is also evidence to show that a sizeable number of

women were found to have committed heinous crimes like murder, murderous assault, dacoity and robbery. It can be safely inferred that in the years to come, criminality amongst women is likely to go up.

2. The broad indications that have emerged from the present study are the following:

Female offenders. The study has revealed that the criminality amongst women did not exhibit a well-defined trend in the period from 1971 to 1975 but the number of women arrested increased 46.8 percent in 1975 when compared with the figures of arrest of 1971 (paragraph 2, Section II). When compared with the base year 1971, the rate of increase of female criminality in 1975 is more or less the same as that for male criminality (paragraph 4, section II). Crimes amongst female juveniles increased at a slower rate than amongst women of and above the age of 21 years. While the rate of increase of crime by female juveniles was 31.6 percent in 1975 compared with 1971, the rate of increase of crime by women of and above the age of 21 years was 48.5 percent in the same period (paragraph 7, section II). Female crime per lakh of female population increased in many other countries including the U.S.A., West Germany, Japan, Ireland, as it has in India and Scotland. In some countries, criminality amongst women has been constantly on the increase since 1971 (paragraphs 10 and 11, section II). Theft constituted the greatest proportion of crimes among women in India. This is true for other countries as well. In 1975, 21.80 percent of the total arrests of women was for theft (paragraph 13, section II). The percentage of arrest of women in murder cases is higher in India than in other countries (paragraph 16, section II). More and more women are being arrested for involvement in white collar crimes (paragraph 2, section II). Women have also been arrested in heinous crimes like dacoity and robbery (paragraph 19, section II). Maharashtra reported the highest number of arrests of women in I.P.C. crimes followed by West Bengal, Kerala, Tamil Nadu, Andhra Pradesh, Gujarat, Madhya Pradesh, Uttar Pradesh, Karnataka, Rajasthan, and Bihar. In the Union Territories, Pondicherry tops the list, followed by Delhi. In other states and Union Territories, the incidence of female criminality is not substantial (paragraphs 36 and 37, section II).

Female Convicts. Of the female convicts, 24.5 percent were undergoing imprisonment for the crime of murder and/or murderous assault. This was followed by the offence of theft/house breaking which accounted for 15 percent of the convicts. If the fact that sentences in murder and murderous asault cases are necessarily of a longer duration is taken into account, it would seem that, like female criminality, theft/burglary cases account for a very large percentage of female involvement (paragraph 4, section III).

Young women in the age group of 21 to 39 years accounted for as high as 40.87% of the convicts. (paragraph 6, section III). Women in the age group of 30 to 39 years were responsible for the commission of the highest number of murders/murderous assault, kidnapping and abduction, illicit distillation, and travelling without a ticket on a train. The highest number of women involved in theft and house breaking cases were found in the age group of 40 to 49 years. (paragraph 8, section III). The maximum number of life convicts were in the age group of 30 to 39 years (paragraph 11, section III). As many as 60 percent of the convicts had been given short sentence of one year or less (paragraph 13, section III). With respect to cases of theft/house breaking, it was found that the courts normally gave short sentence of between three to six months in the majority of cases (paragraph 14, section III). A large number of female convicts who were sentenced to imprisonment up to one month need special attention on release from jail to ward against repeat offence or vagrancy (paragraph 16, section III). Of the women criminals, 86.2 percent were found to be housewives engaged in agriculture and working as laborers (paragraph 17, section III). A majority of the criminals belonged to urban areas (paragraph 18, section III). Married women committed more crimes than unmarried women (paragraph 19, section III). As many as 96.3 percent of the women criminals undergoing sentence were illiterate (paragraph 20, section III). Women used a sharp-edged weapon in as many as 76.7 percent of the cases (paragraph 21, section III).

V. Comments

1. The objective of this study is to focus attention on the extent and nature of criminality amongst women in India. We have demonstrated with the help of published statistics and with the help of the sample study of 641 women convicts that criminality amongst women has increased in recent years and that women have been found to be involved even in heinous crimes like murder, murderous asault, dacoity, and robbery. There is little doubt that the criminality of the female has been increasing in some other countries also. But the comparison ends there. It is common knowledge that other countries have already recognized the necessity and importance of devoting special attention to female crime at all levels: the police, the courts, the jails and the rehabilitational institutions. Some of them, more notably England, have conducted extensive research on the behavior of women criminals in Borstals and Detention Centers with a view to finding out more effective methods for their reform and rehabilitation. Efforts have also been

made in those countries to devise methods and procedures by which repeat offences by women could be reduced to the minimum. Therefore, the problem of rising criminality amonst women may not pose insurmountable and uncontrollable problems in those countries because of their preparedness to deal with the same. In so far as India is concerned, there is no evidence of such preparedness. In our view, it is time that attention was devoted to this problem.

2. Some of the fields in which action should be initiated are mentioned below.

Police. It is evident that policemen will have to deal with an increasing number of women criminals in the years to come. More and more women suspects may have to be interrogated because the largest number amongst them are found to be involved in property offenses. Some of the police manuals have made specific provisions with regard to matters like detention of women. These instructions may require amplification where they exist, or incorporation in the police manuals where they do not exist to prevent misuse of authority and to ensure that any lack of clear instructions does not lead to resentment of the public with regard to the behavior of the police towards women suspects.

Problems of investigation in which women suspects may have to be interrogated also need attention. According to section 160 of the Code of Criminal Procedure, any police officer making an investigation may, by order in writing, require the attendance before himself of any person who appears to be acquainted with the facts and circumstances of the case *provided that* no woman shall be required to attend at any place *other than the place in which such woman resides*. In States and Union Territories where the number of women being arrested for crimes is substantial, there is a case for formulating clear and detailed departmental instructions in this regard laying down the minimum rank of the police officer who should handle investigations involving women or who should handle the interrogation of women in certain cases; the time of the day during which such interrogation should be considered advisable, the type and number of other persons who should be allowed to be present at the time of interrogation or questioning of the female suspect; the method of their transport to jail in case of judicial remand; and the procedure of their interrogation in jail. The role of women police, if they are competent to investigate and if they are readily available, should also be defined in these instructions.

Women have been found perpetrating a large number of property offences. As a matter of fact, the maximum number of arrests of women in India, as in some other countries, has been for the offence of theft, burglary, dacoity, or robbery. It is the duty of the police not only to investigate cases but also to prevent crimes, especially crimes against property. For this purpose, records of criminals are maintained at the police station and there is also a system of surveillance. Serious thought should be given by the police forces to the matter of maintenance of records on female criminals and the mode of their surveillance. Perhaps it will be difficult to follow the same system of surveillance of women criminals as is followed for men criminals.

Social Welfare and other Departments. The Department of Social Welfare should undertake programs to deal with the fact that more and more women are likely to be involved in crimes and sent to jails in the years to come and to tackle problems connected with the protection and rehabilitation of the deviant female. The work of various nongovernment and voluntary organizations engaged in this task should be coordinated.

The Jail Administration should also receive clear instructions dealing with women convicts. Procedures relating to their accommodation, food, privacy, remission, and interview should be redefined.

The possibility of associating experts with efforts of the Jail Administration to re-integrate the women convicts with their families on release should also be considered. It must be remembered that vagrancy in a woman is likely to be fraught with more dangers than vagrancy in a man.

The difficulty of obtaining statistics about female criminality is well understood, but this should not discourage further research and enquiry into this matter. If there is need for more research and further inquiry into any field, it is the field of the female criminal, her treatment, and her rehabilitation.

2. Emancipation of Women and Crime in Japan

K. S. SATO

Kinko Saito Sato is Councilor at the Office of the Prime Minister and has served with the Office of the Public Prosecutor, Ministry of Justice. Her primary interests in the field are criminal justice, criminology, and social criticism. She was a Japanese Government Representative to the Third Committee (Social,

Cultural and Humanitarian Committee) of the United Nations General Assembly (1976–77). Her publications include: *The Bargaining Society—American Criminal Justice (Torihiko-no-Shakai)* (Tokyo: Chuokoron, 1974), *The Yama and Goddess—Justice of the Japanese and the Americans (Enma-to-Megami)* (Kyoto: PHP, 1979).

I. Image of Japanese Women

1. Japanese women, rightly or wrongly, are often considered to be subordinate, polite, gentle, obedient, and tame. It is repeatedly said that happiness consists of living in an American apartment, eating Chinese food, and having a Japanese wife—or, to be exact, a Japanese maid. It is true that, for a long period, Mount Fuji and geisha girls were representative of the Japanese image. This image of Japanese women has a historical background.

During the Edo period (1603–1867), the role of a woman in society was very limited. Women were confined to the earthly mission of females— namely, though they received respect as wives and mothers, they counted for very little as a social-political unit. Women were commonly taught that they had no home of their own in the threefold world: this world, the previous life, and the next world. Therefore, a woman should obey her father as daughter, her husband as wife, and her son after the death of her husband.

Inazo Nitobe (1862–1933) in his noted book, *Bushido: The Soul of Japan,* clearly described an ideal woman under the code of moral principles of the fighting nobles, the samurai (warrior class);

> As daughter, woman sacrificed herself for her father, as wife for her husband, and as mother for her son. Thus, from earliest youth she was taught to deny herself. Her life was not one of independence, but of dependent service. Man's helpmate; if her presence is helpful, she stays on the stage with him; if she hinders his work, she retires behind the curtain.[1]

2. At the beginning of the Meiji period (1868–1912), which followed the Edo period when the so-called Meiji Restoration occurred along with the impact of Western civilization, the government recognized the necessity of education for women in order to transform Japan into a modern, industrial, and wealthy nation. It was the ideal type of women in Bushido, the woman with the ethics of the samurai class, those who experienced the least freedom in the premodern period, that the government adopted as a basis for the

education of women. Thus, the history of modern Japanese women started with the motto, "Good Wife and Wise Mother." The principle was significant because it recognized the value of woman in these two roles. However, it is needless to point out that this ideal type has its limitations. A woman may be a good wife for her husband. A woman may be a wise mother for her son. But she is taught to deny her own needs. Education for women was encouraged as long as such education produced a "Good Wife and Wise Mother." Therefore, education for women did not imply in general any academic development for women. For them, junior high school (*Koto Jogakko*) education was almost all they could receive. Senior high schools were monopolized by boys. There was no coeducation. With rare exceptions, no national or state universities were opened to women. Only a few national normal schools for women (*Joshi Koto Shihan Gakko*) and several private colleges for women (*Joshidai*) were available for their higher education. Even after graduation from higher educational institutions, there were almost no opportunities for women. The kinds of job women could take were severely limited. Women had neither the right to vote in elections nor the right to be elected. Women were inferior to men under the law and were discriminated against in political, economic, and social relations.

A famous leading woman socialist wrote in her autobiography as follows:

> Every road for women ended up as a dead alley. There was no possibility for her to develop her potential ability. I never felt the joy of youth in my younger years. Because of the desperate irritation and impatience, I felt as if I were walking in the dark.[2]

II. Reforms after World War II

1. After World War II, a new Japanese Constitution was enacted in 1946. The new Constitution guarantees equality of men and women under the law (Art. 14, Const.).[3] as well as equal rights of husband and wife in family life (Art. 24, Const.).[4] To comply with the new Constitution, widespread legal reforms in civil, criminal, and public fields were carried out.

In the penal code the crime of adultery was deleted. Under the old penal code, adultery constituted a crime when it was committed by a wife, punishable by imprisonment with hard labor, but it was not a crime when a husband committed it. In the sphere of the civil code regulating marriage, parental relationship, guardianship, support, and succession, fundamental reforms were needed to meet the constitutional requirement of equality of men and women under the law.[5]

Under the old system, the head of a family, usually a male, husband or father, had various kinds of powers over the members who were registered in the family. For example, a member of a family could not marry without the consent of the head of his or her family (Art. 750 I, old civil code). Together with the abolition of the Family (*Iye*) system, inheritance of the headship of a family was also abolished. Under the old civil code, the eldest son was the sole heir to the headship of a family as well as to all the property and estate of the family. Many tragedies took place under these regulations of the old civil code. By way of example, there is the case of a male who had only daughters by his formal wife but had an illegitimate son by his concubine. The illegitimate son was to inherit all the property, leaving nothing to the formal wife and daughters. Under the new civil code, each brother and sister can benefit equally, and the wife cannot be excluded from inheriting her husband's property.

Another main reform of the old civil code under the new Constitution was the establishment of equality between husband and wife. Under the old civil code, a woman lost her legal competency and contractual capacity once she married and could not make several legal transactions stipulated by the code without the permission of her husband (Arts. 14–18, old civil code). A married woman was no different from a minor or a mentally incompetent person. Moreover, a husband could control the property of his wife if they had not decided otherwise by an agreement prior to the marriage (Arts. 801 and 793, old civil code). All these provisions which are discriminatory against women were abolished under the new Constitution.

2. Along with these legal reforms under the new Constitution, far-reaching social changes took place in Japanese society.

a. Women, for the first time, exercised the right to vote and to be elected to public offices in 1946. In this election, 39 women were elected to the National Diet. At the present time, we have 7 women representatives among 486 members of the House of Representatives, and we have 13 among the 250 members of the House of Councillors. There are about 600 women representatives in the local assemblies.

b. Women are holding senior positions in public offices. They have held several ministries in the cabinet. In the judicial field, there are over 50 female judges, about 20 public prosecutors and government lawyers, and about 350 practicing lawyers.

c. However, the most important change was the emancipation of education for women. With few exceptions, the universities which had closed their doors to women for the last hundred years are now open to them. It is hardly necessary to emphasize that with the prevailing higher education for women, their professional horizon has been enlarged. In 1973, the total working population reached over 52 million in Japan. This included over 20 million female workers (38.6 percent). Under the category of skilled and professional occupations, female workers accounted for over 40 percent, although the rate of women among the managerial and supervisory occupations remained low (under 6 percent).

III. Emancipation of Women and Crime

1. In every country the great majority of crimes are committed by male offenders. In general, sex difference has a very close correlation with the incidence of criminality. By way of example, in 1973 throughout Japan, 51,133 female offenders were cleared by the police on the charge of violation of the penal code. On the other hand, the number of men who were cleared by the police in the same year amounted to 357,738. The percentage of female offenders among the total offenders of the penal code was only 14.3 percent.

In addition to the penal code offenses, violators of the special criminal statutes who were cleared and sent to the public prosecutor's office by the police[6] (sochi jinin) amounted to 122,716 persons including 24,394 women (19.9 percent).[7]

In the same year, 51,733 female offenders under the penal code were disposed of by the public prosecutors, with 47.2 percent of the cases prosecuted and 49.2 percent suspended.[8] Of 813,828 male offenders who were disposed of in the same year, 65.7 percent were prosecuted and the rest were suspended. And in 1972 a total of 27,855 male offenders were sent to correctional institutions, while only 568 female offenders were newly received into these facilities.

2. The disparity in the crime rate between men and women has been attributed to differences in the social standings between the two sexes as well as to physical, biological, and psychological differences. It is often pointed out that "the female crime rate shows some tendency to approach closest to the male in countries in which females have the greatest freedom and equality with males. . . . If countries existed in which females were politically and socially dominant, the female rate according to this trend, should exceed the male rate."[9]

As mentioned previously, Japanese women underwent enormous political and social changes after World War II. If the disparity in crime rate is to be attributed to differences in the social standing between both sexes, Japan should have witnessed an explosion in female crimes. However, during the period between 1946 and 1977, though female offenders increased in terms of real numbers and percentages of women among the total offender population, the rates of women offenders per 1,000 population of women 14 years of age or over (criminally responsible or punishable population) remained relatively stable. Compared with 1 : 3 in the year of 1946, the ratio in 1977 was 1 : 5 (as shown by Table 1).

With regard to the qualitative changes of female offenses, Table 2 shows the number of female offenders in 1943 and 1972, respectively, classified by the type of offense. According to statistics, female offenders seem to be getting more violent. For example, there was no woman charged with robbery in 1943. However, in 1972, 69 women were handled by the prosecutor's office under the charge of robbery. The percentage of women in extortion increased from 1.3 to 3.3 percent.

We also have to take notice of the following facts. First, 38 out of 69 robbers, 239 out of 553 assailants, and 354 out of 460 extortionists in 1972 were youthful offenders under 24 years of age. Second, the attitudes of law enforcement agencies and society on the whole toward female offenders might be different from what it was in the prewar period. Just as the increase of indecency offenses does not necessarily justify the conclusion that women became more indecent, so also the increase of violent offenses committed by women needs more precise examination.

Except for professional negligence causing death and/or injury, the most common charges against women were theft. If we compare the proportion of female offenders with the total offender population, by the type of offense, infanticide comes first, followed by negligence causing death and/or injury, desertion and accidental fire, participation in suicide, and murder. These offenses are considered to be "female offenses." They are related to women as mother and housewife, lover, daughter-in-law, and so forth. And these "female offenses" were common both in 1943 and in 1972 (see Table 2). We may conclude, then, that far-reaching postwar changes in women's social positions in the Japanese society seem to have had little influence upon the criminality of women in both qualitative and quantitative perspectives.

3. The rate of women offenders increased until 1950 when it reached 1.9, as shown by Table 1 and Figure 1. It started to decline until 1959. However, after a relatively stable period of the 1960s, it started to rise steadily, from 1.1 in 1972 to 1.5 in 1977. The trend of female criminality is in contradiction with that of male criminality, which seems to continue its decrease since 1950, when it had reached 20.7 per 1,000.

Table 1.   The Rate per Population.

Year	Female Number [1]	Rate [4]	Male Number [2]	Rate [4]	Female Percentage $\frac{(1)}{(1)+(2)} \times 100$
1946	33,819	1.3	408,760	17.8	7.6
1947	35,749	1.3	419,348	16.7	7.9
1948	44,869	1.6	502,122	19.6	8.2
1949	53,605	1.9	526,292	20.1	9.2
1950	54,278	1.9	553,491	20.7	8.9
1951	51,296	1.7	555,390	20.3	8.5
1952	46,918	1.6	510,603	18.3	8.4
1953	43,509	1.4	476,198	16.8	8.4
1954	41,074	1.3	461,989	15.9	8.2
1955	39,667	1.2	475,813	16.0	7.7
1956	31,990	1.0	438,532	14.4	6.8
1957	31,850	1.0	439,750	14.2	6.8
1958	31,995	0.9	425,217	13.4	7.0
1959	31,936	0.9	422,962	13.1	7.0
1960	33,935	1.0	408,592	12.6	7.7
1961	36,711	1.0	414,875	12.5	8.1
1962	42,001	1.2	388,152	11.4	9.8
1963	48,154	1.3	377,319	10.8	11.3
1964	51,183	1.3	398,659	11.1	11.4
1965 [3]	49,724	1.3	390,839	10.7	11.3
1966	46,471	1.2	387,078	10.4	10.7
1967	44,142	1.1	358,596	9.5	11.0
1968	45,573	1.1	348,258	9.1	11.6
1969	45,057	1.1	332,769	8.6	11.9
1970	47,509	1.1	333,341	8.5	12.5
1971	48,234	1.2	313,738	7.9	13.3
1972	47,408	1.1	301,380	7.5	13.6
1973	51,133	1.2	306,605	7.5	14.3
1974	58,261	1.3	305,048	7.4	16.0
1975	61,432	1.4	302,685	7.2	16.9
1976	67,276	1.5	292,084	6.9	18.7
1977	68,919	1.5	294,225	6.9	19.0

Source: Adapted from National Police Agency, *Criminal Statistics Report* (Hanzai Tokei Sho) for 1952 (pp. 76–77, p. 122), 1960 (p. 67, p. 91), and from 1961 to 1977, respectively.

[1] The number of female offenders of the penal code cleared by the police as suspects.

[2] The number of male offenders of the penal code cleared by the police as suspects.

[3] Until 1965, the offenders of professional negligence causing death and/or injury were excluded. Since 1966, the offenders of professional negligence causing deaths and/or injury *due to the traffic accidents* were excluded.

[4] The rates of suspects per 1,000 population of the same sex who are 14 years of age or over.

[5] Percentages of female offenders among the total number of offenses.

Table 2. Female Criminality by Type of Offense.

Type of Offense	1943		1972	
	Number	Percentage	Number	Percentage
Total	30,004 (100.0)	9.4	65,773 (100.0)	6.3
Theft	13,386 (44.6)	12.3	23,542 (35.8)	14.9
Robbery	0 (0)	0	69 (0.1)	3.0
Fraud	1,172 (3.9)	5.1	1,954 (3.0)	8.7
Embezzlement	1,185 (3.9)	6.3	552 (0.8)	5.7
Extortion	27 (0.1)	1.3	471 (0.7)	3.3
Assault	12 (0.0)	3.5	453 (0.7)	1.8
Injury	288 (1.0)	2.2	1,145 (1.7)	1.9
Murder (including murder of ascendent)	138 (0.5)	17.1	486 (0.7)	22.3
Infanticide	186 (0.6)	81.2	45 (0.1)	91.8
Participation in suicide	4 (0.0)	23.5	11 (0.0)	29.7
Arson	109 (0.4)	23.1	157 (0.2)	16.1
Accidental fire	3,601 (12.0)	34.3	1,786 (2.7)	38.0
Indecency	33 (0.1)	5.0	748 (1.1)	14.5
Gambling	6,156 (20.5)	5.8	1,030 (1.6)	6.7
Negligence causing death/injury	1,598 (5.3)	47.7	484 (0.7)	53.5
Professional negligence causing death/injury	166 (0.6)	2.7	30,686 (46.7)	4.6
Desertion	64 (0.2)	42.1	76 (0.1)	54.3
Defamation	65 (0.2)	18.9	163 (0.2)	19.9
Others	1,814 (6.0)	7.7	1,915 (2.9)	3.4

Source: Adapted from The Research and Training Institute of the Ministry of Justice, *White Paper on Crime* (Hanzai Hakusho), Tokyo, 1973, p. 393; National Police Agency, *Criminal Statistical Report for 1943* (Hanzai Tōkei Sho), Tokyo, 1974, p. 3. Due to the limitation of available statistics, the numbers for 1972 represent women offenders who were disposed of by the public prosecutor's office, and the numbers for 1943 represent those of women who were cleared by the police as suspects.

Thus, the increase in the percentage of female offenders among the total offender population is mainly due to the decrease in the number of male offenders.

Figure 1.

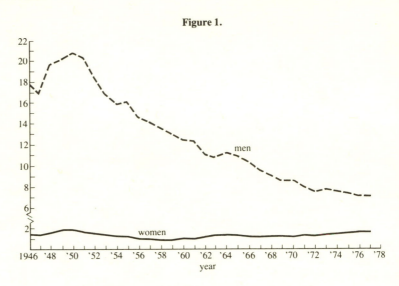

IV. Characteristics of Japanese Society

We need explanations for the decrease of crime in general in Japan and for the stability of crimes committed by women despite the so-called emancipation of women after World War II.

Many answers, such as the efficiency and effectiveness of the police and law enforcement organizations, economic development, the high level of education of the people, the homogeneity of Japanese society, and so forth, are readily given for the general decrease in crime. These can never be more than tentative hypotheses, due to the lack of knowledge about the causation and dynamics of the crime phenomenon.

However, one of the explanations is to be found in the relationship of one person to another in Japanese society. This society is very well integrated, and usually people are not so isolated, not so alienated or rejected that they commit offenses. They are affiliated with a group or to someone with whom they feel a sense of belonging and security. This comes from weak individualism or unassertive self-awareness in the Japanese mentality. These Japanese come out of the Japanese family and vice versa.

Professor Ezra F. Vogel, in his study of the new Japanese middle class, observed the following:

> The life of the modern Japanese family with a husband in the new bureaucratic organization has changed greatly from Japanese family life of an earlier era, but it remains different from the common patterns in the United States and many European countries. The unique features of the salary-man family discussed in the body of this work, the insulation of the family from the firm, the lack of participation of husbands in household tasks, the narrow range of the wife's social participation and her very close relationship with the children show no signs of radical change.[10]

It seems to me that this unique character of the Japanese family may be attributed to the Japanese mentality; namely, the very strong sense of belongingness and affiliation which leads to weak individualism.

1. *Family Relationship*. Figuratively speaking, the core of individuality is weak among the Japanese compared with westerners. Therefore, both husband and wife lose their individuality in the family. A woman should be a good wife and a wife a good mother and keep nothing for herself. She is responsible for housekeeping, cooking, washing, cleaning, and so on; and in particular, she is responsible for the education of the children and for the home economy. In general, the husband is in charge of earning the income to support the family. Almost all Japanese husbands hand over their salary untouched to their wives, although sometimes they secretly keep some extra income for themselves. It is the wives who decide how much money husbands should spend for lunch, drinks, and other things, because she is responsible for the home economy. Often the Japanese home is the castle of the wife. Thus, quite naturally the division of labor between husband and wife is established. Due to the reforms after World War II, husbands and wives are equal but separated. The labor which is divided between the husband and wife is now considered to be equal. *Per contra*, in Western society, where each person is particularly individualistic, again figuratively speaking, each individual lives inside a sort of hard shell.

> The individualism of Anglo-Saxon society cannot let go of the idea that husband and wife are two persons;—hence when they disagree, their separate rights are recognized and when they agree, they exhaust their vocabulary in all sorts of pet names and blandishments. It sounds highly irrational to our ears, when a husband or wife speaks to a third party of his or her other—better or worse—half as being lovely, bright, kind and whatnot.[11]

It is strange for a Japanese to listen to a wife or husband praise the lovely disposition of her or his spouse, but on the other hand, for a westerner it is strange to listen to a Japanese husband refer to his wife as foolish.

Because of individualism alone, the idea that "man and woman shall be one flesh" is very strong in the Anglo-American and some of the European societies. The doctrine of coverture, that the husband and wife are one, has meant that the "one" is the husband and in reality it often resulted in domination of an individualistic husband over an individualistic wife. The conflict of common values of an individualistic society with feminine virtues has been most serious. On the one hand, there is social value placed on being active, independent, unemotional, competitive, and achievement oriented; on the other hand, there are social expectations associated with the traditional role of women, such as adaptability, dependence, unassertiveness, gentleness, and supportiveness.

This conflict is especially acute among women of college graduate level who learn the values of individualism and achievement. In spite of these, when they get married, they are required to be adaptive, dependent, subordinate, and self-denying. Thus, their individualism is squashed. "Women experienced frustration and the ache of vague but constant discontent, even exhibiting at times symptoms of malaise similar to those noted in prisoners-of-war camps, such as extreme apathy, childishness and fear of loss of their sexual potency."[12] Husbands address their wives who are suffering from these symptoms as "my baby."

Though husband and wife should be united as one, in actuality they are two separate individuals. Therefore, to solve the dilemma, the wife and husband should be a couple. Husband and wife "must always appear together as a couple, must share the same friends and forsake those the other cannot tolerate, must always share vacations and most hobbies, must always be available for each other's whim and loneliness."[13]

Japanese society has never been a coupled society. Due to the strong belongingness and weak individualism, the husband and wife are one from the beginning. Wives are not invited to social occasions, partly because most of them are business oriented and partly because husbands represent the whole family. Thus, Japanese wives, fortunately or unfortunately, are more free and independent from their husbands compared with their Western counterparts in a coupled society.

2. *Motherhood.* As the result of weak individualism among the Japanese, the relationship between mother and child, and especially the relationship of mother and son is very close. He is her life, her love, her hope, and an extension of herself. She provides him with continuous attention and protec-

tion. This close relationship between mother and child provides, on the one hand, a sense of the security which children need most in their childhood, but on the other hand, it "tends to arouse in the child a fear of making independent decisions and to create anxiety about being isolated from family or friends."[14] Thus, the relationship helps to create a weak, soft Japanese with strong group identification. Thus, weak individualism and the strong sense of groupism among the Japanese is the cause and product of the relationship between mother and child.

The international comparison of marriage rates, shown in Table 3, illustrates the remarkable characteristics of the Japanese family. The marriage rate in Japan is second highest next to that of the United States of America. However, the rates of married people in their twenties are very low, if they are compared with those of other countries. In particular, with regard to Japanese men between 20 and 24, the rate was only 9.8 percent, while in the case of Americans it was over 44 percent in 1970. It is clear that the Japanese youth get married much later than the youth in any other country. There must be various reasons for this remarkable difference, but one of the most important factors is that children are well-integrated members of the family and protected by their parents. They are never as isolated nor independent from parents as in Western society where each individual person is separate and independent, and the tie of "one flesh" between husband and wife does not include their children. In the coupled society children marry young. "Examining their motives [of marriage], they found that they had married because of social pressure, because adult society is organized almost

Table 3. Marriage and Divorce Rates in 1970.

| | Marriage Rate[1] | Divorce Rate[2] | Rates of Married Person | | | |
| | | | Male | | Female | |
			20–24	25–29	20–24	25–29
U.S.A.	10.7	3.51	44.2	81.6	62.5	83.1
Japan	10.0	0.93	9.8	52.9	27.7	80.4
England and Wales	8.5	1.17	32.4	72.7	58.1	84.3
France	7.7	0.76[3]	20.6	66.6	43.4	80.2
W. Germany	7.2	1.24	18.1	61.3	49.0	80.6
Sweden	5.4	1.61	16.5	57.4	39.0	73.4

Sources: The Council for Population Problems, *Trends of Japanese Population* (Nihon Jinkō no Dōkō), Tokyo, 1974, p. 89; The Bureau of Statistics, Prime Minister's Office, *The Handbook of International Statistics 1973*, (Kokusai Tokei Yōran), Tokyo, 1973, pp. 24–25.

[1] Marriage rate is the number of formal marriages per 1,000 persons.
[2] Divorce rate is the number of registered divorces per 1,000 persons.
[3] This number is the divorce rate of 1969 in France.

completely in terms of couples, because they had become sexually involved and decided to live together. Some had wanted to escape from their parents. In these circumstances, making a mistake had seemed almost inevitable.''[15]

Thus, the belated marriage in Japan is the result of weak individualism and a strong sense of belongingness and affiliation. The second factor contributing to this phenomenon is that Japanese youth marry only after they have taken fixed employment in some organization where they will probably work throughout their lives. In general, they marry only after they are ready to support their family, to play a role of husband, and eventually a role of father. Thus, from the beginning, Japanese marriage has a solid base which is conducive to a low rate of divorce in spite of easy and liberal divorce procedures.

3. *Familiarization.* People learn fundamental human relationships in the family. "There is a continuity and compatibility between the child's dependence on his immediate family and the dependence which he later feels toward his school and work groups."[16] As he was dependent on his mother, so also is he dependent on his wife. (The husband is a big son for his wife.) He is dependent on his work organization. He tends to see the human relationships as being analogous to those of a family.)

The company in which a man works is a family for him. The president or chief of staff is his father figure, the vice-president or deputy chief is his mother, and coworkers are his brothers and sisters. Correspondingly, the senior members of the company regard workers as children for whom they should care. The Japanese concept of family extends even further. They regard the society as a family and the state as a family. Therefore, Japanese society as a whole is characterized by a strong sense of belongingness and weak individualism.

If Japanese society fares better with a strong sense of belongingness, the Japanese mother should be praised. If Japanese society fails without strong individualism, the Japanese mother should be blamed.

4. *Epilogue.* The increase of female offenders in spite of the decrease of male offenders in recent years is sometimes attributed to the changes in the status of Japanese women. The theory goes that Japan's period of rapid economic growth propelled women into society too suddenly, causing tensions and dislocations for which neither they nor society were prepared. But this argument does not adequately explain the following facts. First, a breakdown of the types of crimes committed by women shows that the overwhelming majority are crimes of theft. The number of women cleared by the police for theft increased from 37,392 in 1970, to 47,122 in 1974, to 51,711 in 1975. Thus, the increase of women offenders is due to the increase of women who were cleared by the police for theft. Second, approx-

imately 80 percent of thefts committed by women are shoplifting, and offenders in this category are again about 80 percent housewives, students, and others without regular employment. Over 40 percent of the women arrested for theft are middle-aged or over.

The rise in female crime may be a symptom of the frustration of women with their marriage, family, and society. Still, female criminality in both the quantitative and the qualitative perspective shows that Japanese women and the Japanese society as a whole have preserved their unique features.

Notes

1. Inazo Nitobe Bushido, *The Soul of Japan* (Tokyo, 1935), p. 152.

2. Kikue Yamakawa, *Onna Nidai no Ki* (the record of two generations of women) (Tokyo, 1972) p. 310. But it will be misleading to consider the period as totally dark. There were pioneering women with unusual talent who distinguished themselves in various professional fields.

3. Article 14. All of the people are equal under the law and there shall be no discrimination in political, economic or social relations because of race, creed, sex, social status or family origin.

4. Article 24. Marriage shall be based only on the mutual consent of both sexes and it shall be maintained through mutual cooperation with the equal rights of husband and wife as a basis.

With regard to choice of spouse, property rights, inheritance, choice of domicile, divorce and other matters pertaining to marriage and the family, laws shall be enacted from the standpoint of individual dignity and the essential equality of the sexes.

5. One of the most important reforms was the abolition of the so-called family system (*Iye-Seido*).

6. A judicial police officer who has conducted the investigation of a crime shall send the case together with the documents and items of evidence to a public prosecutor, except as otherwise provided in law. However, this shall not apply to the case which is specially designated (Art. 246. C. Cr. P.).

7. The breakdown of major violations of the special criminal statutes was shown in the table.

Statutes	Women	Men	Percentage of Women
Anti-prostitution law	2,662	659	80.1
Controlling entertainment businesses regulations	5,745	4,780	54.6
Registration of aliens regulation	5,184	8,710	37.3
Child welfare law	404	743	35.2
Public office election law	4,893	13,885	26.0
Narcotics control law	25	300	7.7
Stimulant drug control law	1,179	7,122	14.2
Opium law	181	85	68.0

8. Japanese public prosecutors control the power of the Institution of Criminal Public Prosecution (Art. 247. C. Cr. P.). In addition, they have the power to suspend public prosecution. Article 248 reads as follows: "If, after considering the character, age and situation of the offenders, the gravity of the offence, the circumstances under which the offence was committed, and the conditions subsequent to the commission of the offence prosecution is deemed unnecessary, prosecution may not be instigated."

9. F. H. Sutherland and D. R. Cressey, *Principles of Criminology*, 6th ed. (New York, 1960), p. 112. They point out further that the "female crime rate shows some tendency to approach closest to the male in countries in which females have the greatest freedom and equality with males, such as Western Europe, Australia, and the United States, and to vary most from the male rate in countries in which females are closely supervised, such as Japan and Algiers."

10. Ezra F. Vogel, *Japan's New Middle Class: The Salary Man and His Family in Tokyo Suburb* (California, 1963), p. 265.

11. Inazo Nitobe, *op. cit.*, p. 162.

12. Neal O'Neil and George O'Neil, *Open Marriage; A New Life Style for Couples* (New York, 1973), p. 27.

13. *Ibid.*, p. 31.

14. Vogel, *op. cit.*, p. 233.

15. Leslie A. Westoff, Tying the Knot More Than Once, Remarriage Is a Growing Trend," *New York Times,* Sunday, August 10, 1975, p. 8.

16. Vogel, *op. cit.*, p. 235.

INDEX

Africa
  Statistics lacking, 11
American experience, 1-13
  Concern of international community, 5-10
  Contemporary scene, 1-5
  Female increase in crime, 1 *et seq.*
  International concern in, 1-13
  Juvenile delinquency, 4
  Men and women compared, 2-3
  Regional distribution by sex, 7
  Sexist oppression, 4
  Statistics,
    Meager sources for, 10, 11
    Problem with, 9
  Women in prison, 4, 5
Argentina, 188-214
  Comparative statistics of criminal acts with intervention, 209-213
  Females sentenced, 193-208
  Incarcerated population, 214
  Lesser criminality of women, 189
  Menopause, 190
  Statistics, 188-214
Egypt, 176-187
  Categories of women, 177
  Fear of getting involved in crime, 178
  Place in society, 178
  Statistical analysis, 178-187
    Age arrested and sentenced, 179, 180
    Age of deviation, 180
    Educational status, 181

Father and mother, 181
    Friends, 183
    Other motives, 185
    Religion, 184
    Social condition, 180, 181
    Television, 184
    Unmatched marriages, 183
England and Wales, 102-121
  Abortion, 118
  Contraceptives, 118
  Discussion, 116-121
  Drugs, 109
  Menstruation, 116-117
  Mental abnormality, 113-116
  Penology, 110-113
    Prostitutes, 112
  Shoplifting, 105, 115
  Terrorism, 109
  Violence, 107
Finland, 64-84
  Defamation, 75
  Drunken driving, 72
  Female criminality in, 64-84
  Hidden criminality, 78-79
  Infanticide, 72, 78
  Prison population, 66, 67
  Property offenses, 68
  Sentencing, 80
  Statistics, 64-84
  Violent offenders, 70
Germany, 122-133

Germany (*continued*)
  Alcoholism, 123
  Baader-Meinhof gang, 125-131
  Bank robbery, 124
  Changing pattern of, 122-133
  Ensslin, Gudrun, 126-129
  Female aggression, 131-132
  Search for causes, 129-131
  Statistical picture, 122-125
  Terrorism and political murder, 125-131
Hungary, 145-157
  Crimes against life, 145-157
    Burdensome obligation, escape from, 148, 149
    Personal relationship factor, 147
    Poor environment, 151, 152
    Profit, for, 150
    Psychological factors, 153
    Weapons, types of, 155
India, 228-258
  Comments, 256-258
  Conclusion, 254-256
  Female convicts, 243-254
  Introduction, 228-230
  Women offenders, 230
    Abduction, 242
    Burglary, 237
    Dacoity, 240
    Increase in some countries, 233
    Juvenile offenders, 231
    Kidnapping, 242
    Male and female criminality, 231
    Nature of criminality, 233-235
    Robbery, 241
    Trends, 230
      Other countries, 232
      State and union territories, 236
    White collar crime, 243
Japan, 258-271
  Adultery, 260
  Characteristics of Japanese society, 266-271
  Education, 261
  Emancipation of women and crime, 262-266
  Familiarization, 270
  Family relationship, 267
  Image of Japanese women, 259-260
  Motherhood, 268
  Reforms, 260-262

  Theft, 263
Netherlands
  Commitment to government care, 42
  Convictions and dismissals, 23
  Differences between men and women, 16-28
    Arrest rates, 16
    Boys and girls, 20
    Convictions and dismissals, 23
  Differences in female categories, 28-41
  Differential treatment of women, 41-43
  Discussion, 43-54
  Education
    Crimes by A and B students, 39
  Emancipation, 46, 53
  Employment, criminal behavior and, 37
  Female criminality in, 14-63
  Grades and crime, 39
  Housewife, 41
  Introduction, 15, 16
  Official crime figures, 30-31
  Self report studies, 26, 39
  Shoplifting, 35, 52
  Testosterone, 47
Nigeria, 158-171
  Abortion, 161
  Blackmarket, 168
  Child stealing, 162
  Conclusion, 168-169
  Female, role of, 160-161
  Introduction, 158-168
  Juveniles, 163
  Lack of data, 159
  Recidivism, 168
  Shoplifting, 163
Norway, 84-101
  Lawbreaking activity, 89-98
    Drugs and alcohol, 91-95
  Oslo, 89
    Females in city court, 90
  Penal system, 96-99
    Prison and children, 97-98
    Punishment—drugs and alcohol, 98-99
  Social background, 86-89
  Summary, 99-101
  Women in court, 84-101
Poland, 134-145
  Abortion, 138, 143

Decrease rather than increase in crime, 138
  Opposite trend in West, 138
Emancipation of women, 134 *et seq.*
No "female crimes" in Poland, 138
Nonviolent and nondangerous characteriza-
  tion, 142
Occupational orientation, 136
Prostitution, 138
Shoplifting, 138-139
Traffic offenses, 141
Violence in home, 141
Venezuela, 215-227

Abortion, 222
Adultery, 224
Diversity and marginality, 215-227
Juveniles, 222-223
Latin American women, 217-218
Methodology, 215-217
Official data, 220-223
Societal reaction, 223-225
Summary, 225
Venezuelan women, 218-220
Very low rate of criminality, 221